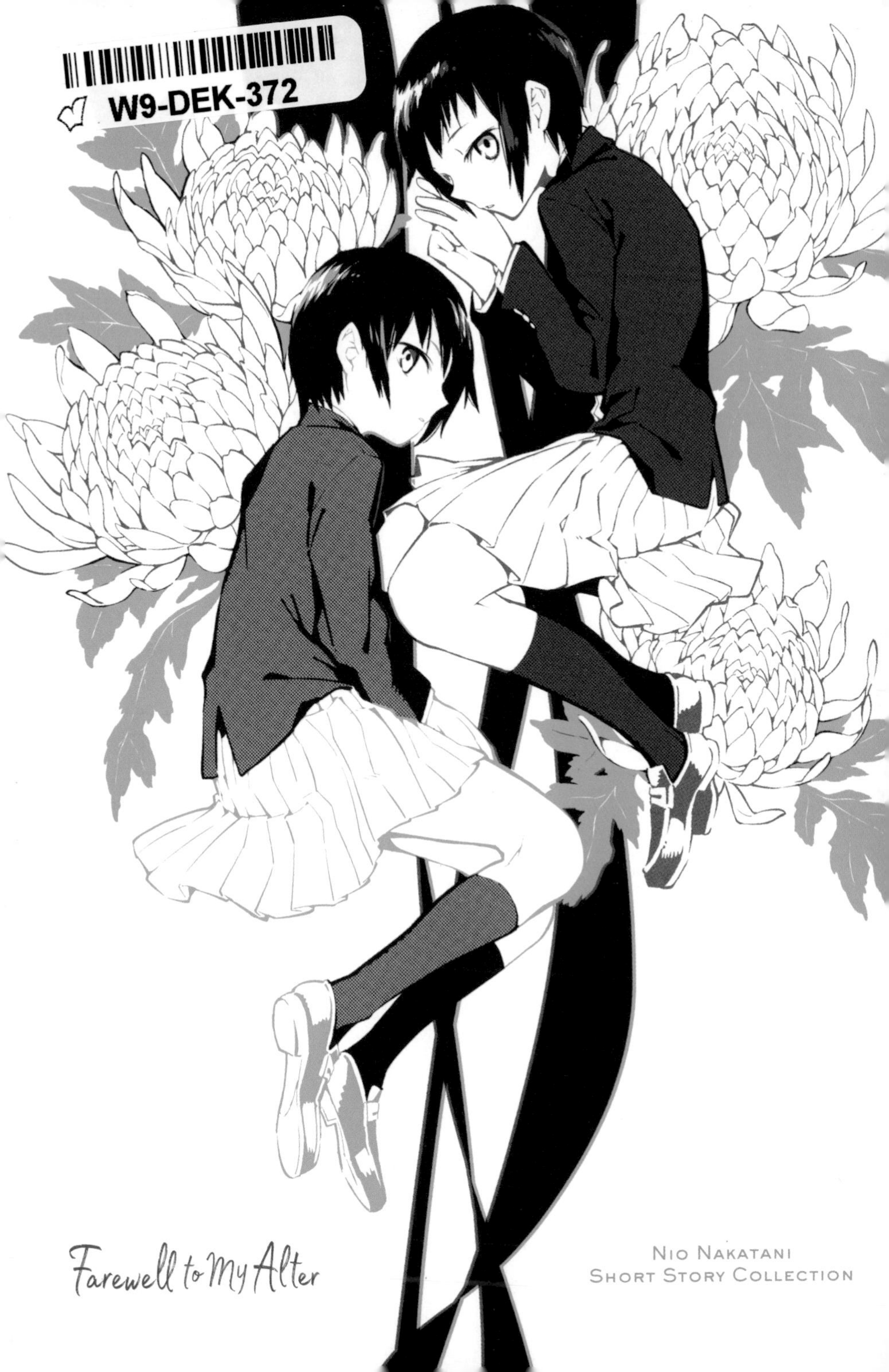

Farewell to My Alter

Nio Nakatani
Short Story Collection

CONTENTS

Farewell to My Alter — 3

The Hero Saves the World Three Times — 31

Tear-Flavored Escargot — 47

Happiness in the Shape of a Scar — 61

Always in Profile — 77

Comm-ear-ication — 85

I Am Custom-Made — 95

Double Bed — 107

I Want to Be Kind — 121

Afterword — 144

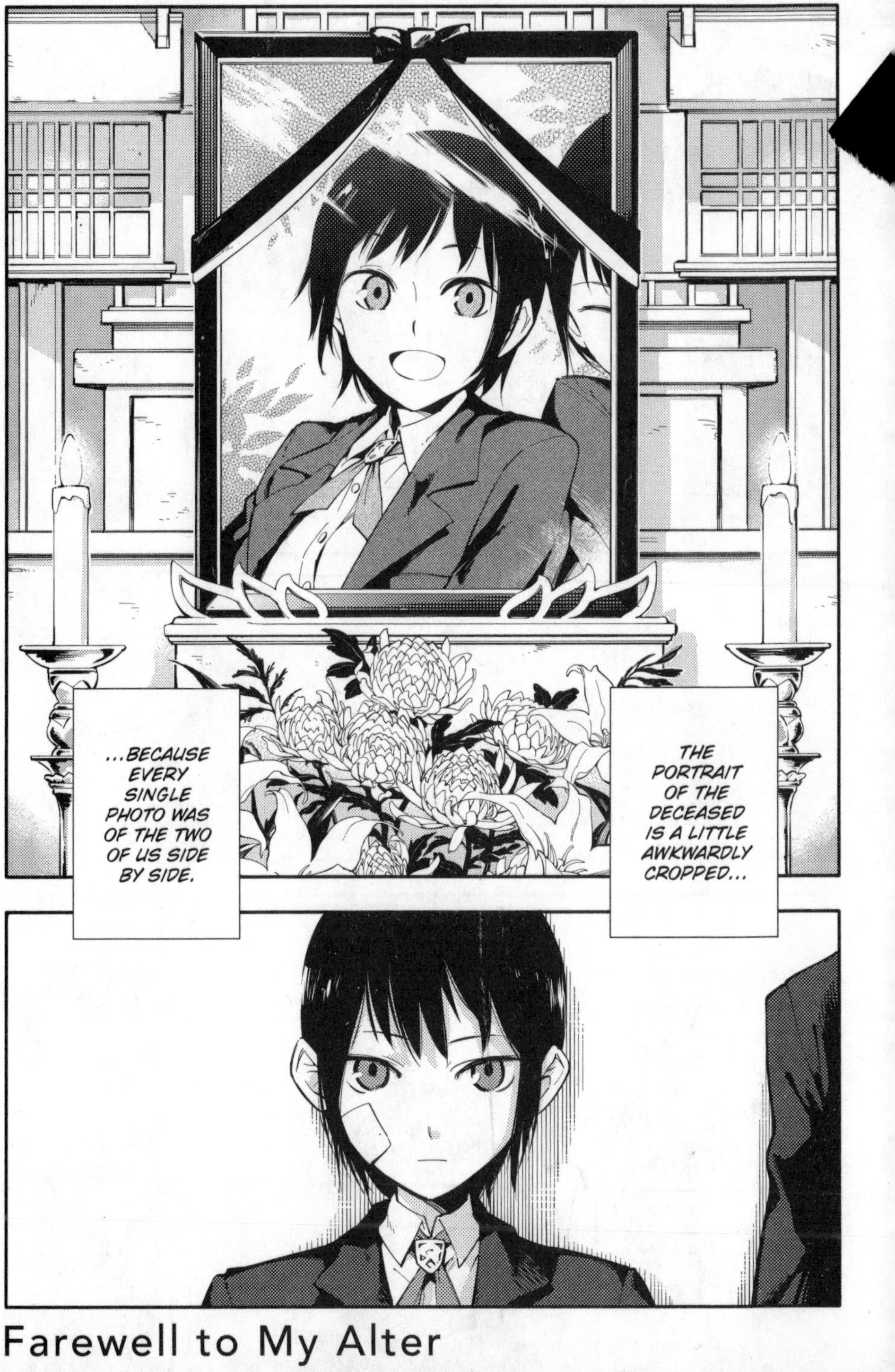
THE PORTRAIT OF THE DECEASED IS A LITTLE AWKWARDLY CROPPED...
...BECAUSE EVERY SINGLE PHOTO WAS OF THE TWO OF US SIDE BY SIDE.

Farewell to My Alter

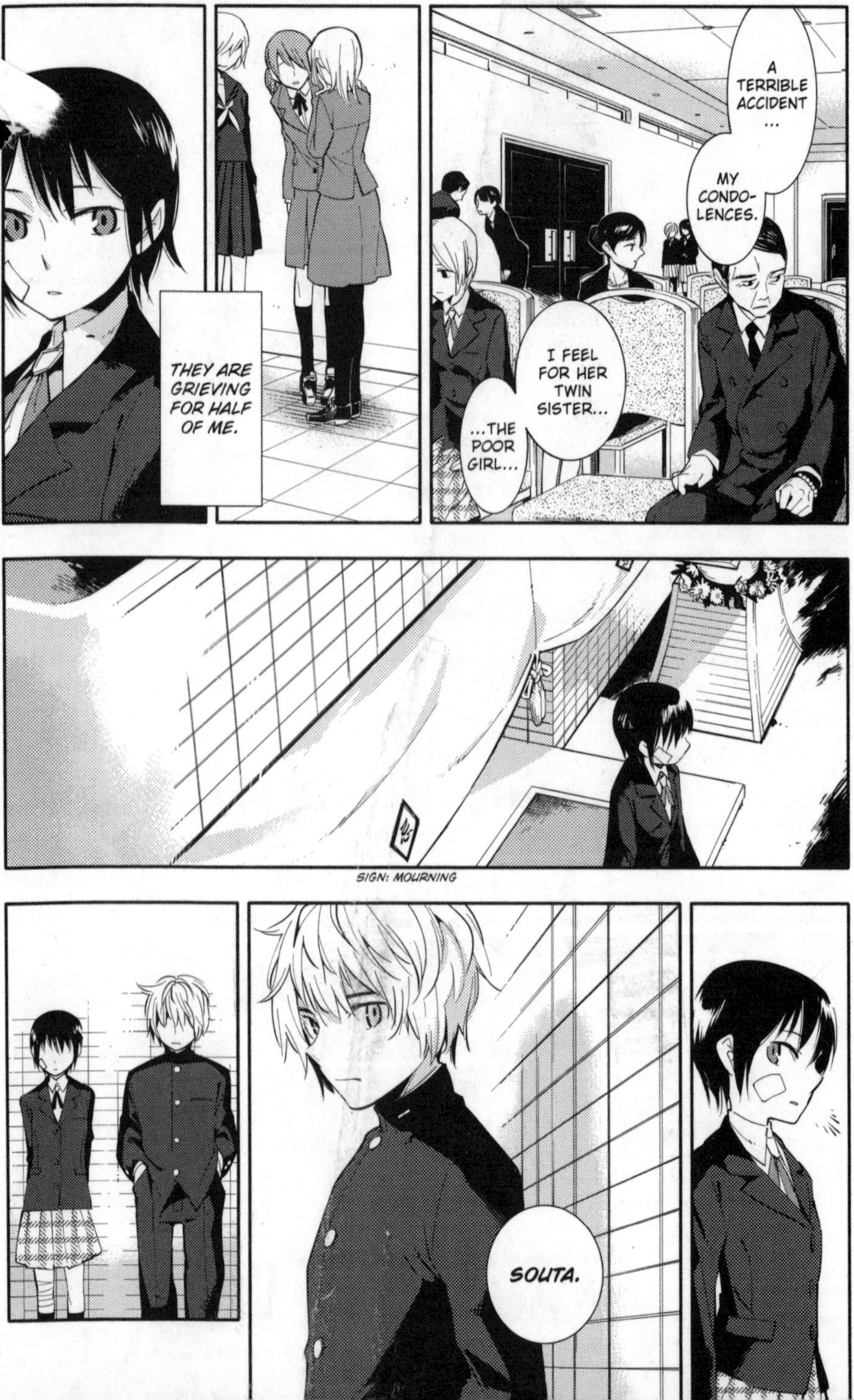
A TERRIBLE ACCIDENT...
MY CONDOLENCES.
I FEEL FOR HER TWIN SISTER...
...THE POOR GIRL...
THEY ARE GRIEVING FOR HALF OF ME.
SIGN: MOURNING
SOUTA.

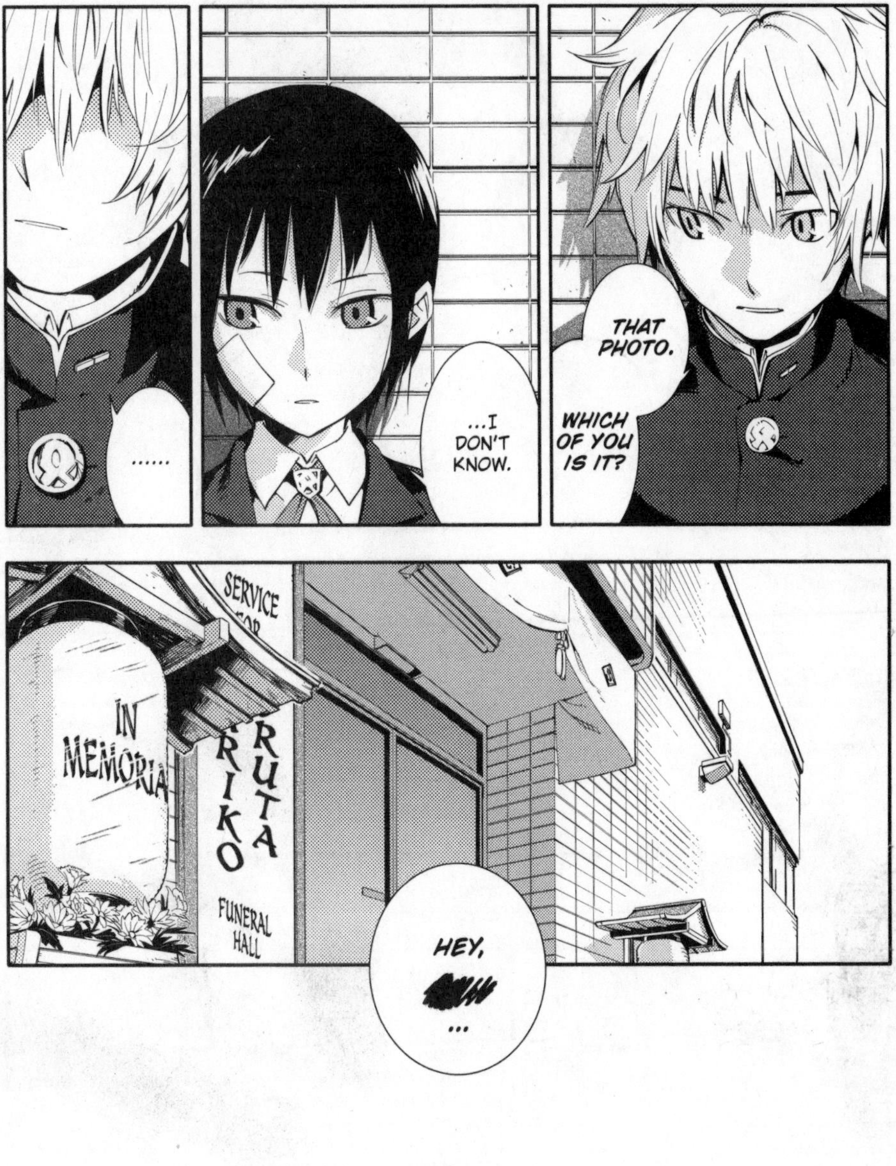
THAT PHOTO.
WHICH OF YOU IS IT?
...I DON'T KNOW.
......
SERVICE
RIKO
RUTA
FUNERAL HALL
IN MEMORIA
HEY, [redacted] ...

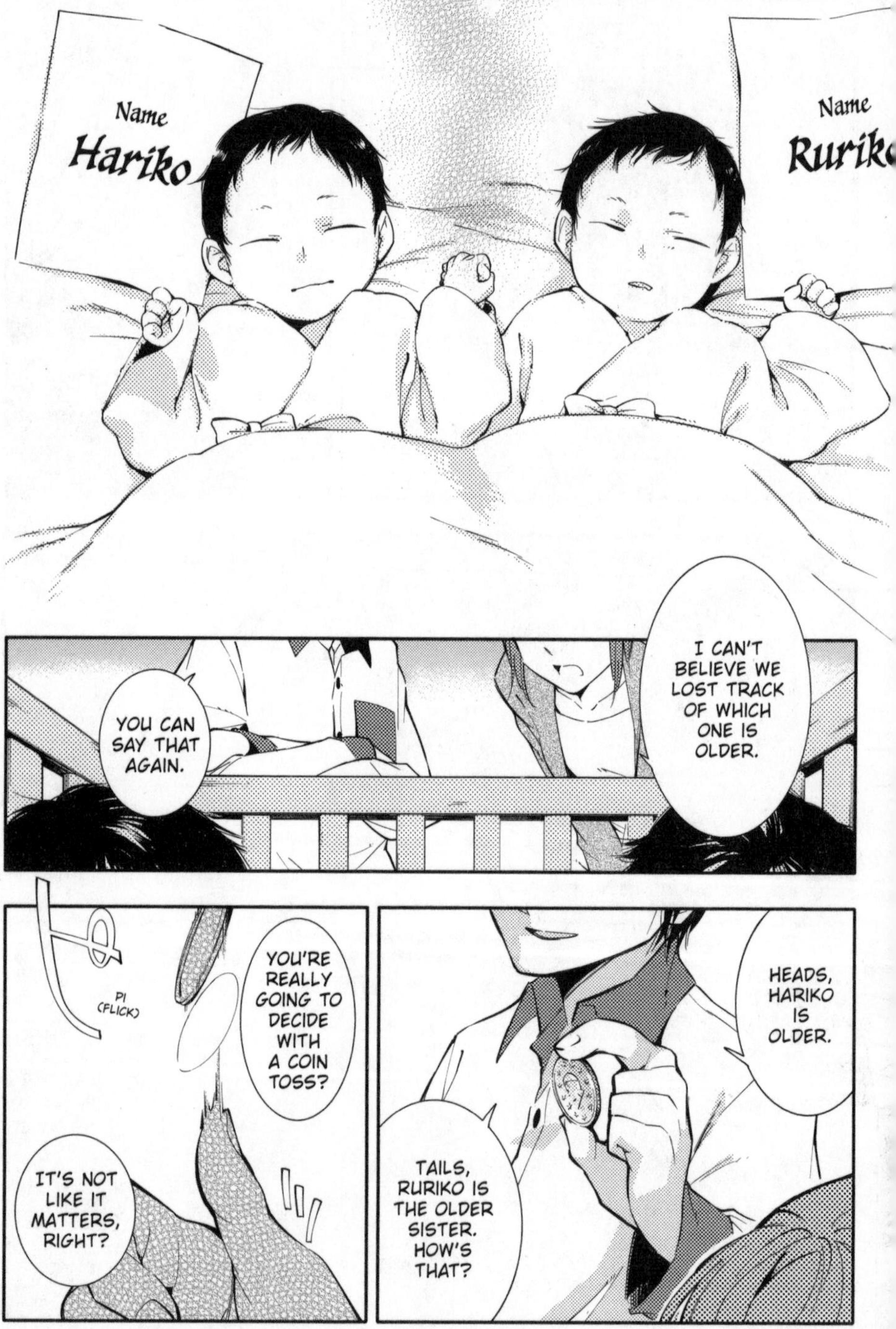
Name
Rurik
Name
Hariko
I CAN'T BELIEVE WE LOST TRACK OF WHICH ONE IS OLDER.
YOU CAN SAY THAT AGAIN.
HEADS, HARIKO IS OLDER.
TAILS, RURIKO IS THE OLDER SISTER. HOW'S THAT?
YOU'RE REALLY GOING TO DECIDE WITH A COIN TOSS?
PI (FLICK)
IT'S NOT LIKE IT MATTERS, RIGHT?

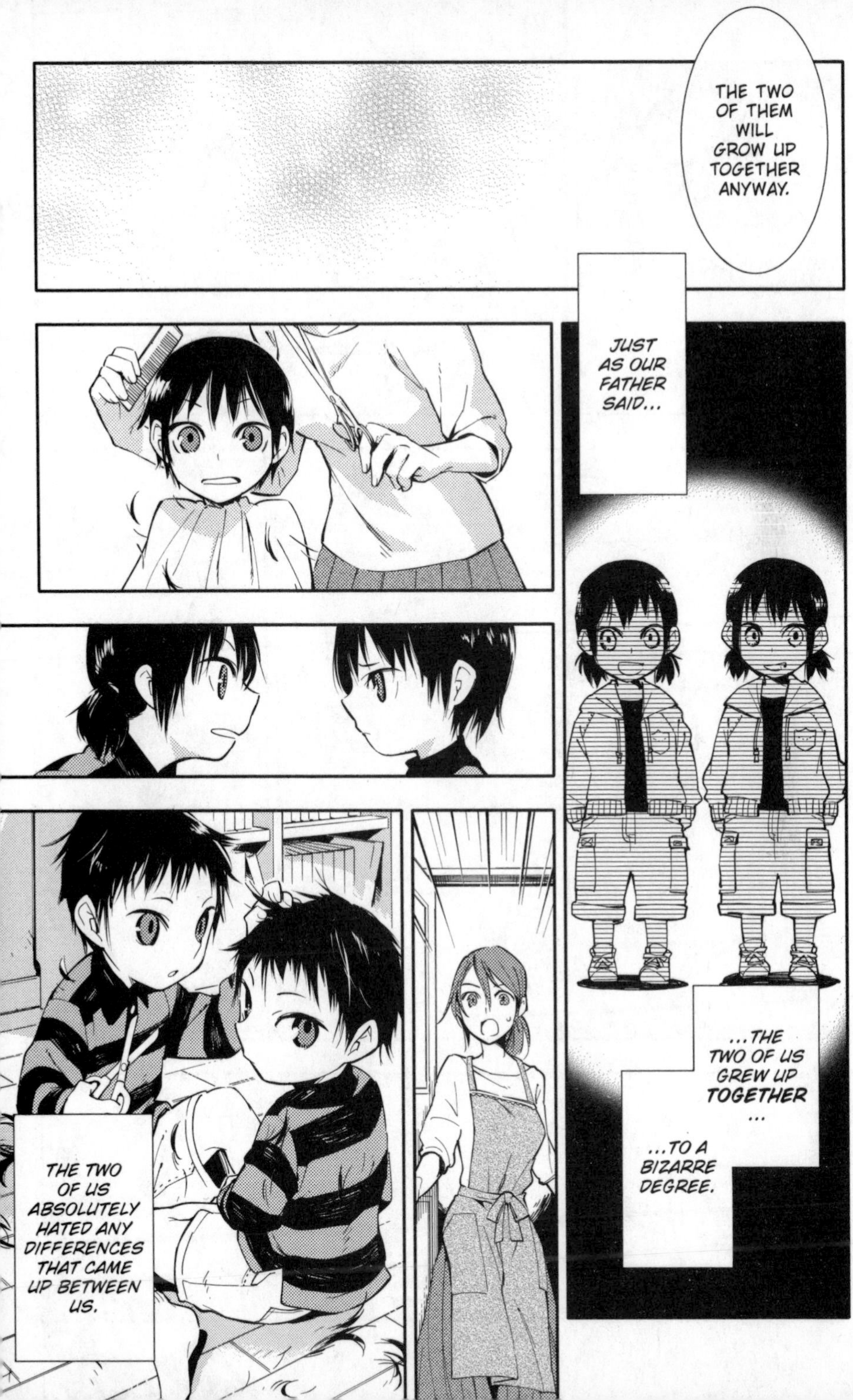
THE TWO OF THEM WILL GROW UP TOGETHER ANYWAY.
JUST AS OUR FATHER SAID...
...THE TWO OF US GREW UP TOGETHER...
...TO A BIZARRE DEGREE.
THE TWO OF US ABSOLUTELY HATED ANY DIFFERENCES THAT CAME UP BETWEEN US.

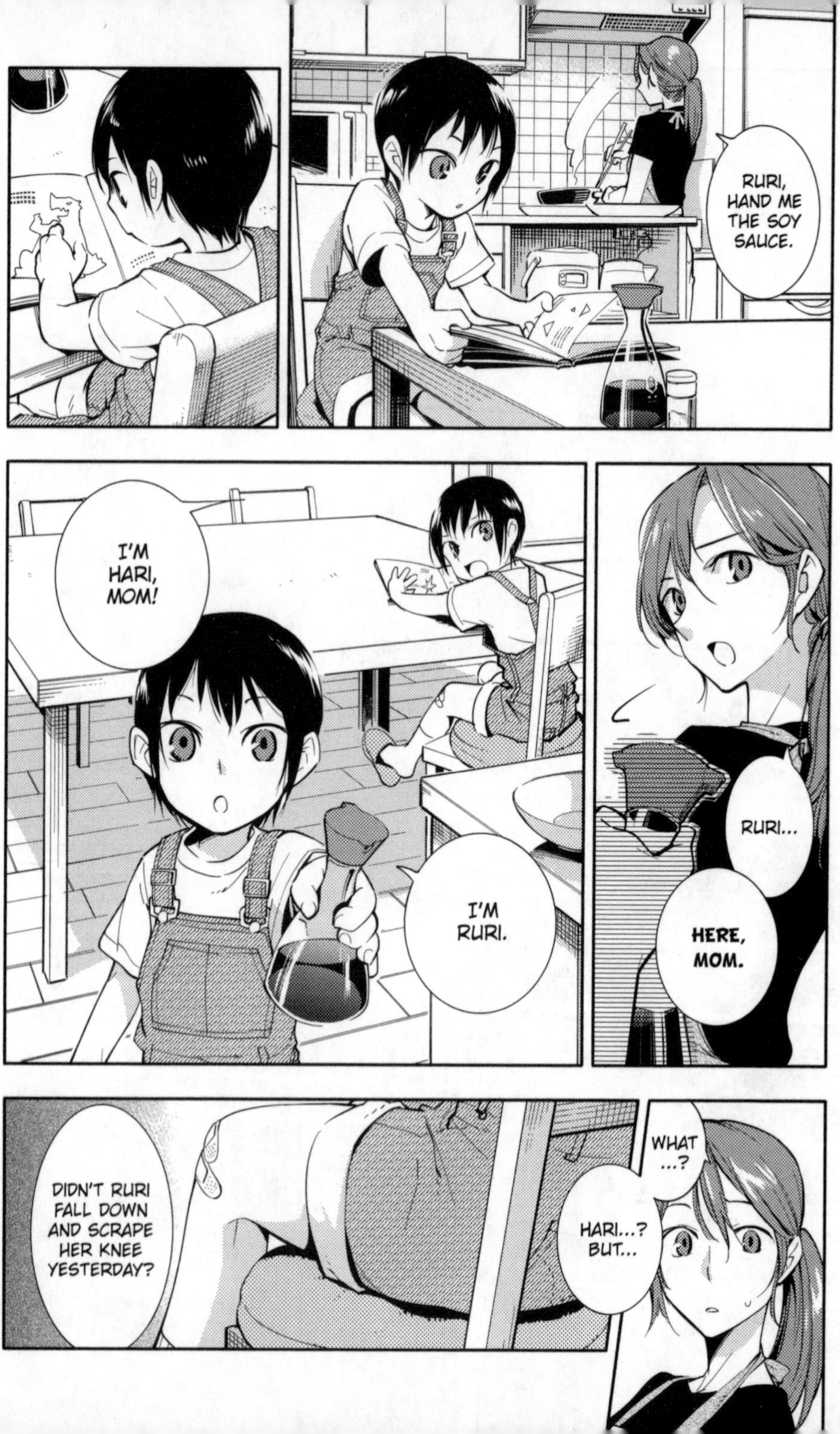
RURI, HAND ME THE SOY SAUCE.
RURI...
HERE, MOM.
I'M HARI, MOM!
I'M RURI.
WHAT ...?
HARI...? BUT...
DIDN'T RURI FALL DOWN AND SCRAPE HER KNEE YESTERDAY?

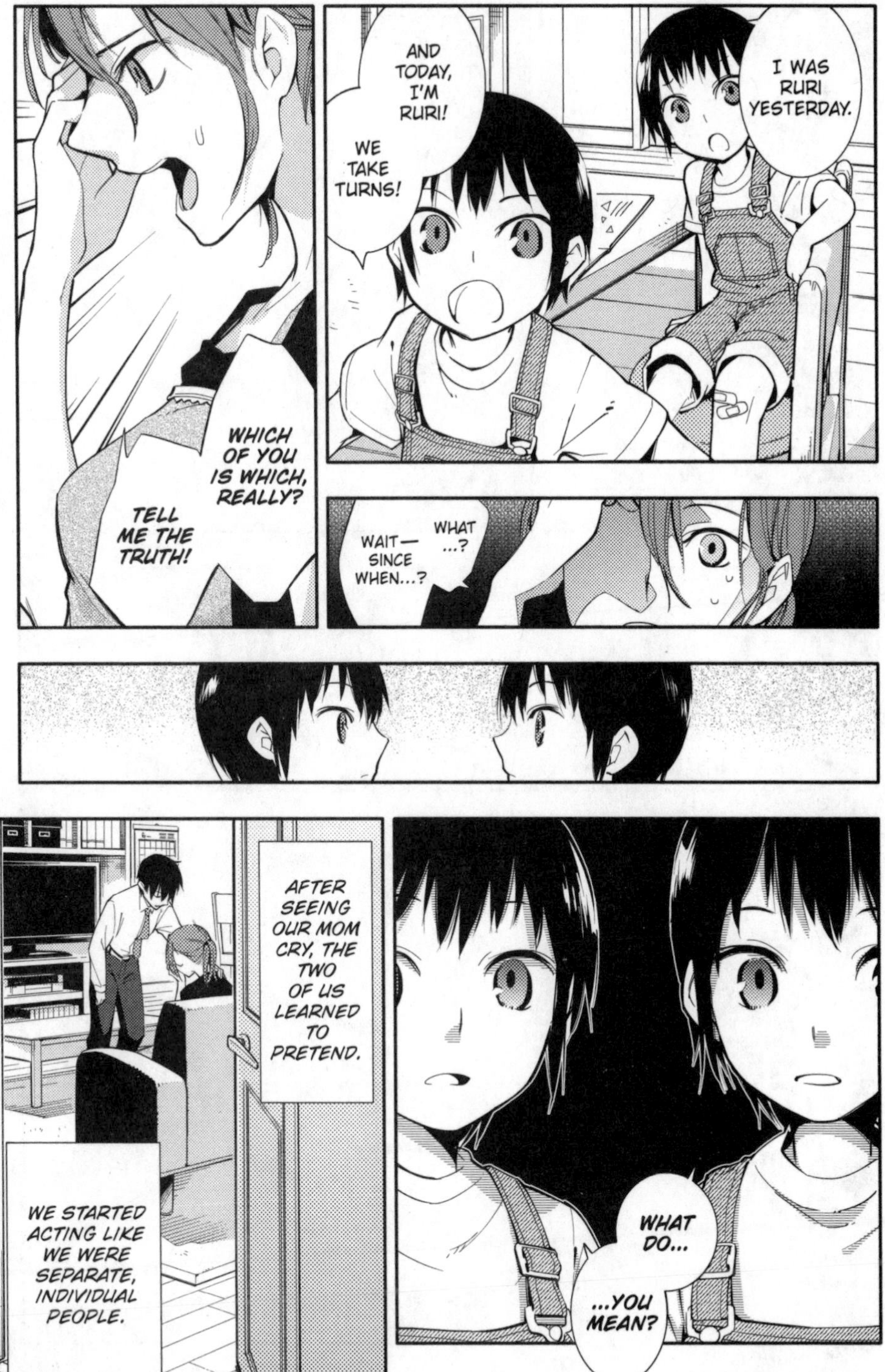
I WAS RURI YESTERDAY.
AND TODAY, I'M RURI!
WE TAKE TURNS!
WHAT ...?
WAIT— SINCE WHEN...?
WHICH OF YOU IS WHICH, REALLY?
TELL ME THE TRUTH!
WHAT DO...
...YOU MEAN?
AFTER SEEING OUR MOM CRY, THE TWO OF US LEARNED TO PRETEND.
WE STARTED ACTING LIKE WE WERE SEPARATE, INDIVIDUAL PEOPLE.

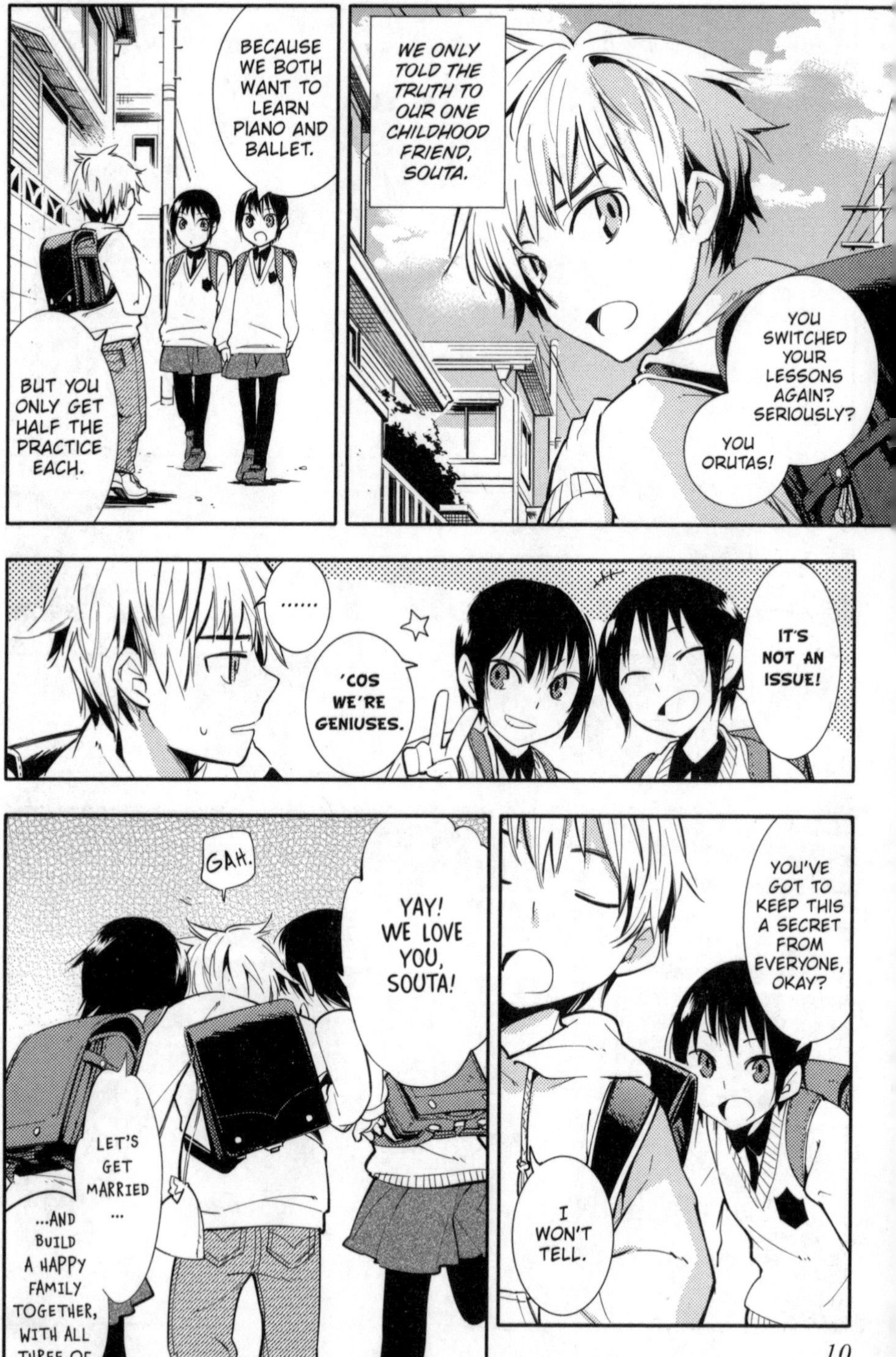
WE ONLY TOLD THE TRUTH TO OUR ONE CHILDHOOD FRIEND, SOUTA.
YOU SWITCHED YOUR LESSONS AGAIN? SERIOUSLY?
YOU ORUTAS!
BECAUSE WE BOTH WANT TO LEARN PIANO AND BALLET.
BUT YOU ONLY GET HALF THE PRACTICE EACH.
IT'S NOT AN ISSUE!
'COS WE'RE GENIUSES.
......
YOU'VE GOT TO KEEP THIS A SECRET FROM EVERYONE, OKAY?
I WON'T TELL.
YAY! WE LOVE YOU, SOUTA!
GAH.
LET'S GET MARRIED...
...AND BUILD A HAPPY FAMILY TOGETHER, WITH ALL THREE OF US!

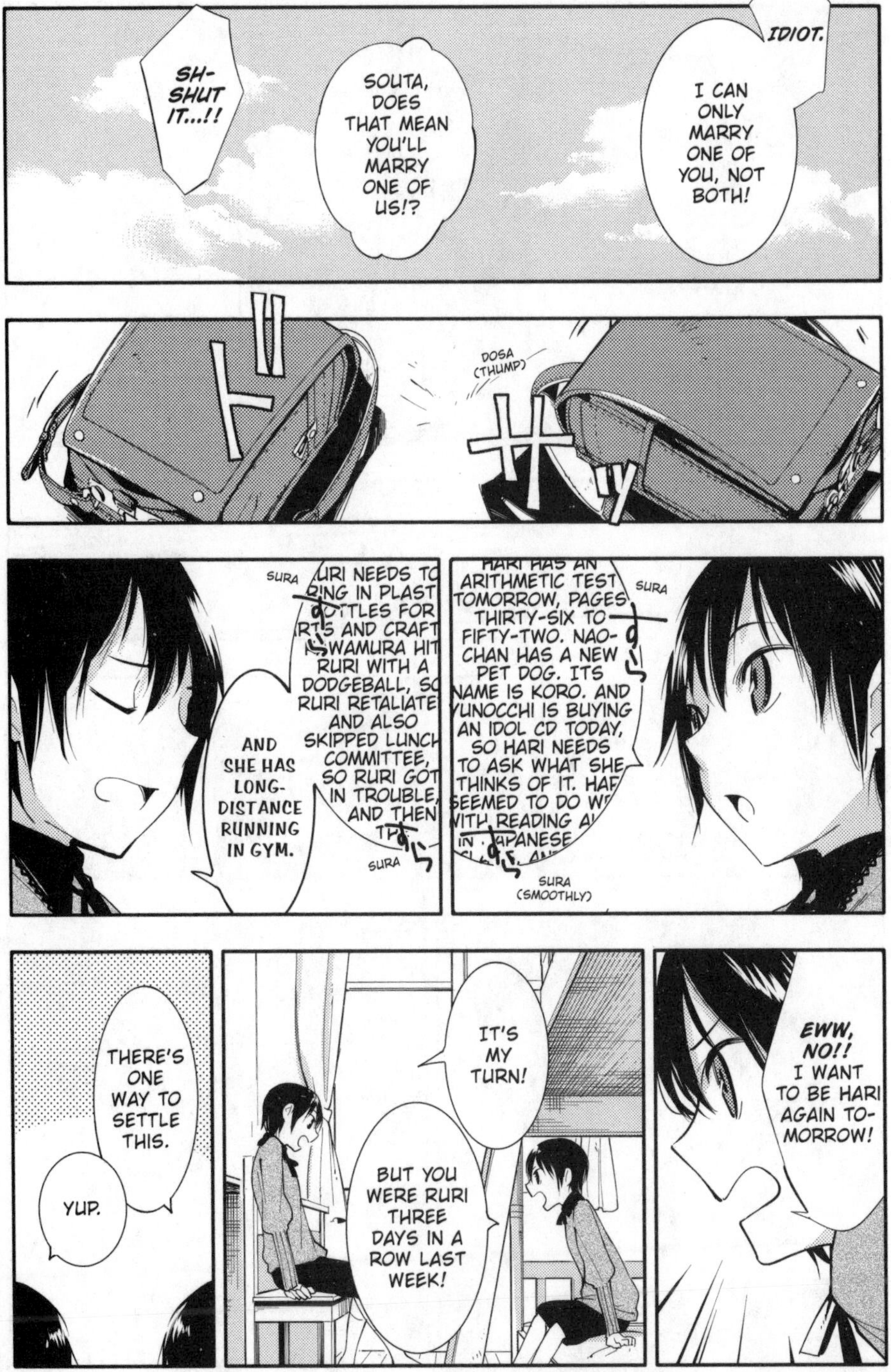
IDIOT.
I CAN ONLY MARRY ONE OF YOU, NOT BOTH!
SOUTA, DOES THAT MEAN YOU'LL MARRY ONE OF US!?
SH-SHUT IT...!!
DOSA (THUMP)
SURA
HARI HAS AN ARITHMETIC TEST TOMORROW, PAGES THIRTY-SIX TO FIFTY-TWO. NAO-CHAN HAS A NEW PET DOG. ITS NAME IS KORO. AND YUNOCCHI IS BUYING AN IDOL CD TODAY, SO HARI NEEDS TO ASK WHAT SHE THINKS OF IT.
SURA (SMOOTHLY)
SURA
RURI NEEDS TO
RURI WITH A DODGEBALL, SO
AND ALSO SKIPPED LUNCH COMMITTEE, SO RURI GOT IN TROUBLE, AND THEN
SURA
AND SHE HAS LONG-DISTANCE RUNNING IN GYM.
EWW, NO!! I WANT TO BE HARI AGAIN TO-MORROW!
IT'S MY TURN!
BUT YOU WERE RURI THREE DAYS IN A ROW LAST WEEK!
THERE'S ONE WAY TO SETTLE THIS.
YUP.

HEADS, I'M HARI!

OKAY. TAILS, I AM.

PASHI (SLAP)

PIN (FLICK)

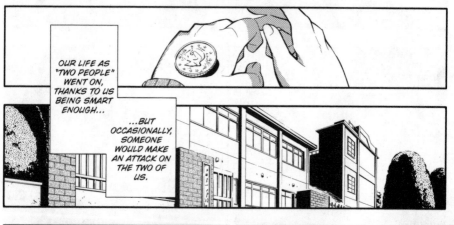

OUR LIFE AS "TWO PEOPLE" WENT ON, THANKS TO US BEING SMART ENOUGH...

...BUT OCCASIONALLY, SOMEONE WOULD MAKE AN ATTACK ON THE TWO OF US.

RURIKO

......

THERE. YOU'RE MUCH EASIER TO TELL APART NOW.

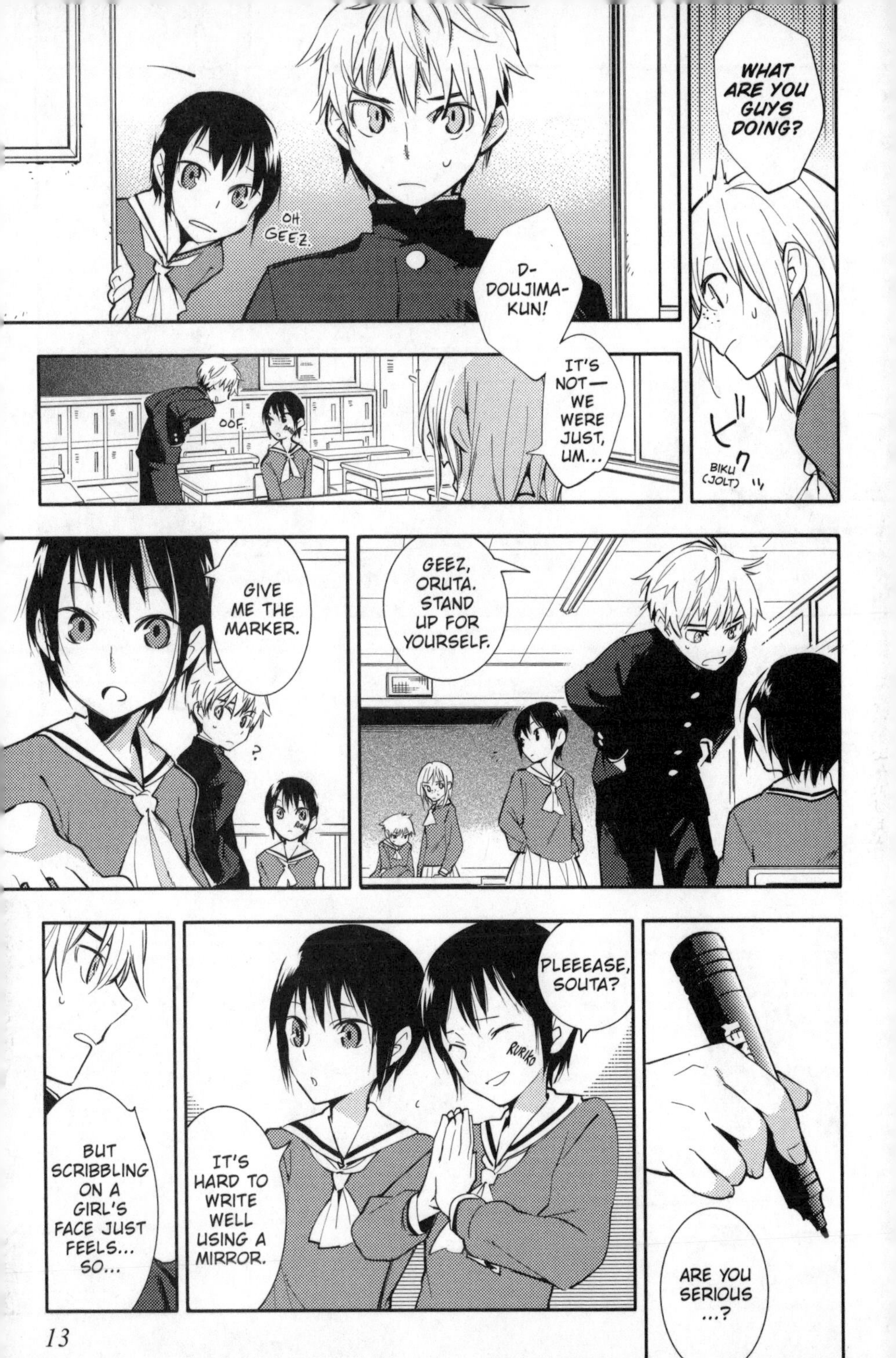
WHAT ARE YOU GUYS DOING?
BIKU (JOLT)
D-DOUJIMA-KUN!
OH GEEZ.
IT'S NOT— WE WERE JUST, UM...
OOF.
GEEZ, ORUTA. STAND UP FOR YOURSELF.
GIVE ME THE MARKER.
?
ARE YOU SERIOUS ...?
PLEEEASE, SOUTA?
RURIKO
IT'S HARD TO WRITE WELL USING A MIRROR.
BUT SCRIBBLING ON A GIRL'S FACE JUST FEELS... SO...

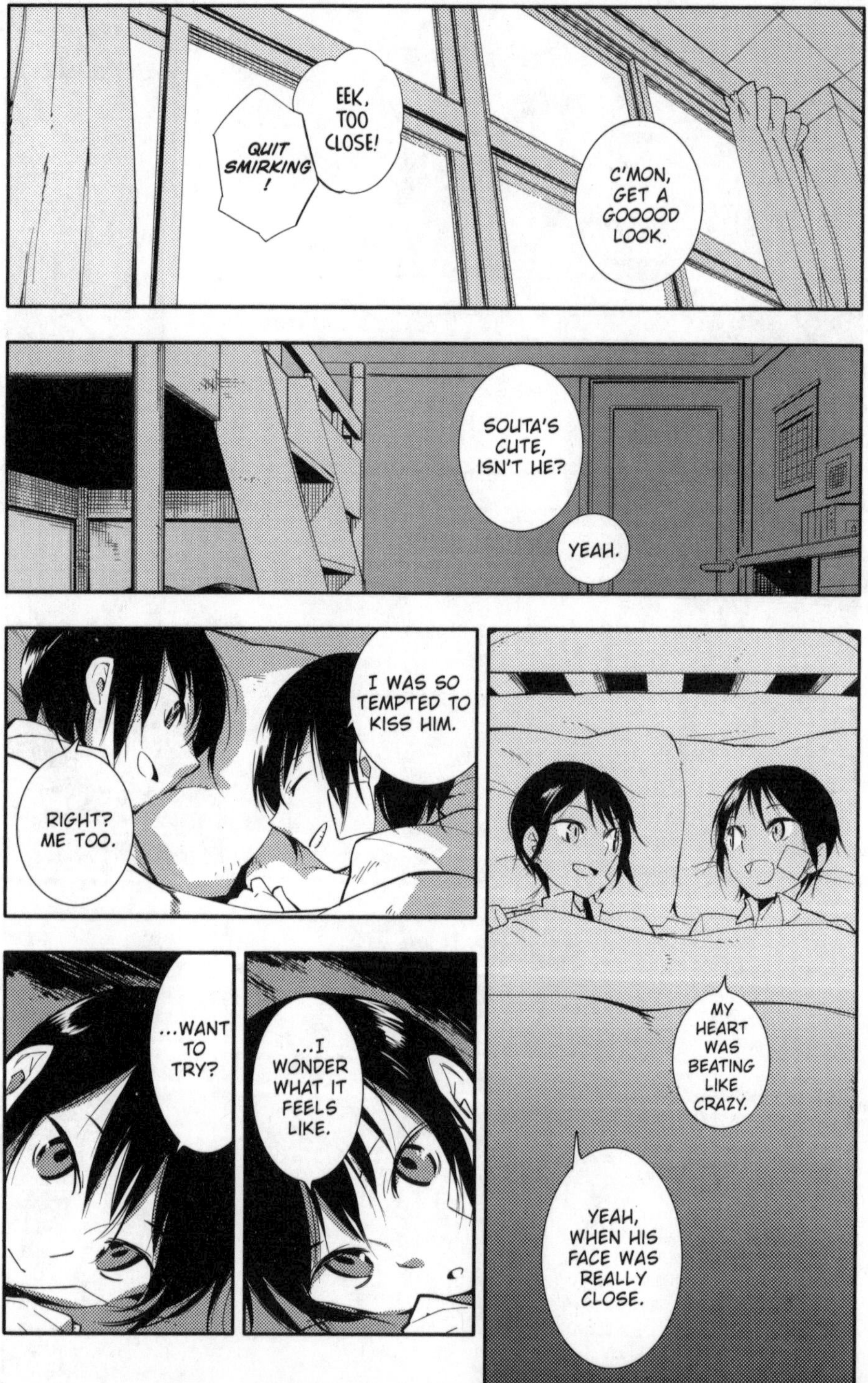
C'MON, GET A GOOOOD LOOK.
EEK, TOO CLOSE!
QUIT SMIRKING!
SOUTA'S CUTE, ISN'T HE?
YEAH.
MY HEART WAS BEATING LIKE CRAZY.
YEAH, WHEN HIS FACE WAS REALLY CLOSE.
I WAS SO TEMPTED TO KISS HIM.
RIGHT? ME TOO.
...I WONDER WHAT IT FEELS LIKE.
...WANT TO TRY?

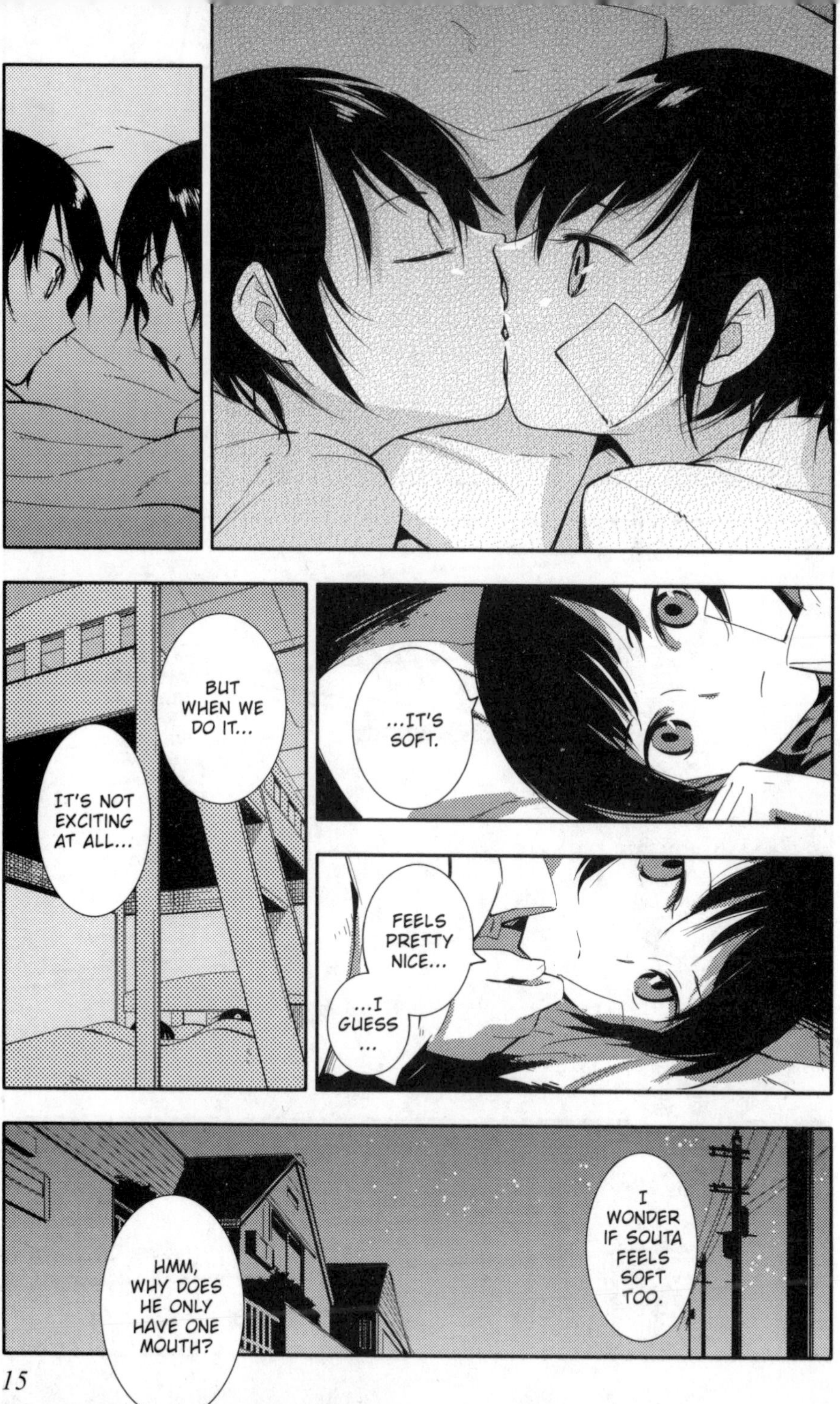
...IT'S SOFT.
FEELS PRETTY NICE...
...I GUESS ...
BUT WHEN WE DO IT...
IT'S NOT EXCITING AT ALL...
I WONDER IF SOUTA FEELS SOFT TOO.
HMM, WHY DOES HE ONLY HAVE ONE MOUTH?

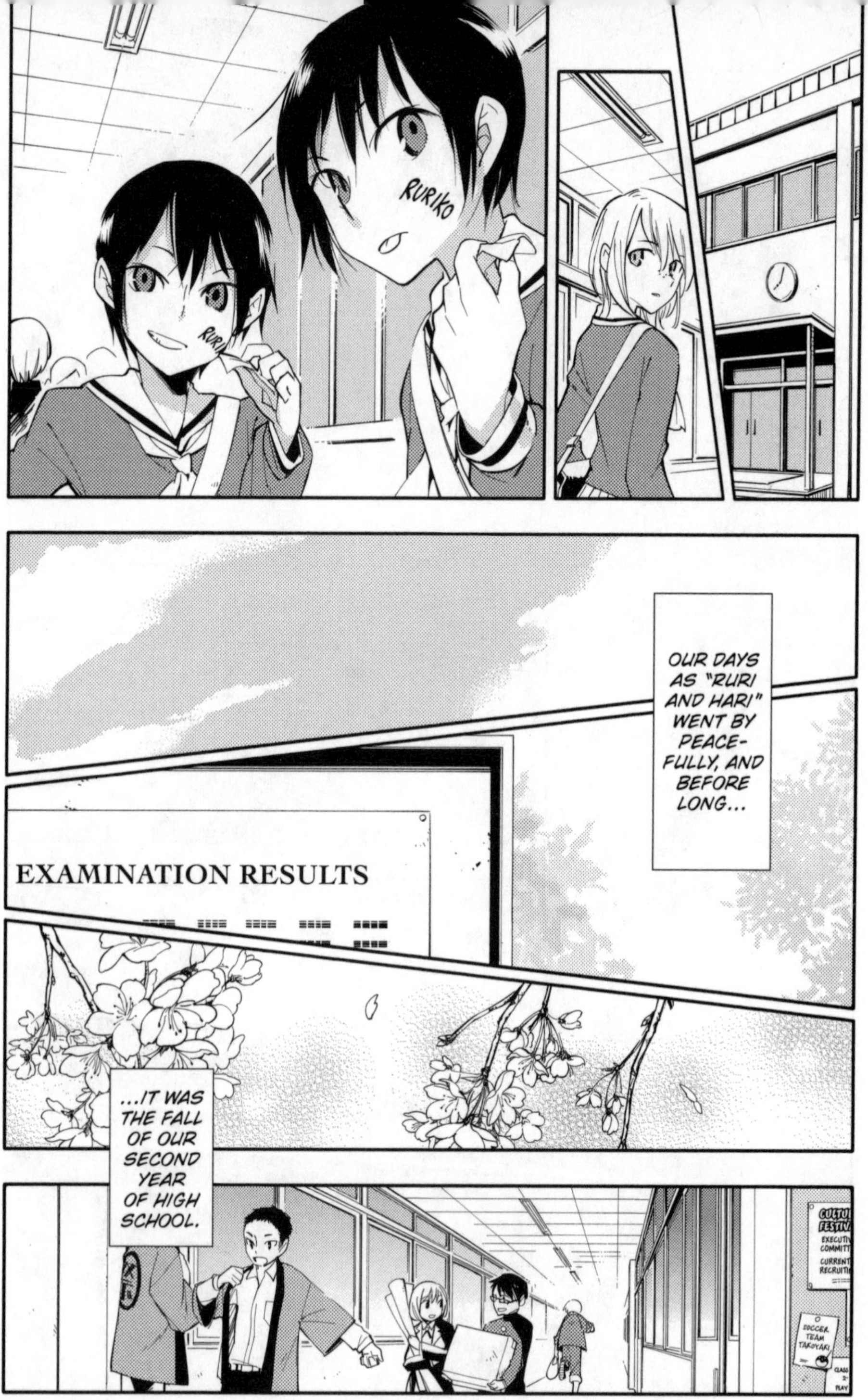
RURIKO
RURI
OUR DAYS AS "RURI AND HARI" WENT BY PEACE-FULLY, AND BEFORE LONG...
EXAMINATION RESULTS
...IT WAS THE FALL OF OUR SECOND YEAR OF HIGH SCHOOL.

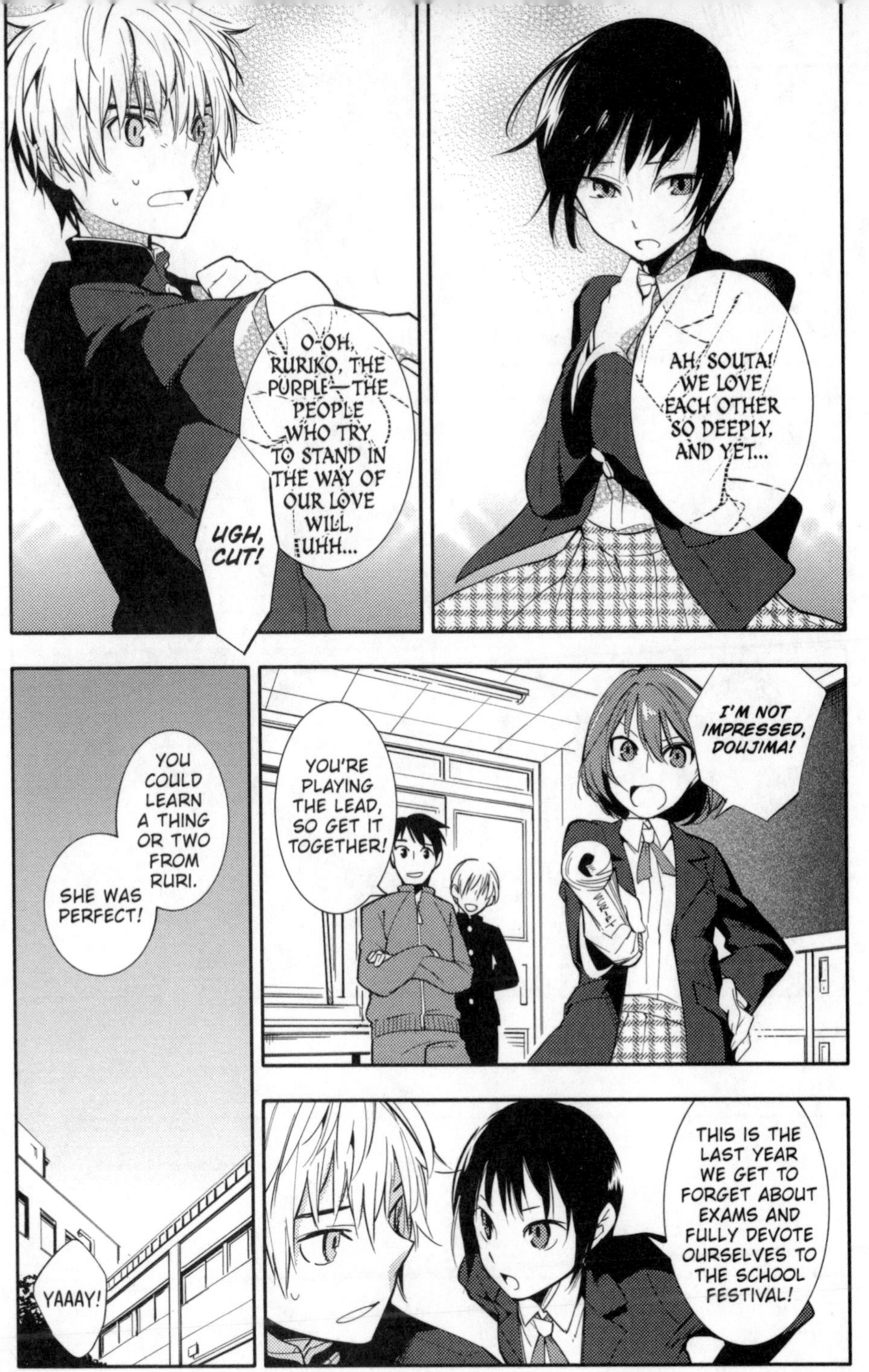
AH, SOUTA! WE LOVE EACH OTHER SO DEEPLY, AND YET...
O-OH, RURIKO, THE PURPLE—THE PEOPLE WHO TRY TO STAND IN THE WAY OF OUR LOVE WILL, UHH...
UGH, CUT!
I'M NOT IMPRESSED, DOUJIMA!
YOU'RE PLAYING THE LEAD, SO GET IT TOGETHER!
THIS IS THE LAST YEAR WE GET TO FORGET ABOUT EXAMS AND FULLY DEVOTE OURSELVES TO THE SCHOOL FESTIVAL!
YOU COULD LEARN A THING OR TWO FROM RURI.
SHE WAS PERFECT!
YAAAY!

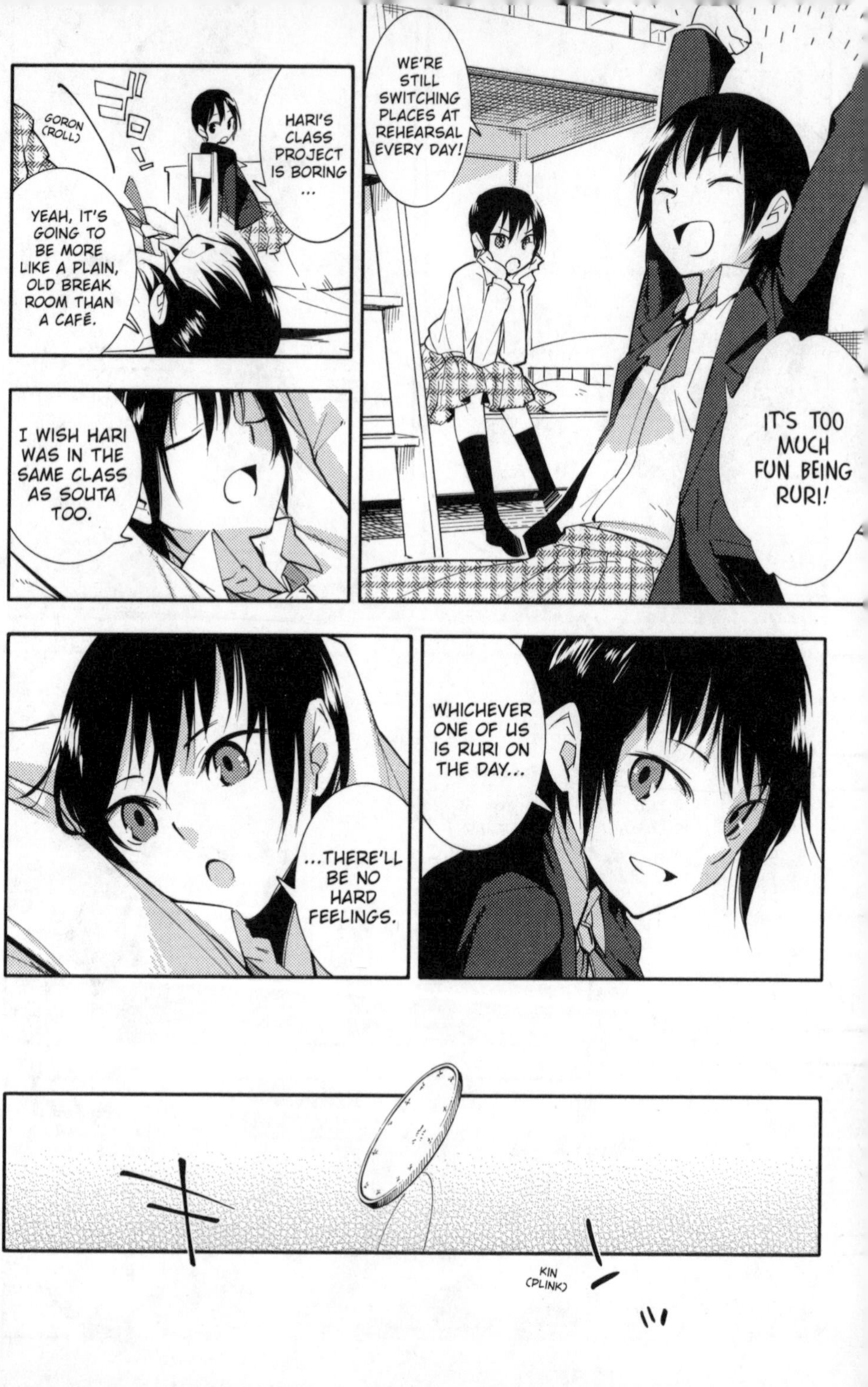
WE'RE STILL SWITCHING PLACES AT REHEARSAL EVERY DAY!
IT'S TOO MUCH FUN BEING RURI!
HARI'S CLASS PROJECT IS BORING ...
GORON (ROLL)
YEAH, IT'S GOING TO BE MORE LIKE A PLAIN, OLD BREAK ROOM THAN A CAFÉ.
I WISH HARI WAS IN THE SAME CLASS AS SOUTA TOO.
WHICHEVER ONE OF US IS RURI ON THE DAY...
...THERE'LL BE NO HARD FEELINGS.
KIN (PLINK)

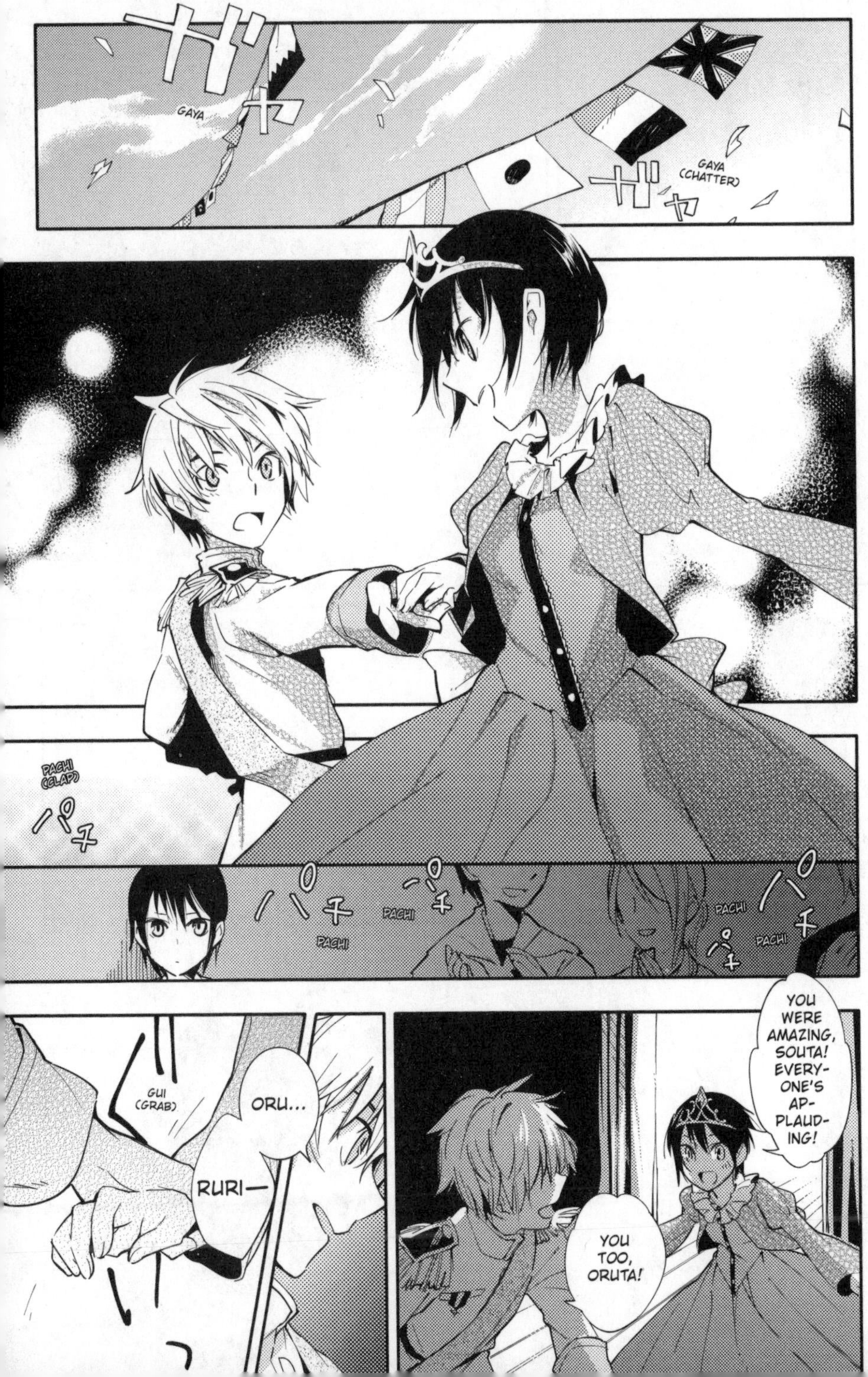
GAYA (CHATTER)
GAYA
PACHI (CLAP)
PACHI
PACHI
PACHI
PACHI
YOU WERE AMAZING, SOUTA! EVERYONE'S AP-PLAUD-ING!
YOU TOO, ORUTA!
ORU...
RURI—
GUI (GRAB)

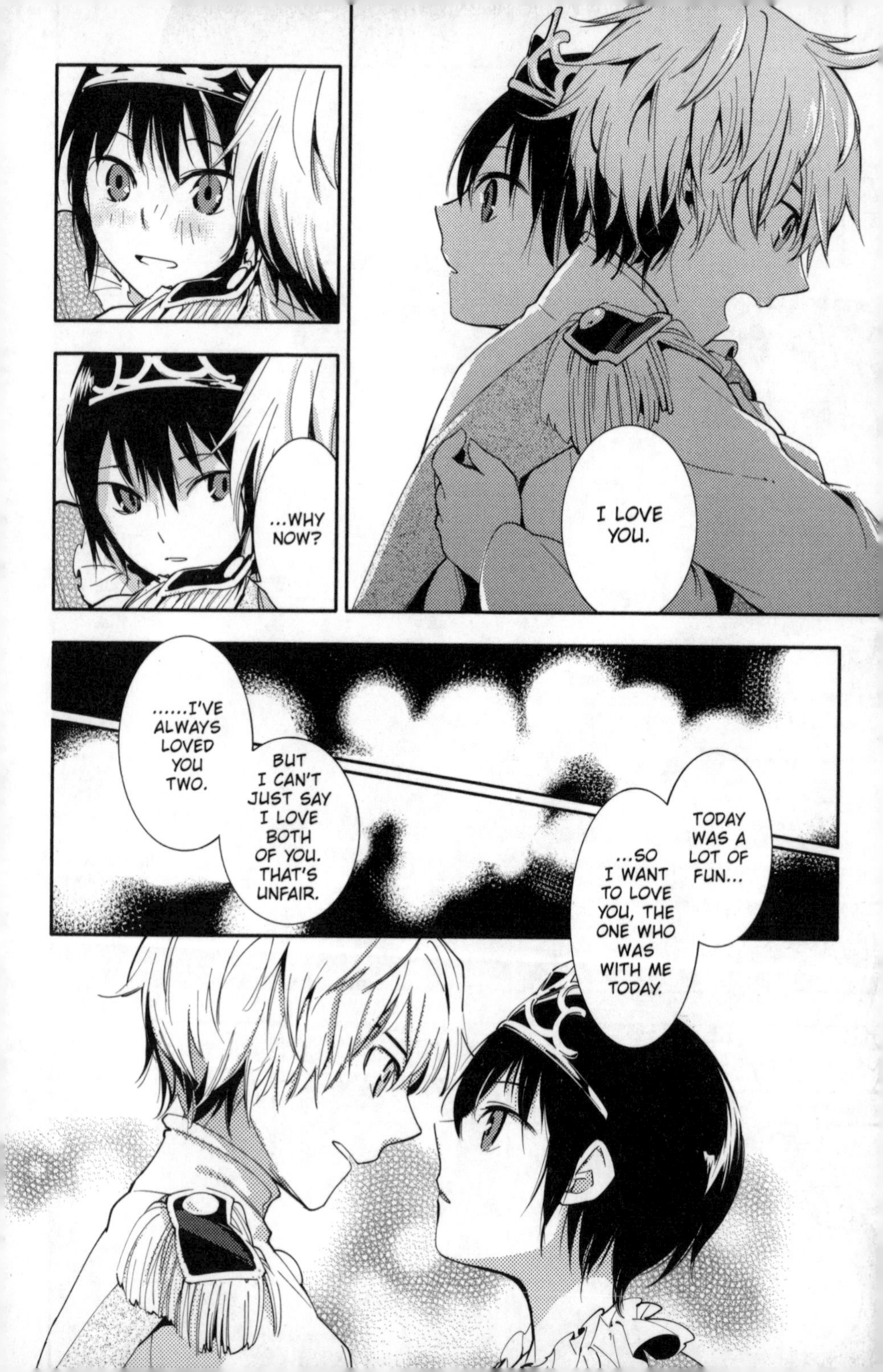
I LOVE YOU.
...WHY NOW?
......I'VE ALWAYS LOVED YOU TWO.
BUT I CAN'T JUST SAY I LOVE BOTH OF YOU. THAT'S UNFAIR.
TODAY WAS A LOT OF FUN...
...SO I WANT TO LOVE YOU, THE ONE WHO WAS WITH ME TODAY.

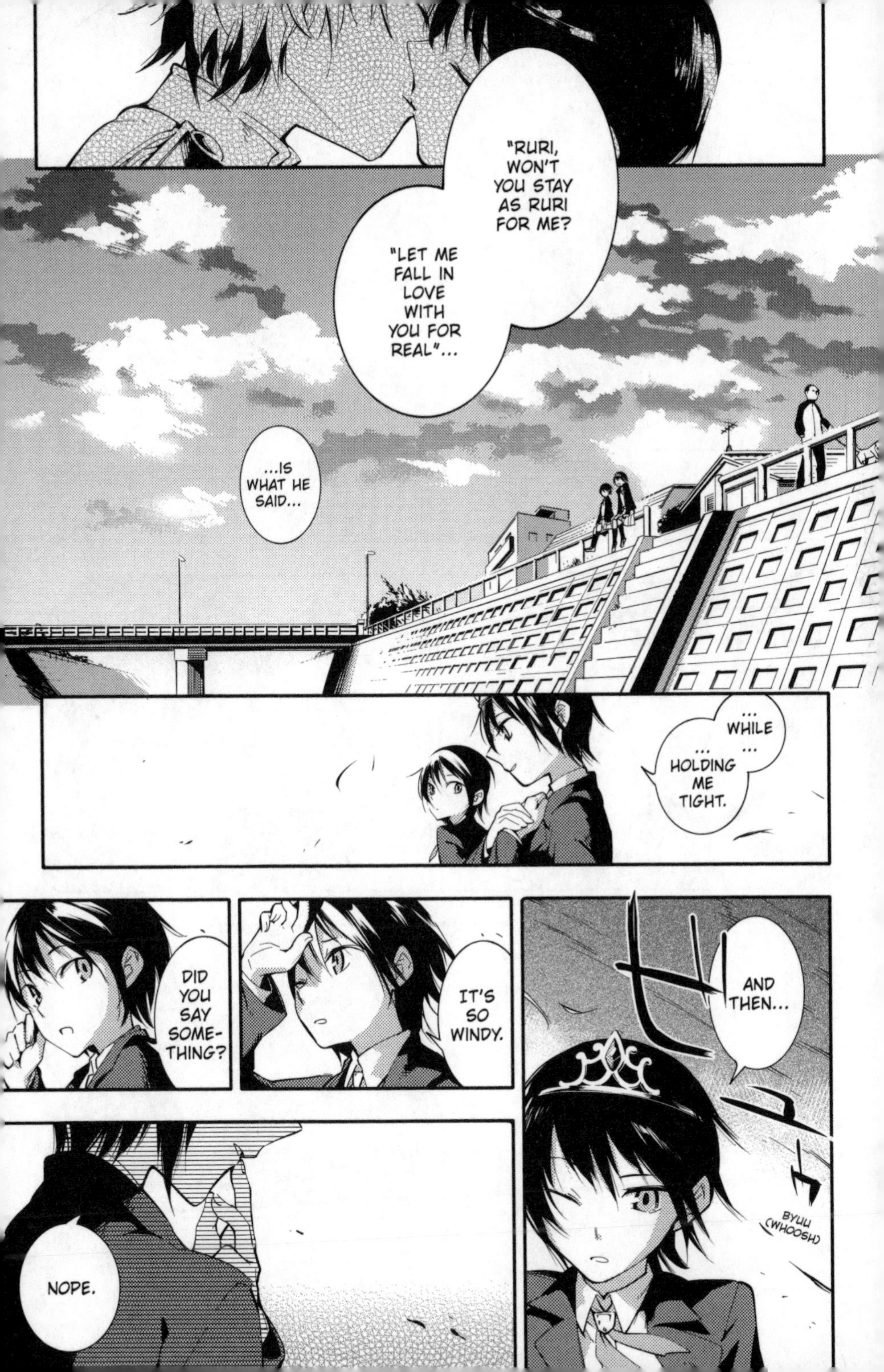
"RURI, WON'T YOU STAY AS RURI FOR ME?
"LET ME FALL IN LOVE WITH YOU FOR REAL"...
...IS WHAT HE SAID...
... WHILE ... ... HOLDING ME TIGHT.
AND THEN...
BYUU (WHOOSH)
IT'S SO WINDY.
DID YOU SAY SOME-THING?
NOPE.

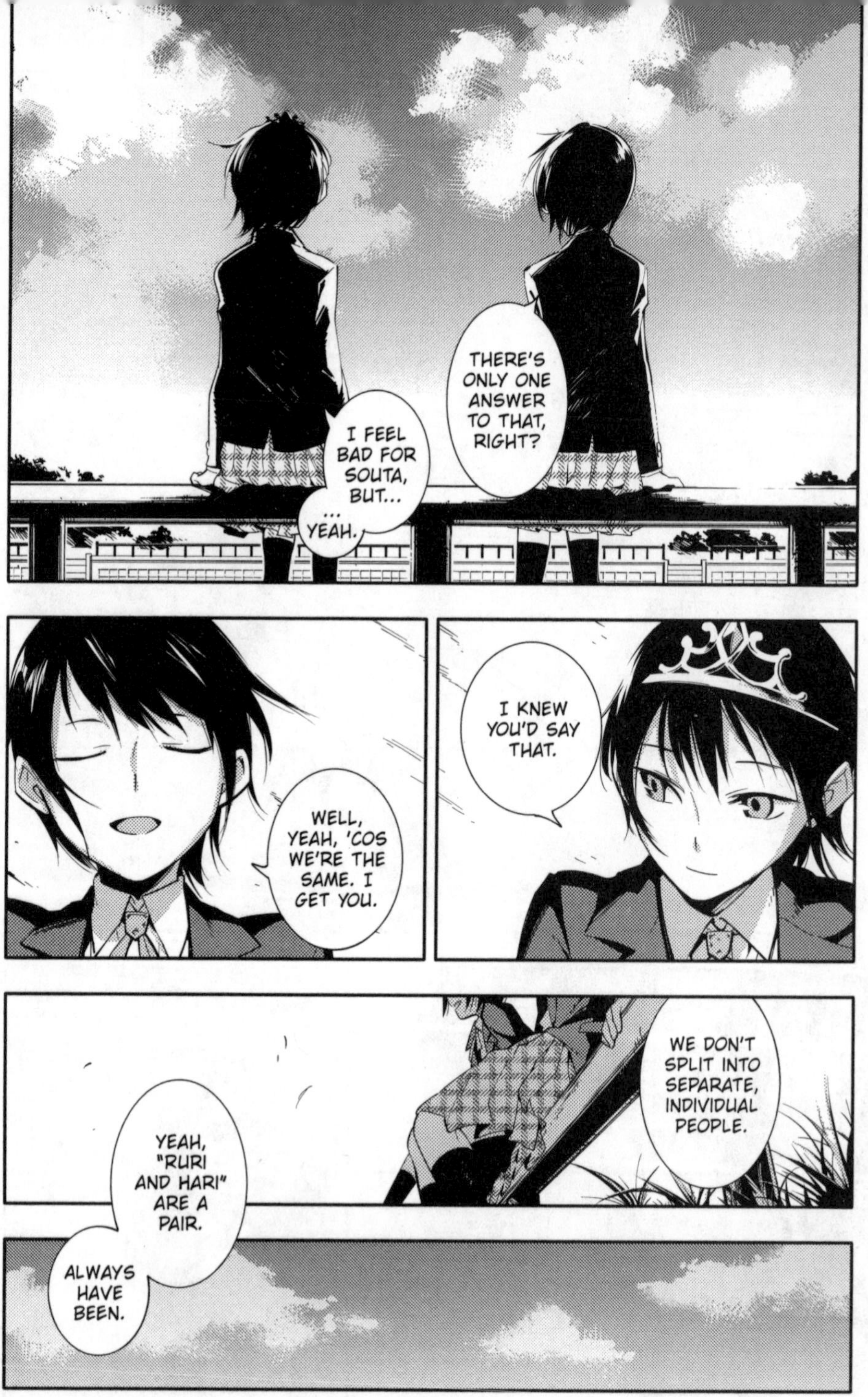
THERE'S ONLY ONE ANSWER TO THAT, RIGHT?
I FEEL BAD FOR SOUTA, BUT...
... YEAH.
I KNEW YOU'D SAY THAT.
WELL, YEAH, 'COS WE'RE THE SAME. I GET YOU.
WE DON'T SPLIT INTO SEPARATE, INDIVIDUAL PEOPLE.
YEAH, "RURI AND HARI" ARE A PAIR.
ALWAYS HAVE BEEN.

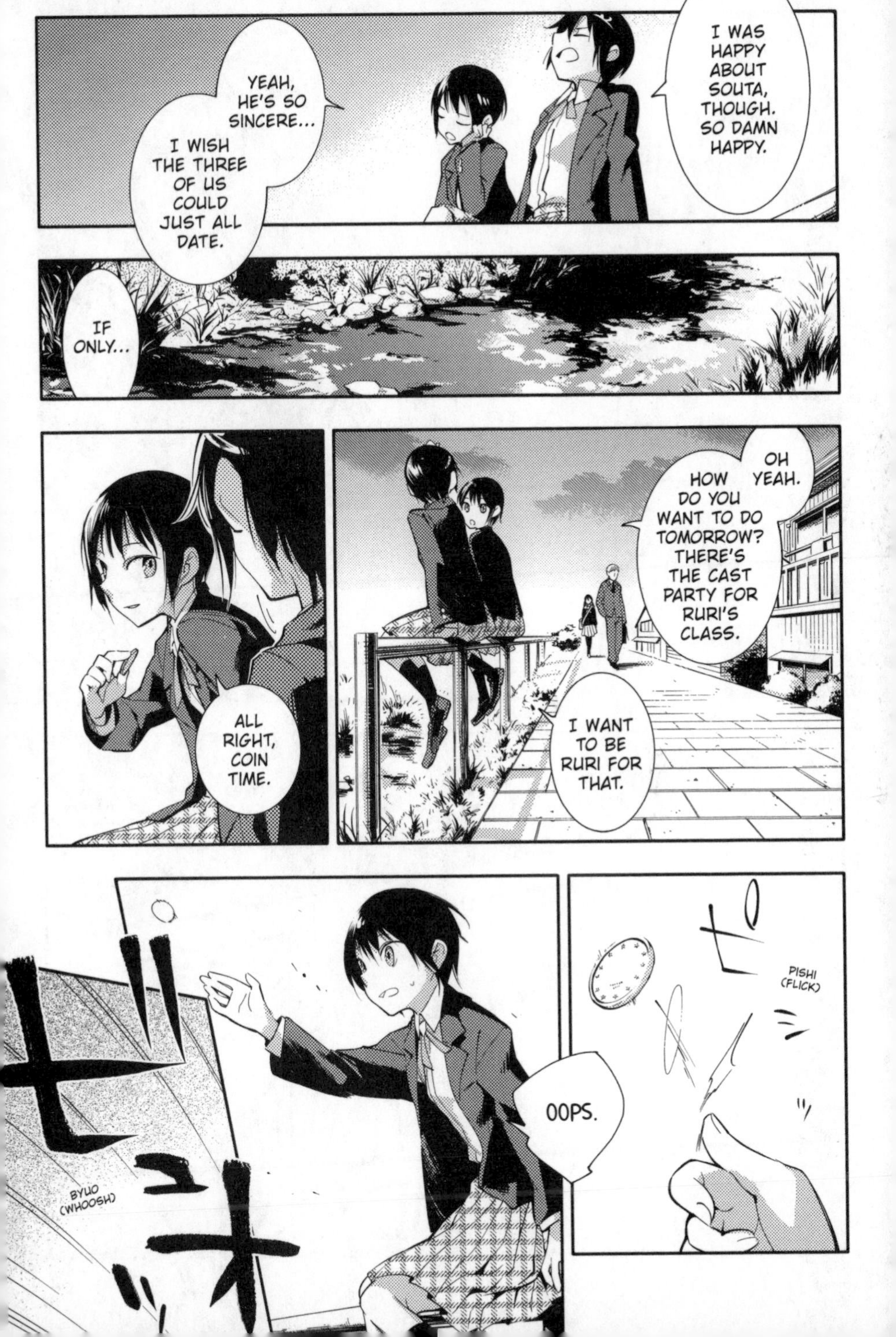
I WAS HAPPY ABOUT SOUTA, THOUGH. SO DAMN HAPPY.
YEAH, HE'S SO SINCERE...
I WISH THE THREE OF US COULD JUST ALL DATE.
IF ONLY...
OH YEAH. HOW DO YOU WANT TO DO TOMORROW? THERE'S THE CAST PARTY FOR RURI'S CLASS.
I WANT TO BE RURI FOR THAT.
ALL RIGHT, COIN TIME.
PISHI (FLICK)
OOPS.
BYUO (WHOOSH)

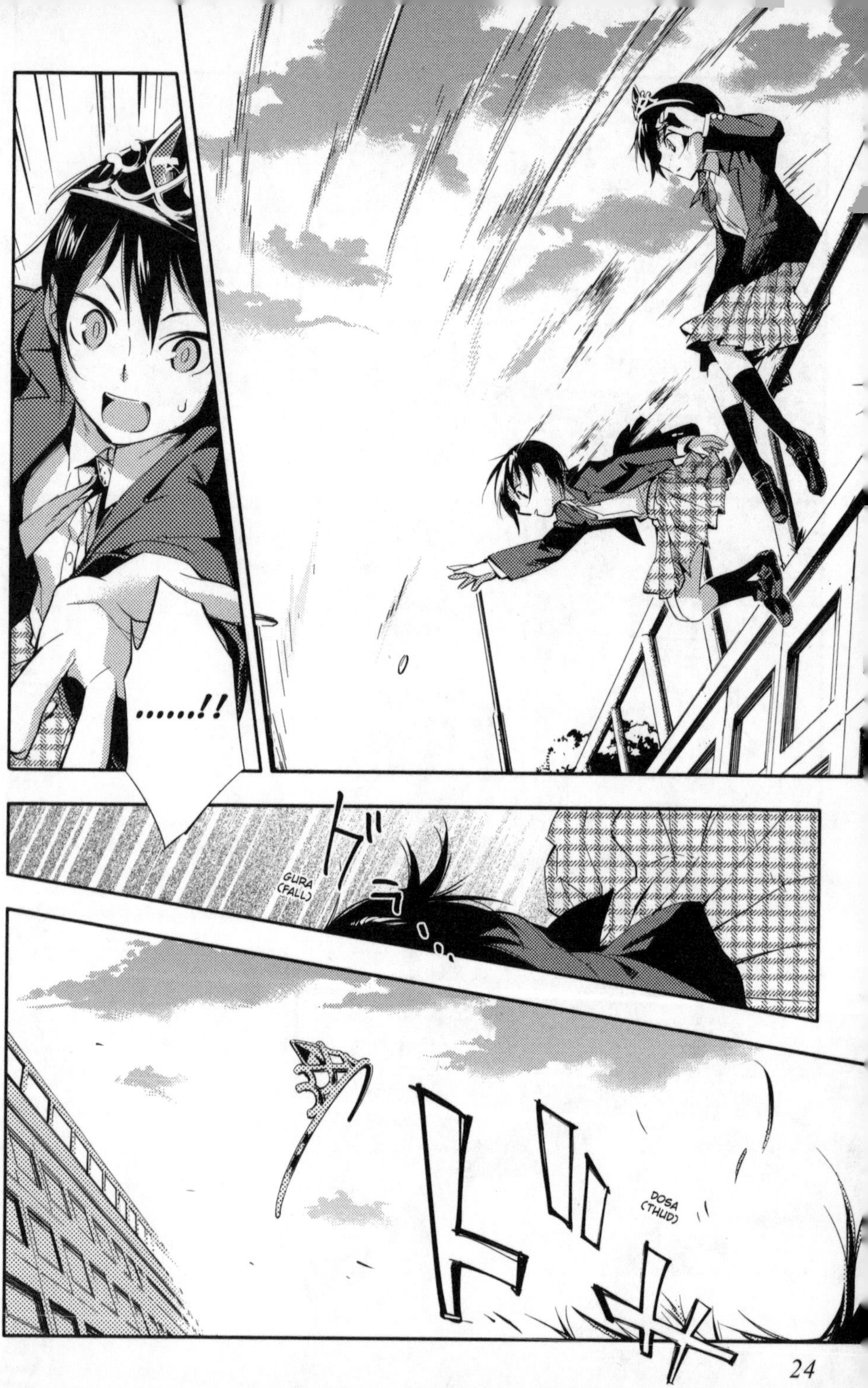
......!!
GURA (FALL)
DOSA (THUD)

OW...
YOU OKAY?
MUKURI (TURN)
むくり
HUH?

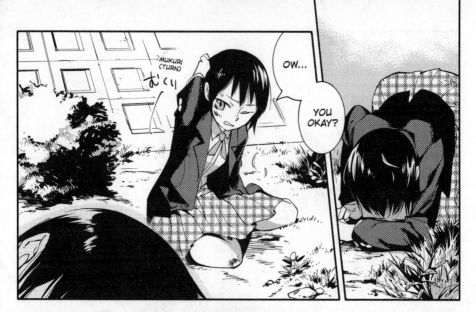

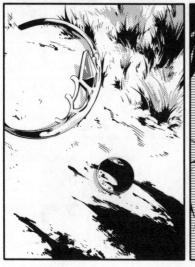

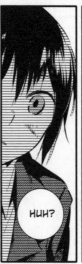

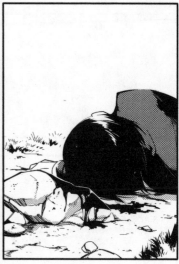

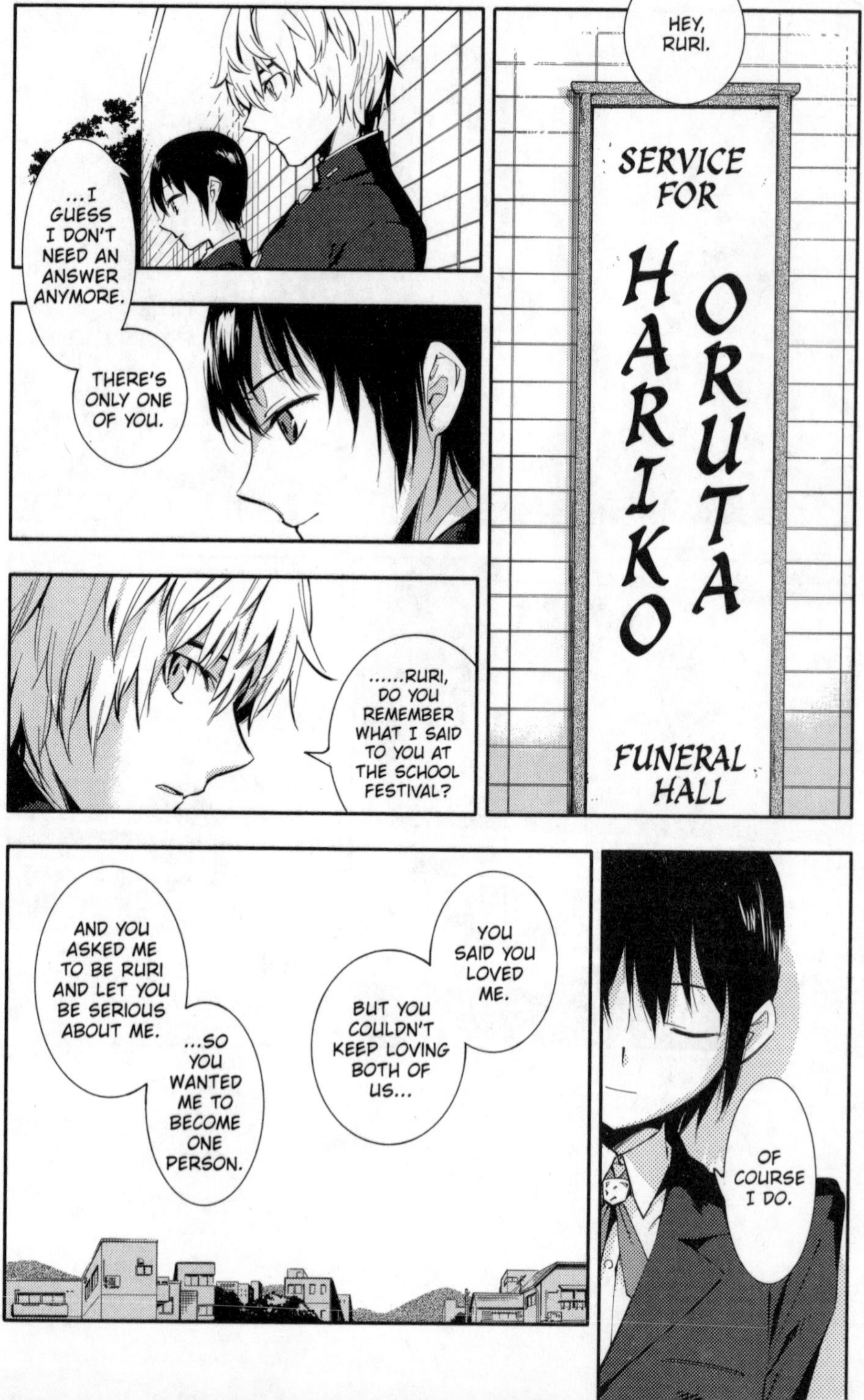
HEY, RURI.
SERVICE FOR HARIKO ORUTA FUNERAL HALL
...I GUESS I DON'T NEED AN ANSWER ANYMORE.
THERE'S ONLY ONE OF YOU.
......RURI, DO YOU REMEMBER WHAT I SAID TO YOU AT THE SCHOOL FESTIVAL?
OF COURSE I DO.
YOU SAID YOU LOVED ME.
BUT YOU COULDN'T KEEP LOVING BOTH OF US...
AND YOU ASKED ME TO BE RURI AND LET YOU BE SERIOUS ABOUT ME.
...SO YOU WANTED ME TO BECOME ONE PERSON.

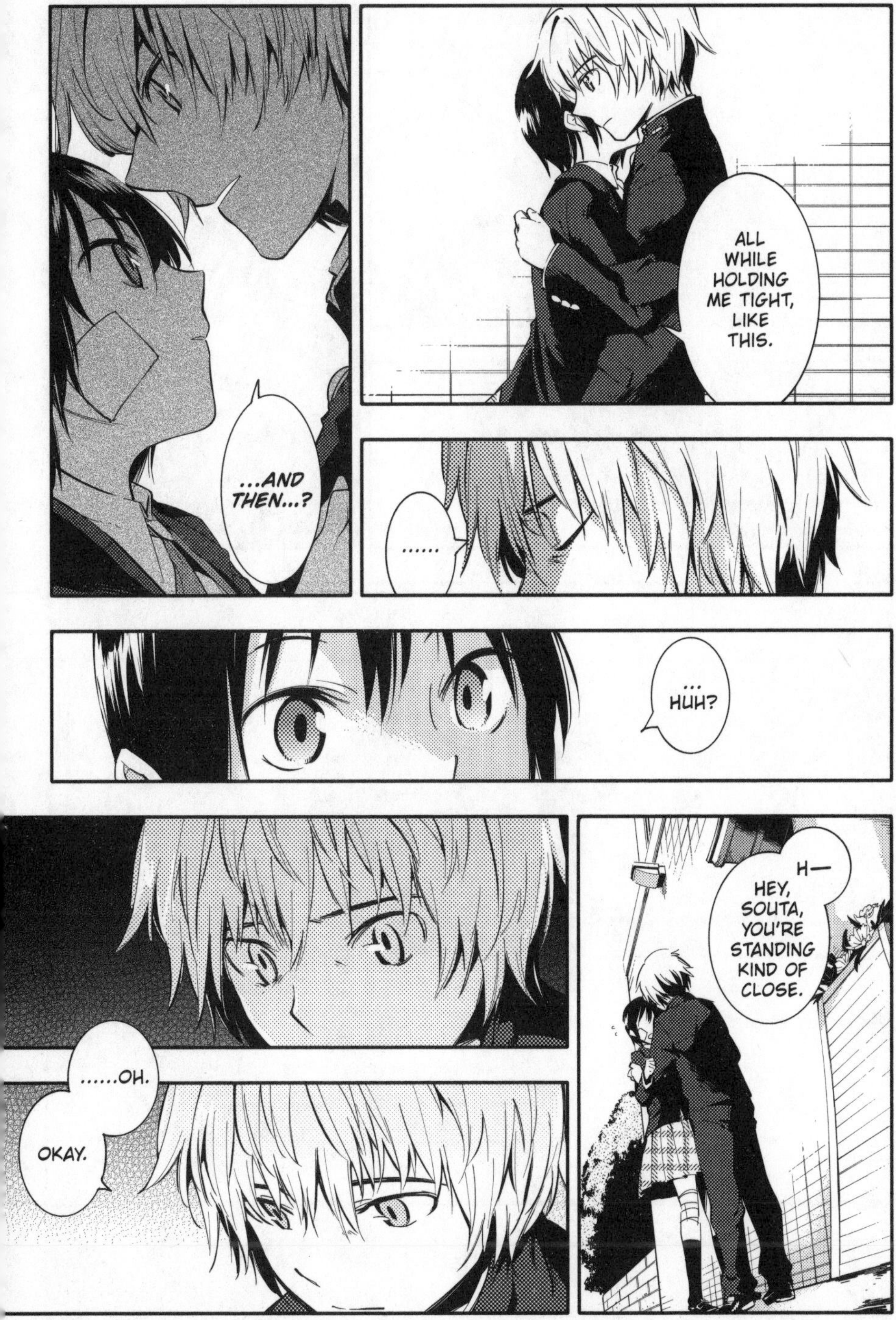
ALL WHILE HOLDING ME TIGHT, LIKE THIS.
......
...AND THEN...?
... HUH?
H— HEY, SOUTA, YOU'RE STANDING KIND OF CLOSE.
......OH.
OKAY.

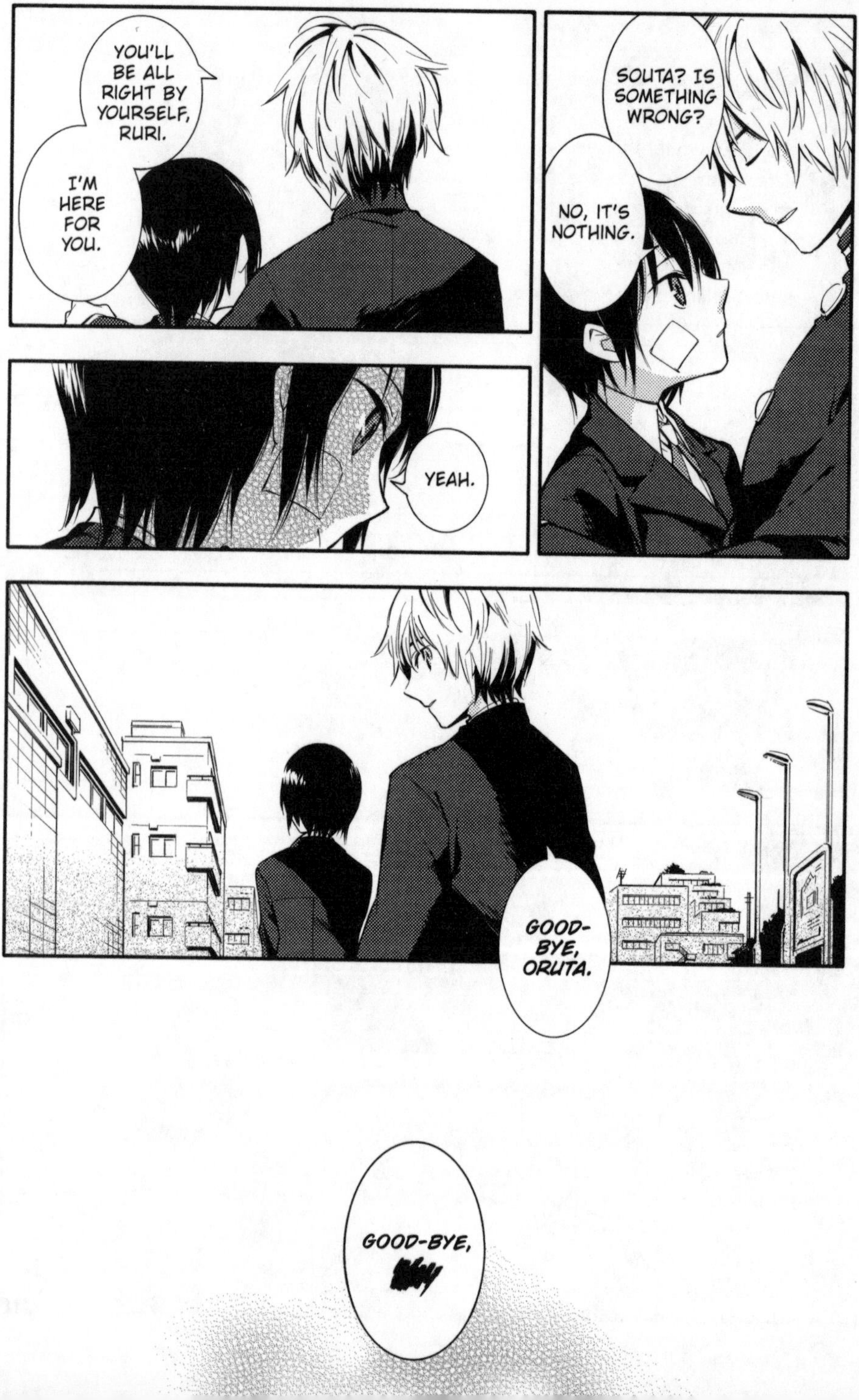
SOUTA? IS SOMETHING WRONG?
NO, IT'S NOTHING.
YOU'LL BE ALL RIGHT BY YOURSELF, RURI.
I'M HERE FOR YOU.
YEAH.
GOOD-BYE, ORUTA.
GOOD-BYE,

【Farewell to My Alter】

I originally published this manga as a doujinshi and then
later submitted it to the Dengeki Awards, making this
my commercial debut. I had previously written several
volumes of original manga to post online, but *Alter* was
the first to be read by the general public. My series *Bloom
Into You* also deals with the idea of a person trying to
become someone else, so perhaps that theme is somehow
important to me.

Initial release: *Dengeki Daioh*, October 2014 issue
Original version initial release: author's doujinshi (published February 3, 2013)

Translation Note:

Page 16
Takoyaki are cooked balls of batter that are traditionally filled with
pieces of octopus. They started off as popular type of street food
and are often sold at festivals and events that have food stalls,
including high school culture festivals.

Page 29
Doujinshi is the Japanese term for self-published comics, including
both fan comics and original stories.

Farewell to My Alter

NIO NAKATANI SHORT STORY COLLECTION

The Hero Saves the World Three Times

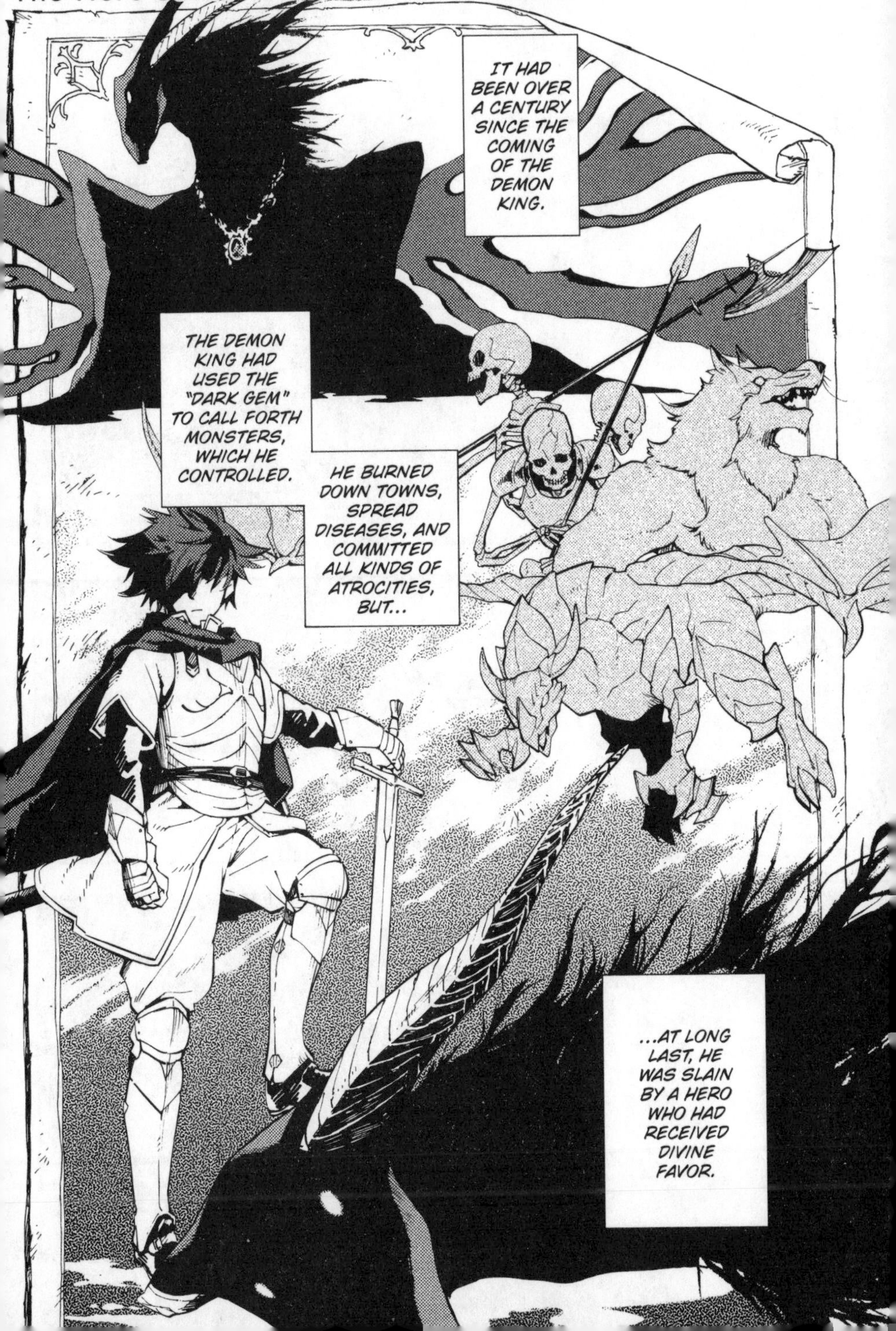
IT HAD BEEN OVER A CENTURY SINCE THE COMING OF THE DEMON KING.
THE DEMON KING HAD USED THE "DARK GEM" TO CALL FORTH MONSTERS, WHICH HE CONTROLLED.
HE BURNED DOWN TOWNS, SPREAD DISEASES, AND COMMITTED ALL KINDS OF ATROCITIES, BUT...
...AT LONG LAST, HE WAS SLAIN BY A HERO WHO HAD RECEIVED DIVINE FAVOR.

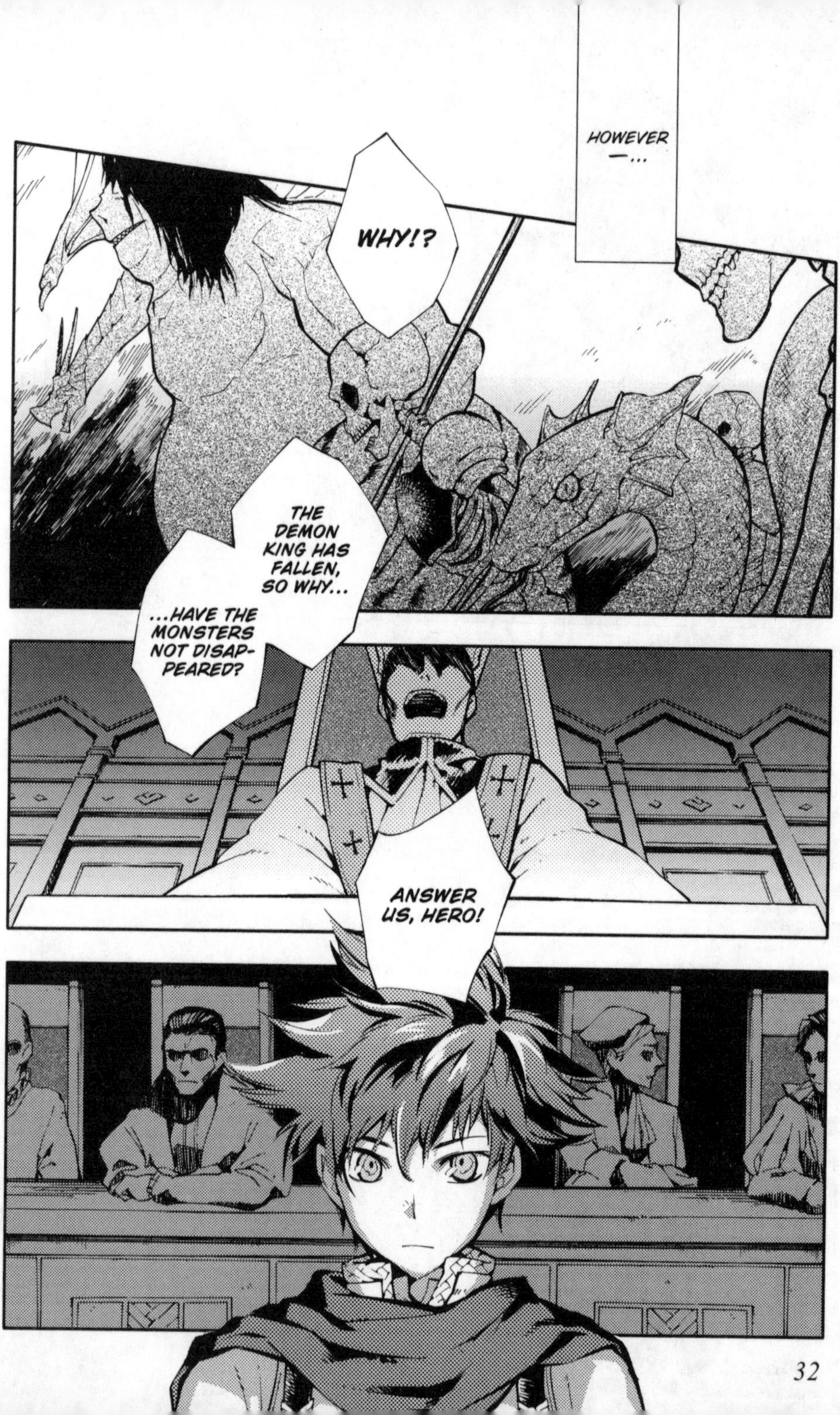
HOWEVER —...
WHY!?
THE DEMON KING HAS FALLEN, SO WHY...
...HAVE THE MONSTERS NOT DISAP-PEARED?
ANSWER US, HERO!

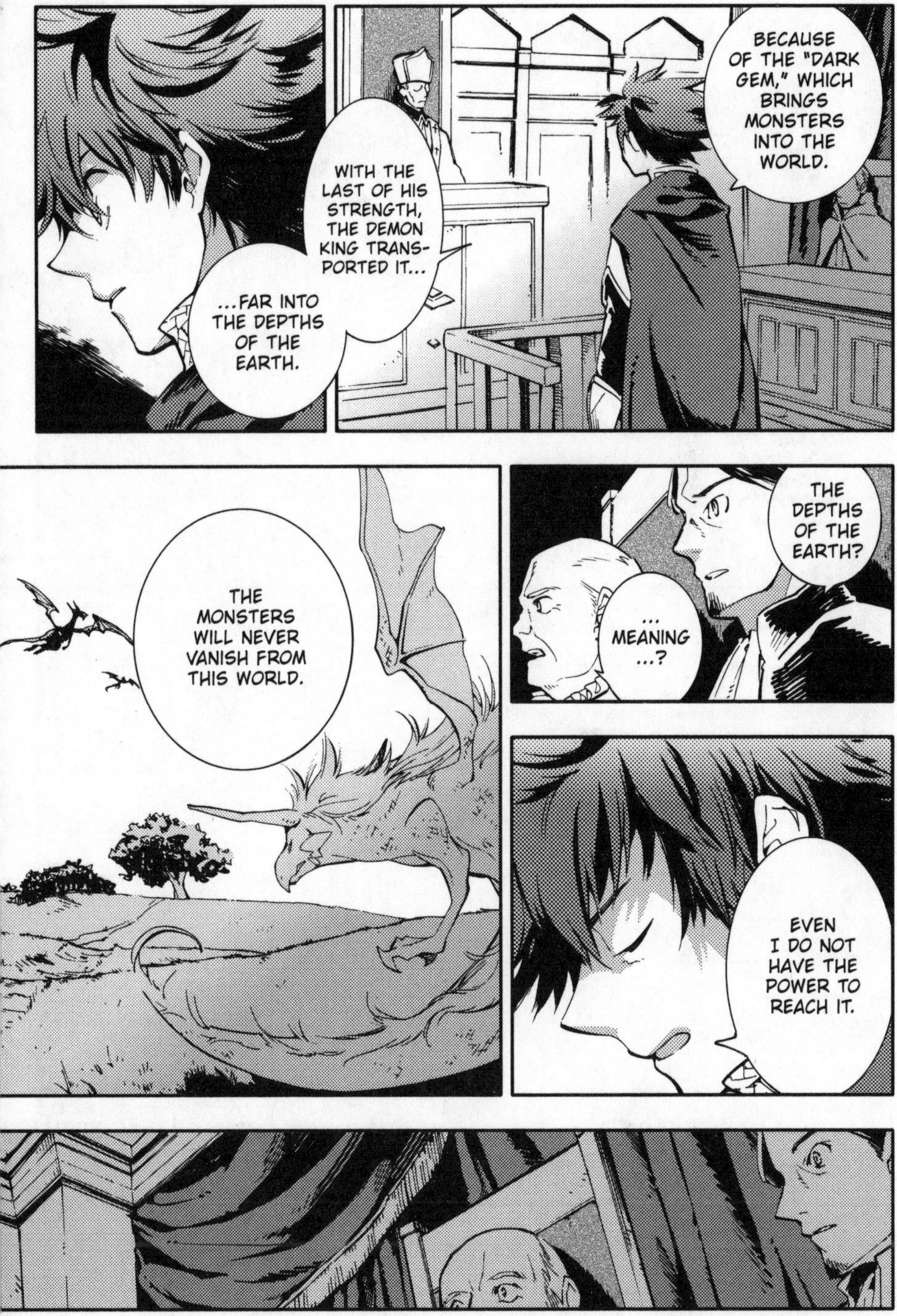
BECAUSE OF THE "DARK GEM," WHICH BRINGS MONSTERS INTO THE WORLD.
WITH THE LAST OF HIS STRENGTH, THE DEMON KING TRANSPORTED IT...
...FAR INTO THE DEPTHS OF THE EARTH.
THE DEPTHS OF THE EARTH?
...MEANING...?
EVEN I DO NOT HAVE THE POWER TO REACH IT.
THE MONSTERS WILL NEVER VANISH FROM THIS WORLD.

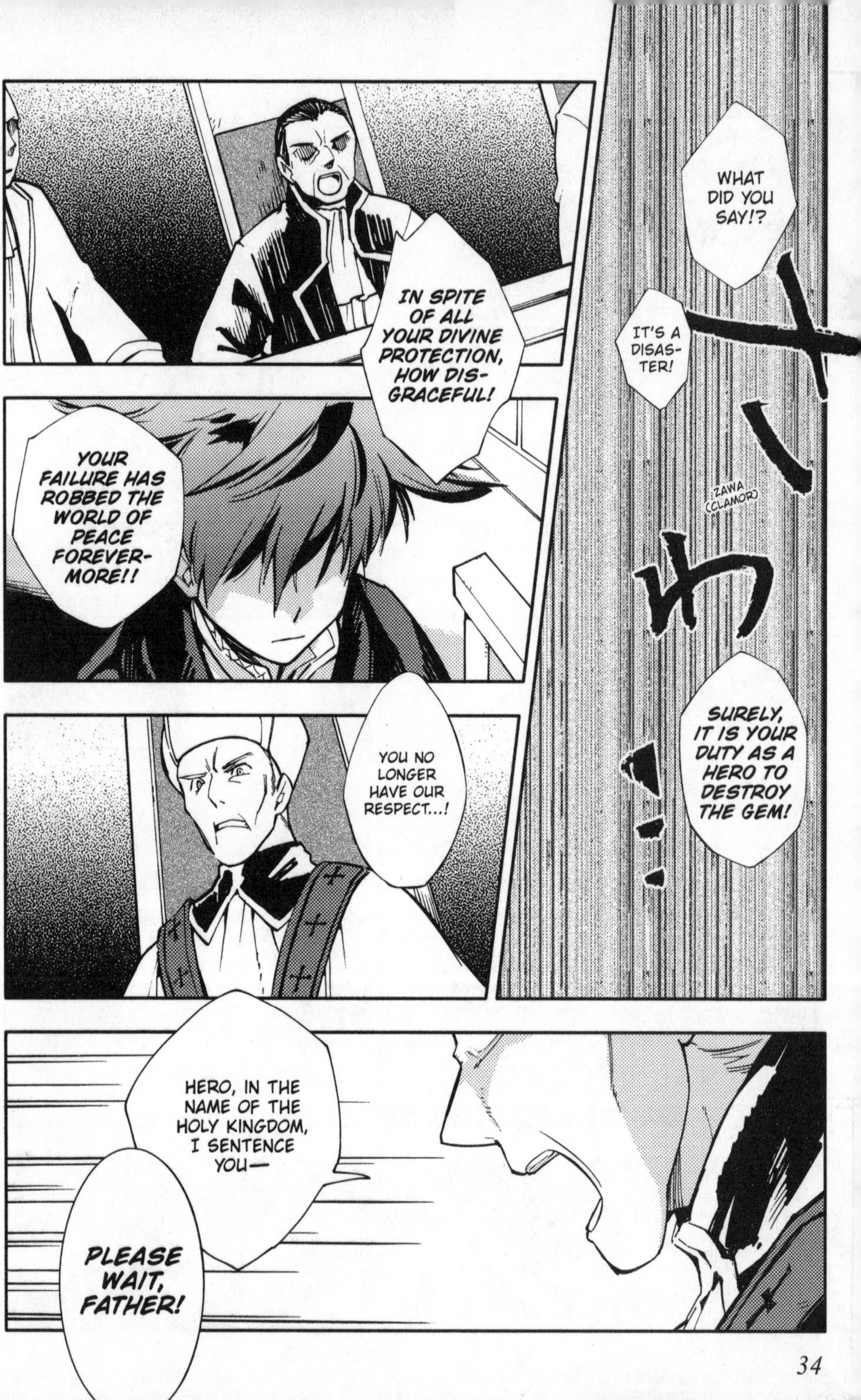
WHAT DID YOU SAY!?
IT'S A DISAS-TER!
ZAWA (CLAMOR)
SURELY, IT IS YOUR DUTY AS A HERO TO DESTROY THE GEM!
IN SPITE OF ALL YOUR DIVINE PROTECTION, HOW DIS-GRACEFUL!
YOUR FAILURE HAS ROBBED THE WORLD OF PEACE FOREVER-MORE!!
YOU NO LONGER HAVE OUR RESPECT...!
HERO, IN THE NAME OF THE HOLY KINGDOM, I SENTENCE YOU—
PLEASE WAIT, FATHER!

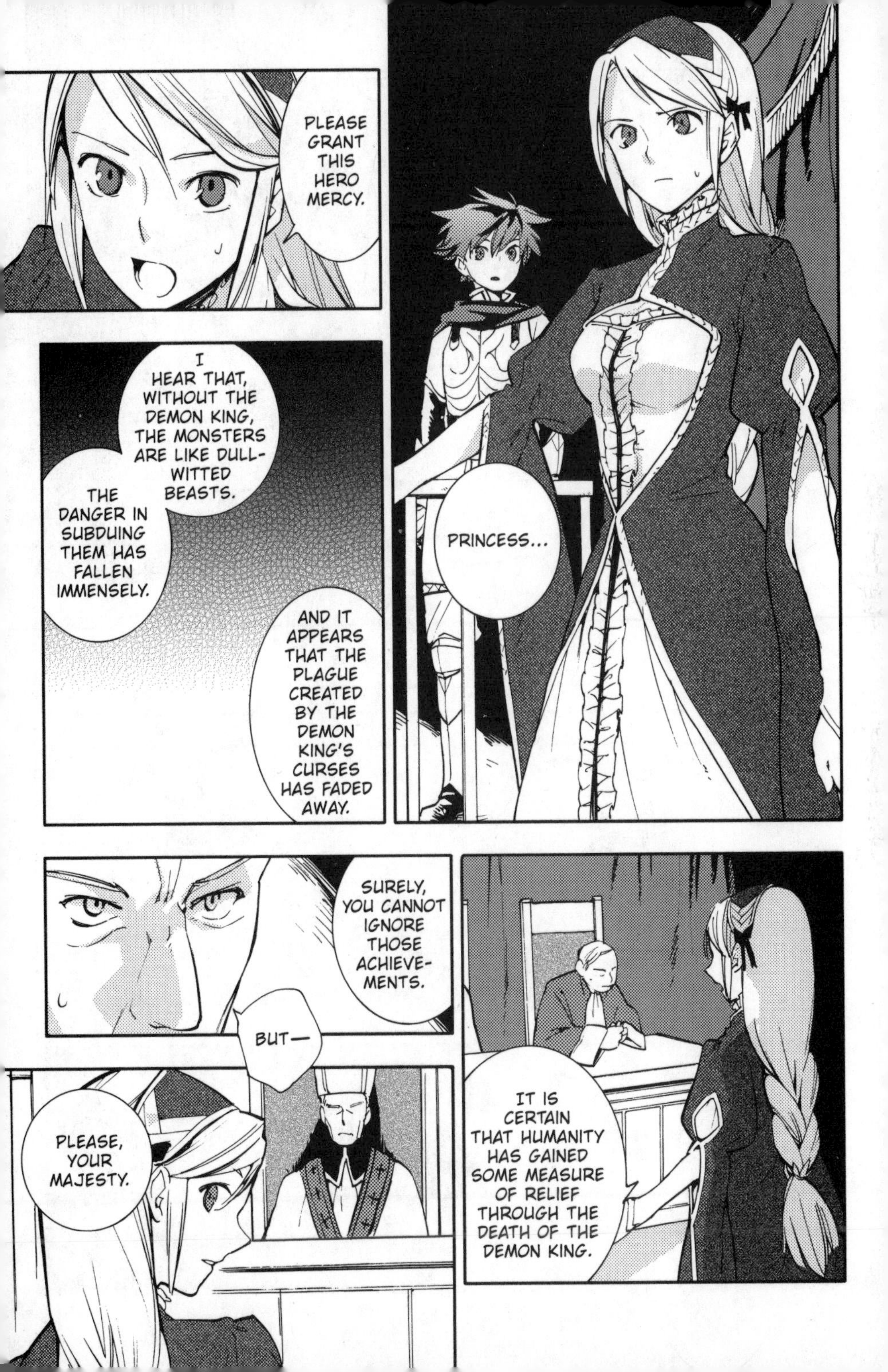
PRINCESS...
PLEASE GRANT THIS HERO MERCY.
I HEAR THAT, WITHOUT THE DEMON KING, THE MONSTERS ARE LIKE DULL-WITTED BEASTS.
THE DANGER IN SUBDUING THEM HAS FALLEN IMMENSELY.
AND IT APPEARS THAT THE PLAGUE CREATED BY THE DEMON KING'S CURSES HAS FADED AWAY.
IT IS CERTAIN THAT HUMANITY HAS GAINED SOME MEASURE OF RELIEF THROUGH THE DEATH OF THE DEMON KING.
SURELY, YOU CANNOT IGNORE THOSE ACHIEVEMENTS.
BUT—
PLEASE, YOUR MAJESTY.

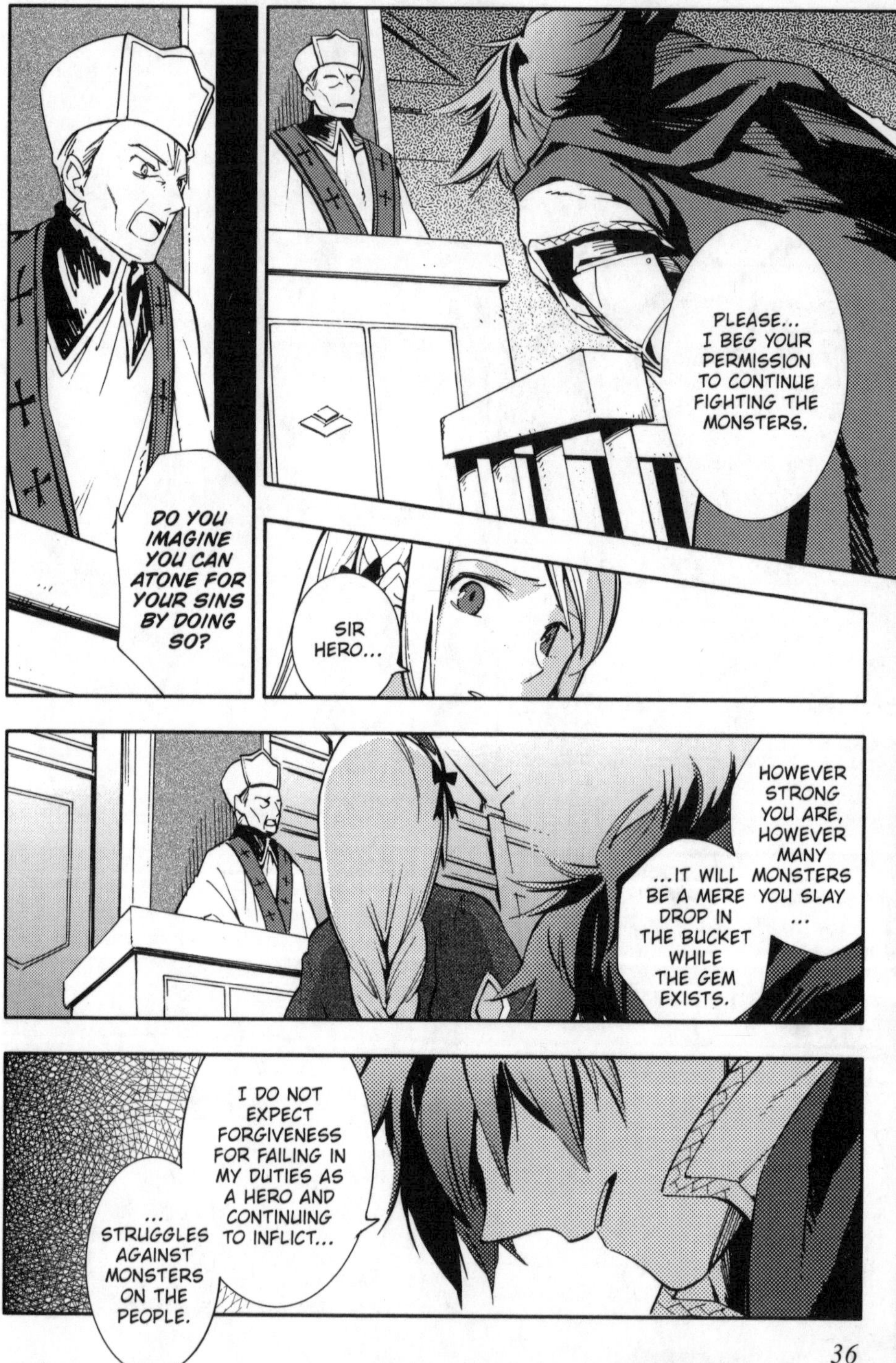
PLEASE... I BEG YOUR PERMISSION TO CONTINUE FIGHTING THE MONSTERS.
SIR HERO...
...
DO YOU IMAGINE YOU CAN ATONE FOR YOUR SINS BY DOING SO?
HOWEVER STRONG YOU ARE, HOWEVER MANY MONSTERS YOU SLAY...
...IT WILL BE A MERE DROP IN THE BUCKET WHILE THE GEM EXISTS.
I DO NOT EXPECT FORGIVENESS FOR FAILING IN MY DUTIES AS A HERO AND CONTINUING TO INFLICT...
...STRUGGLES AGAINST MONSTERS ON THE PEOPLE.

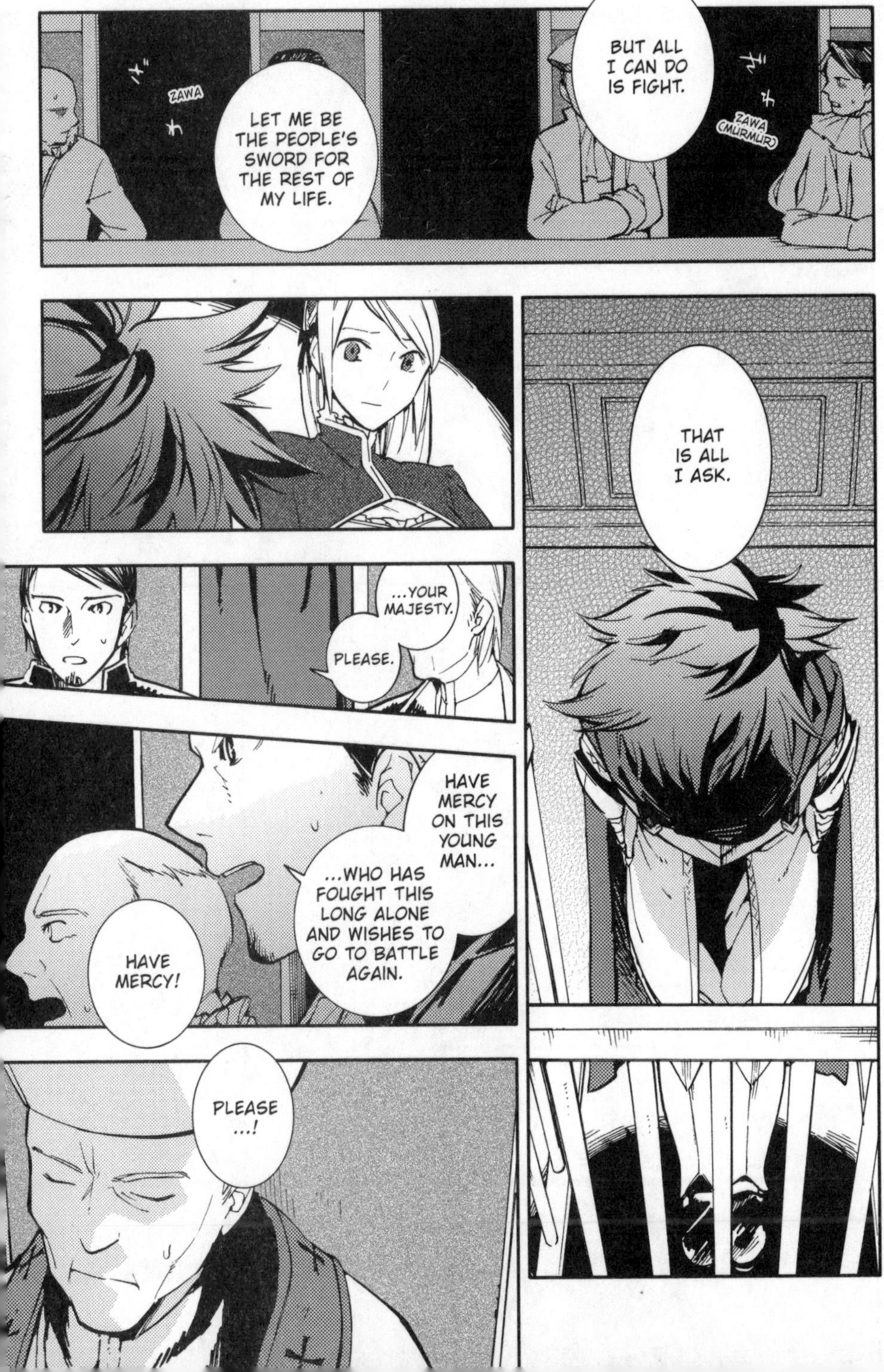
ZAWA (MURMUR)
BUT ALL I CAN DO IS FIGHT.
LET ME BE THE PEOPLE'S SWORD FOR THE REST OF MY LIFE.
ZAWA
THAT IS ALL I ASK.
...YOUR MAJESTY.
PLEASE.
HAVE MERCY ON THIS YOUNG MAN...
...WHO HAS FOUGHT THIS LONG ALONE AND WISHES TO GO TO BATTLE AGAIN.
HAVE MERCY!
PLEASE ...!

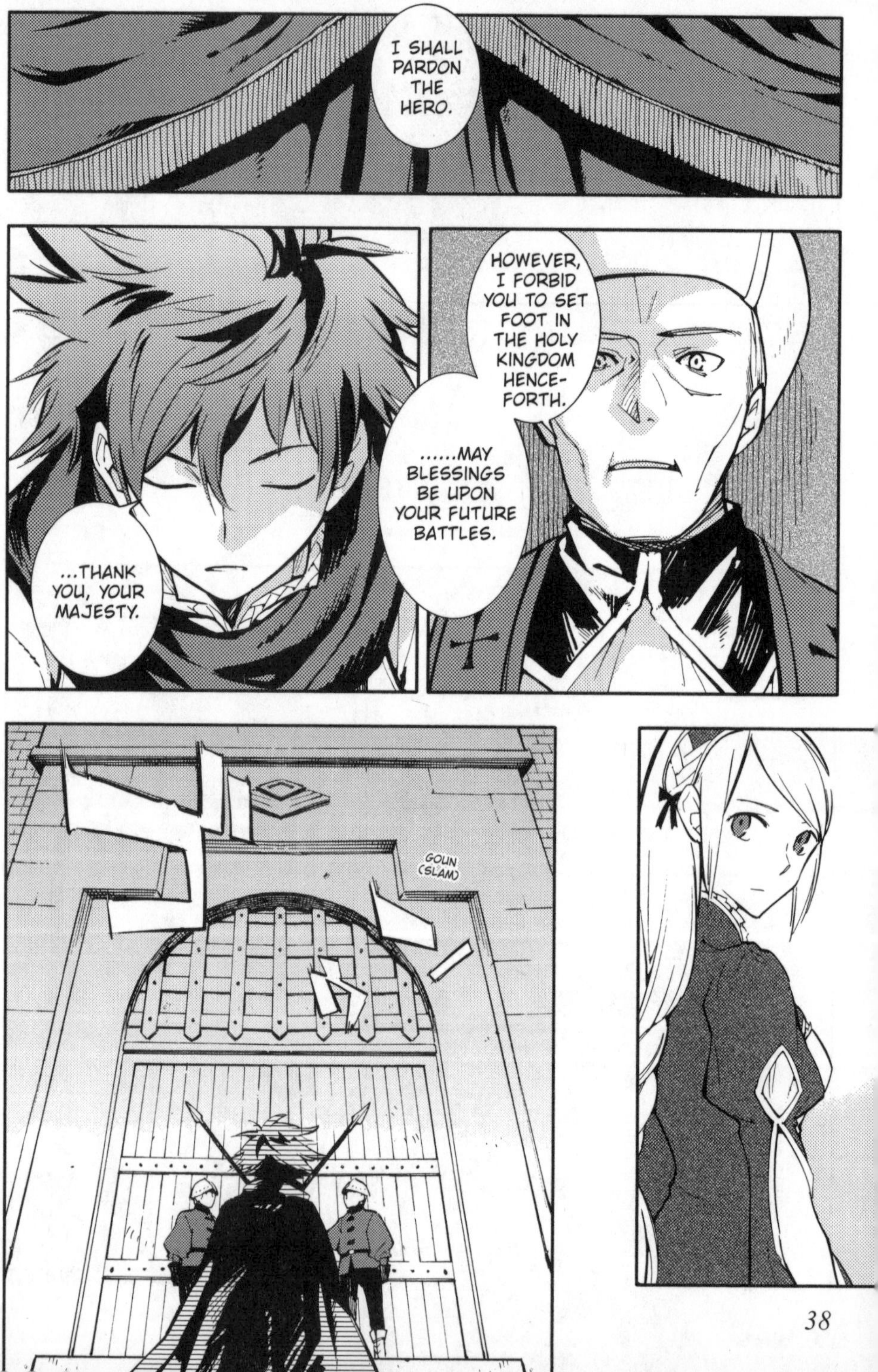
I SHALL PARDON THE HERO.
HOWEVER, I FORBID YOU TO SET FOOT IN THE HOLY KINGDOM HENCE-FORTH.
......MAY BLESSINGS BE UPON YOUR FUTURE BATTLES.
...THANK YOU, YOUR MAJESTY.
GOUN (SLAM)

...SIR HERO.

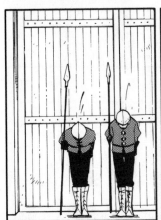

NOTH-ING, SIR. JUST...

HMM?

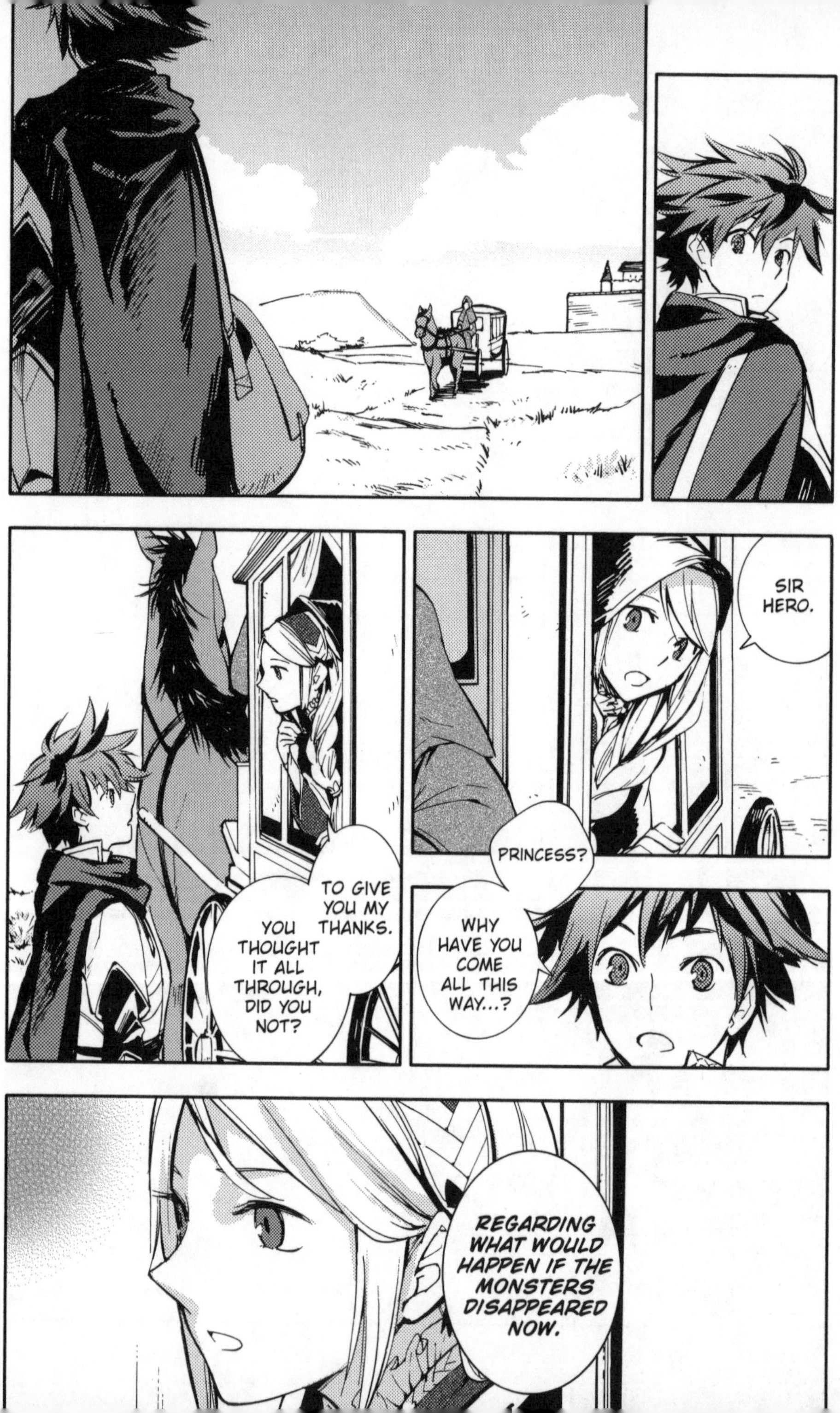
SIR HERO.
PRINCESS?
WHY HAVE YOU COME ALL THIS WAY...?
TO GIVE YOU MY THANKS.
YOU THOUGHT IT ALL THROUGH, DID YOU NOT?
REGARDING WHAT WOULD HAPPEN IF THE MONSTERS DISAPPEARED NOW.

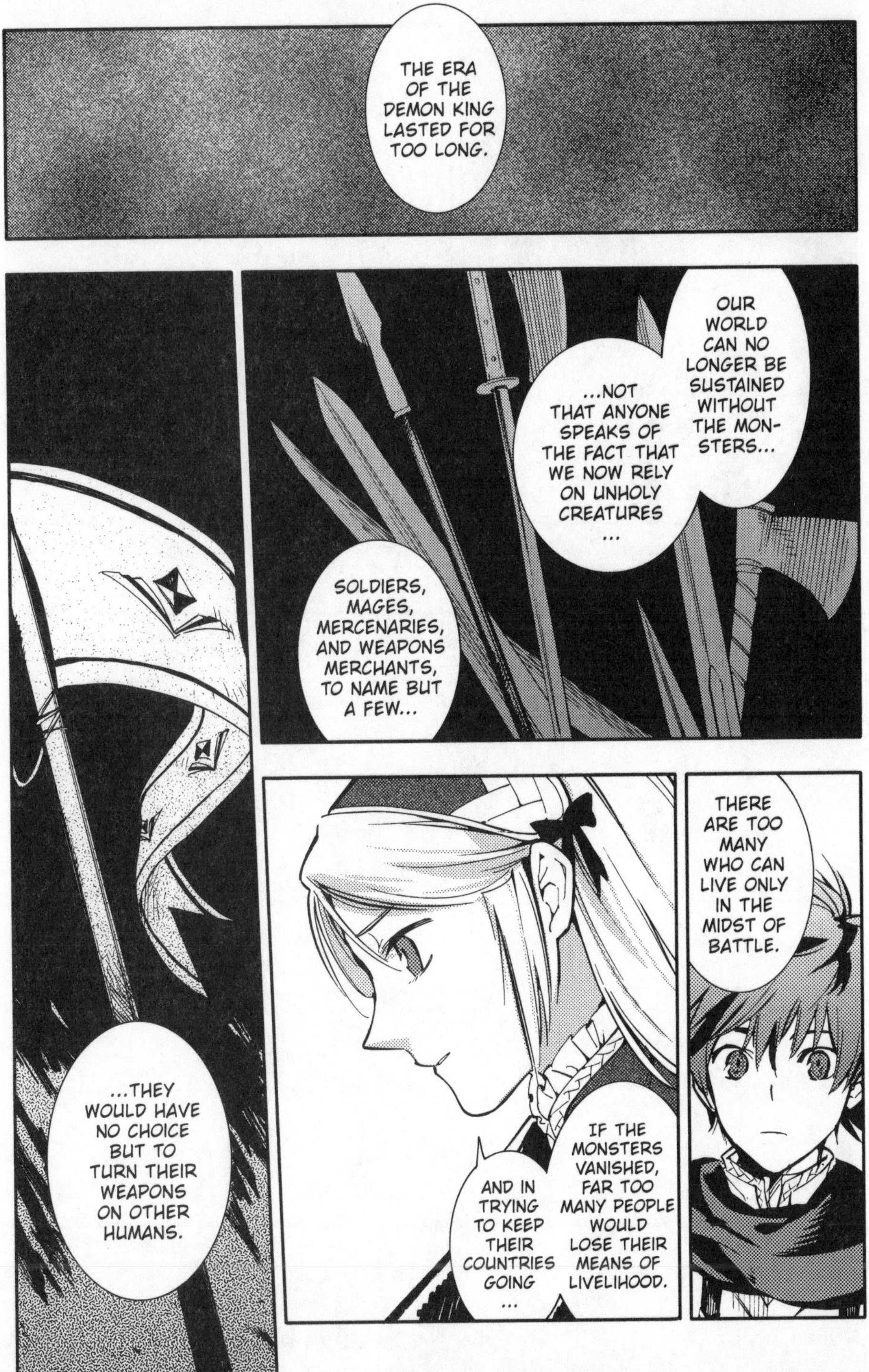
THE ERA OF THE DEMON KING LASTED FOR TOO LONG.
OUR WORLD CAN NO LONGER BE SUSTAINED WITHOUT THE MON-STERS...
...NOT THAT ANYONE SPEAKS OF THE FACT THAT WE NOW RELY ON UNHOLY CREATURES ...
SOLDIERS, MAGES, MERCENARIES, AND WEAPONS MERCHANTS, TO NAME BUT A FEW...
THERE ARE TOO MANY WHO CAN LIVE ONLY IN THE MIDST OF BATTLE.
IF THE MONSTERS VANISHED, FAR TOO MANY PEOPLE WOULD LOSE THEIR MEANS OF LIVELIHOOD.
AND IN TRYING TO KEEP THEIR COUNTRIES GOING ...
...THEY WOULD HAVE NO CHOICE BUT TO TURN THEIR WEAPONS ON OTHER HUMANS.

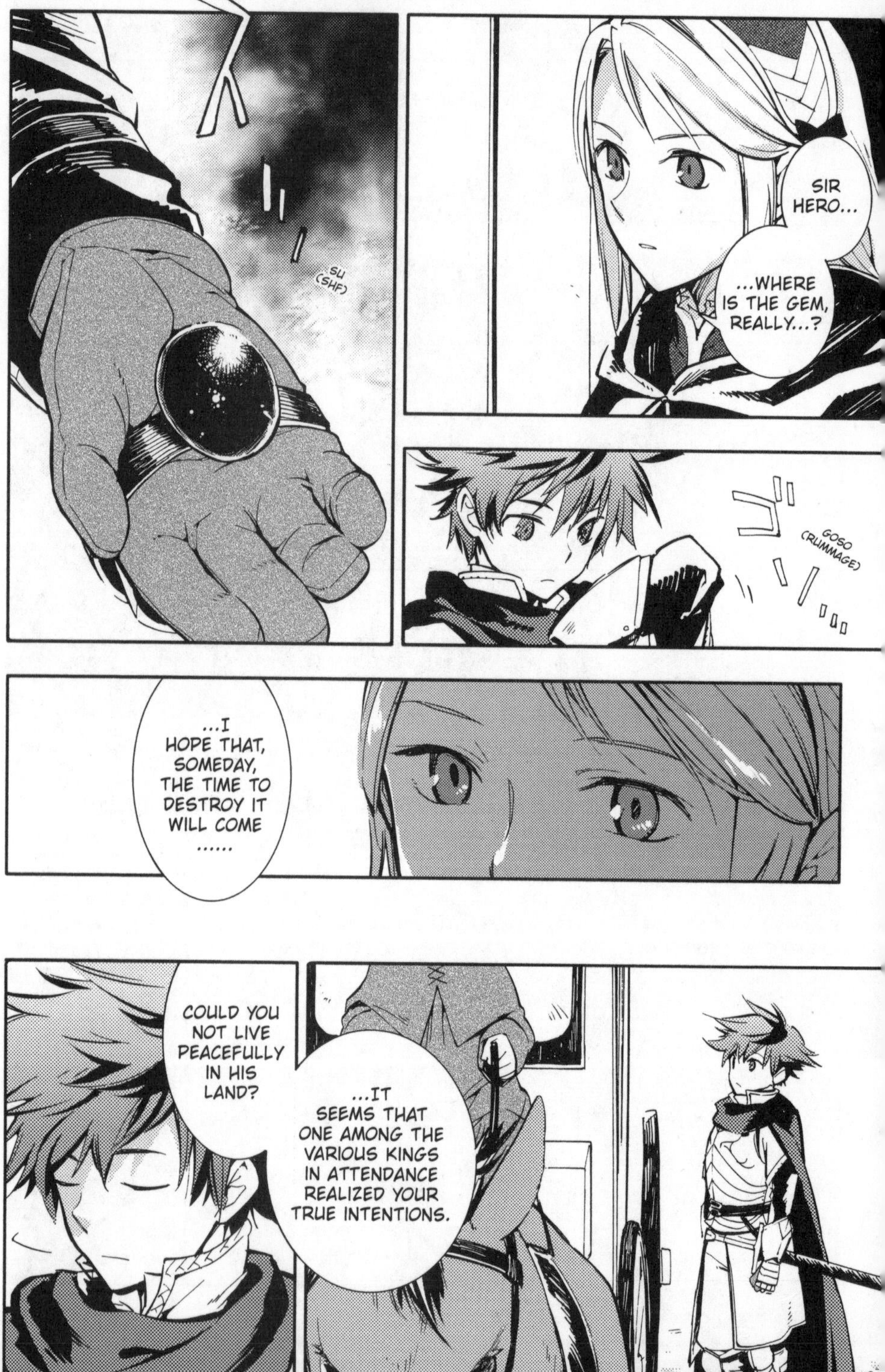
SIR HERO...
...WHERE IS THE GEM, REALLY...?
GOSO (RUMMAGE)
SU (SHF)
...I HOPE THAT, SOMEDAY, THE TIME TO DESTROY IT WILL COME ......
...IT SEEMS THAT ONE AMONG THE VARIOUS KINGS IN ATTENDANCE REALIZED YOUR TRUE INTENTIONS.
COULD YOU NOT LIVE PEACEFULLY IN HIS LAND?

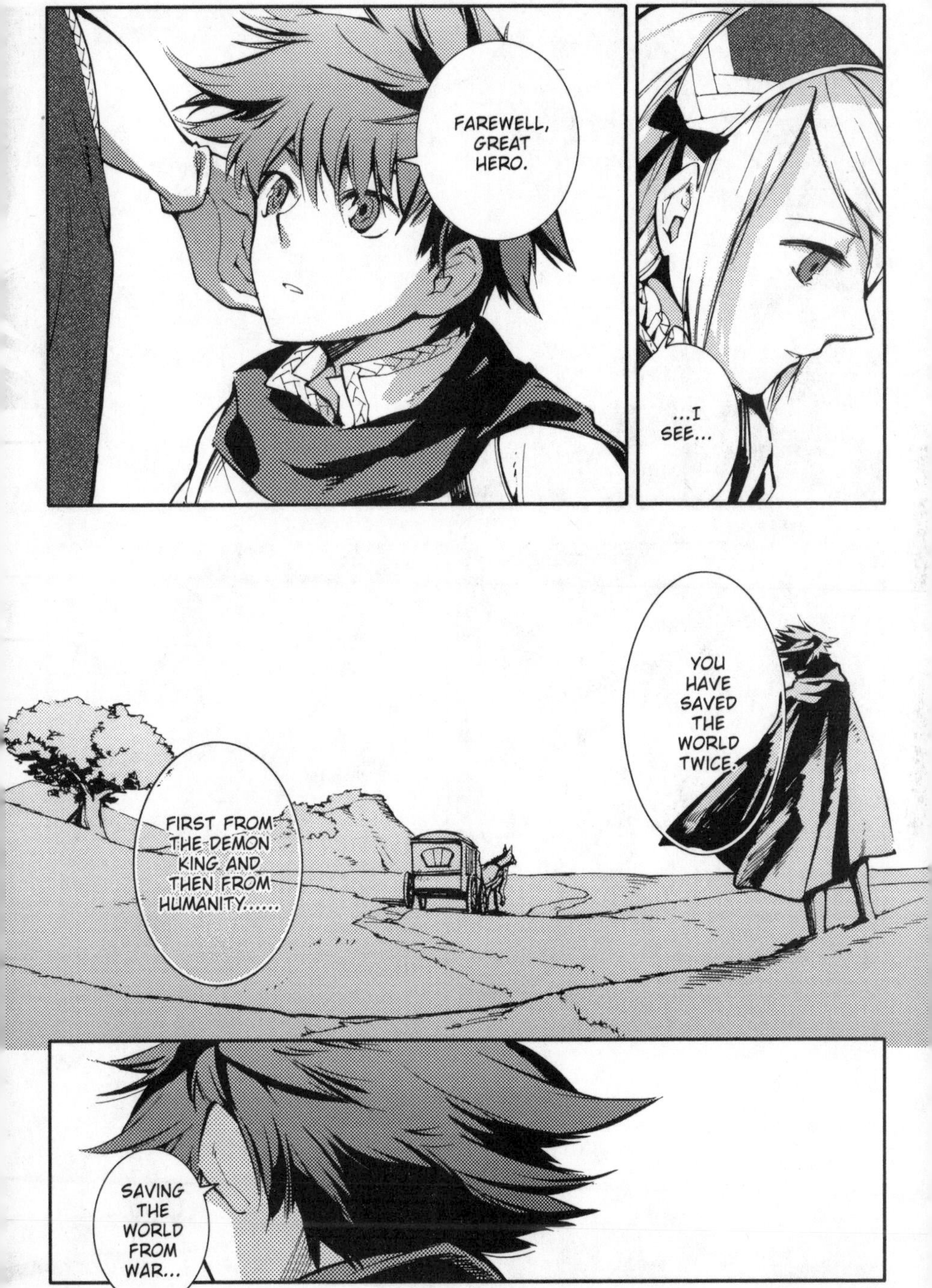
...I SEE...
FAREWELL, GREAT HERO.
YOU HAVE SAVED THE WORLD TWICE.
FIRST FROM THE DEMON KING AND THEN FROM HUMANITY......
SAVING THE WORLD FROM WAR...

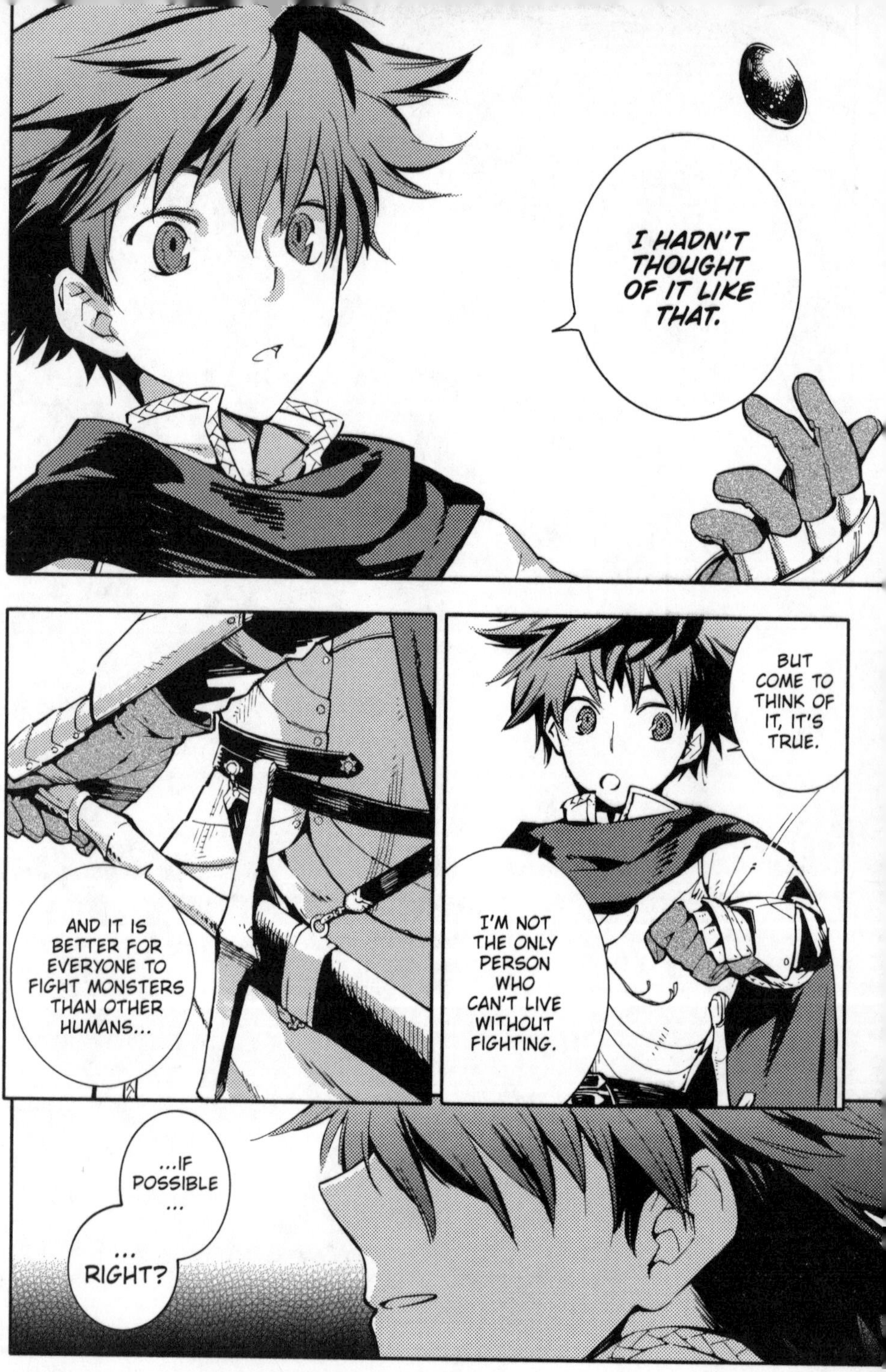
I HADN'T THOUGHT OF IT LIKE THAT.
BUT COME TO THINK OF IT, IT'S TRUE.
I'M NOT THE ONLY PERSON WHO CAN'T LIVE WITHOUT FIGHTING.
AND IT IS BETTER FOR EVERYONE TO FIGHT MONSTERS THAN OTHER HUMANS...
...IF POSSIBLE...
...RIGHT?

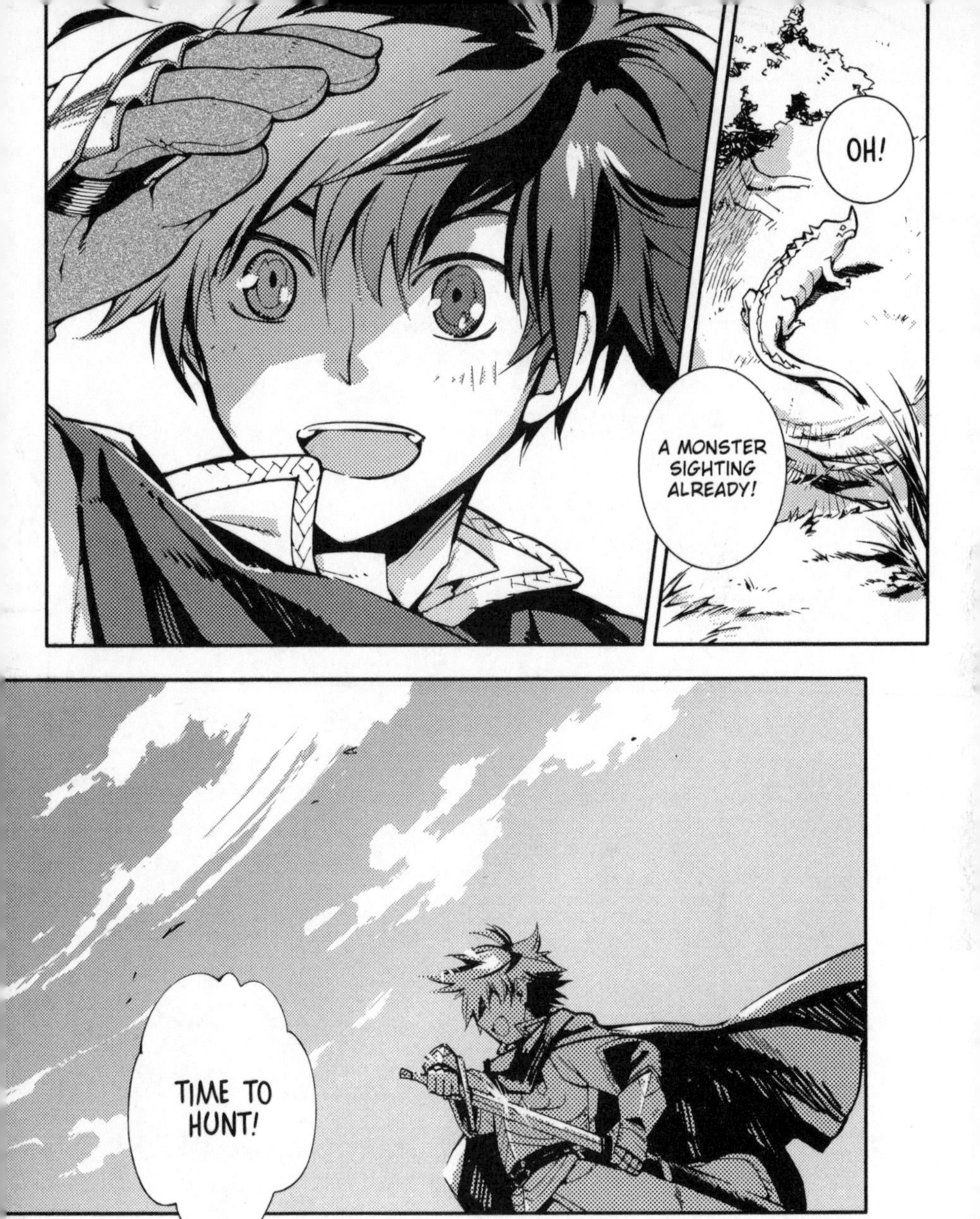
OH!
A MONSTER SIGHTING ALREADY!
TIME TO HUNT!

【The Hero Saves the World Three Times】

It feels as though I was late to the...trend, so to speak, of writing about heroes and demon lords, but as someone who grew up on RPGs, I was determined to use this theme. This story is the only one in the book that I inked traditionally, but it doesn't feel as out of place beside the others as I had expected.

Initial release: self-published doujinshi (published May 5, 2013)

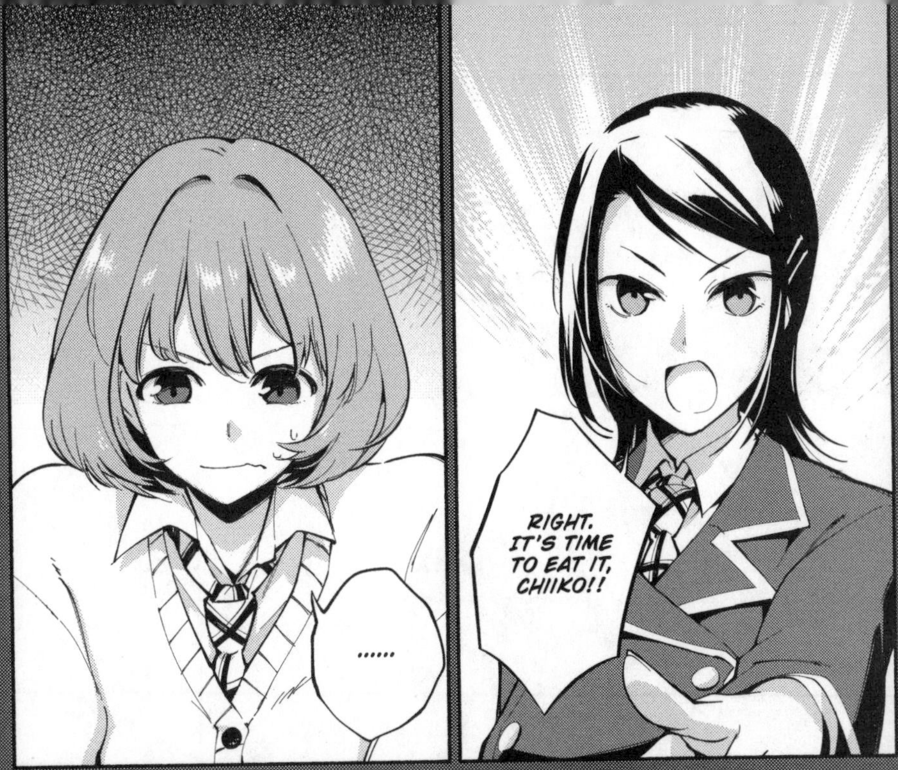
RIGHT. IT'S TIME TO EAT IT, CHIIKO!!
......

Tear-Flavored Escargot

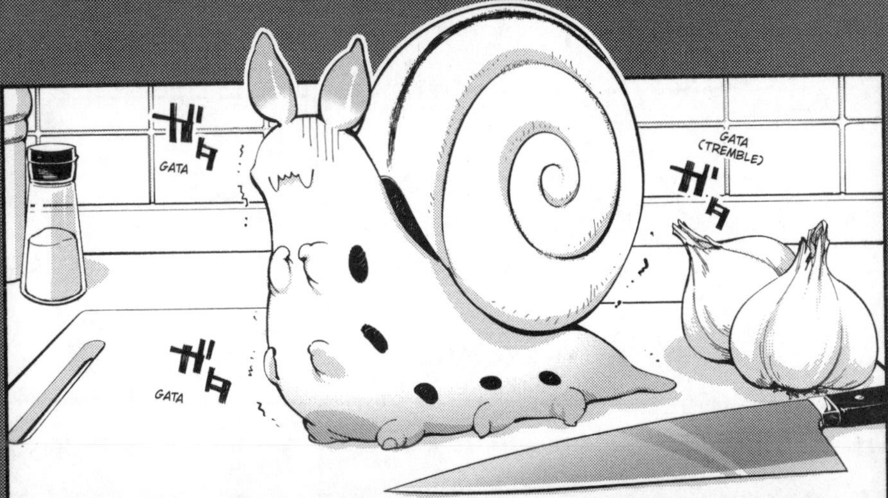
ガタ
GATA (TREMBLE)
ガタ
GATA
ガタ
GATA

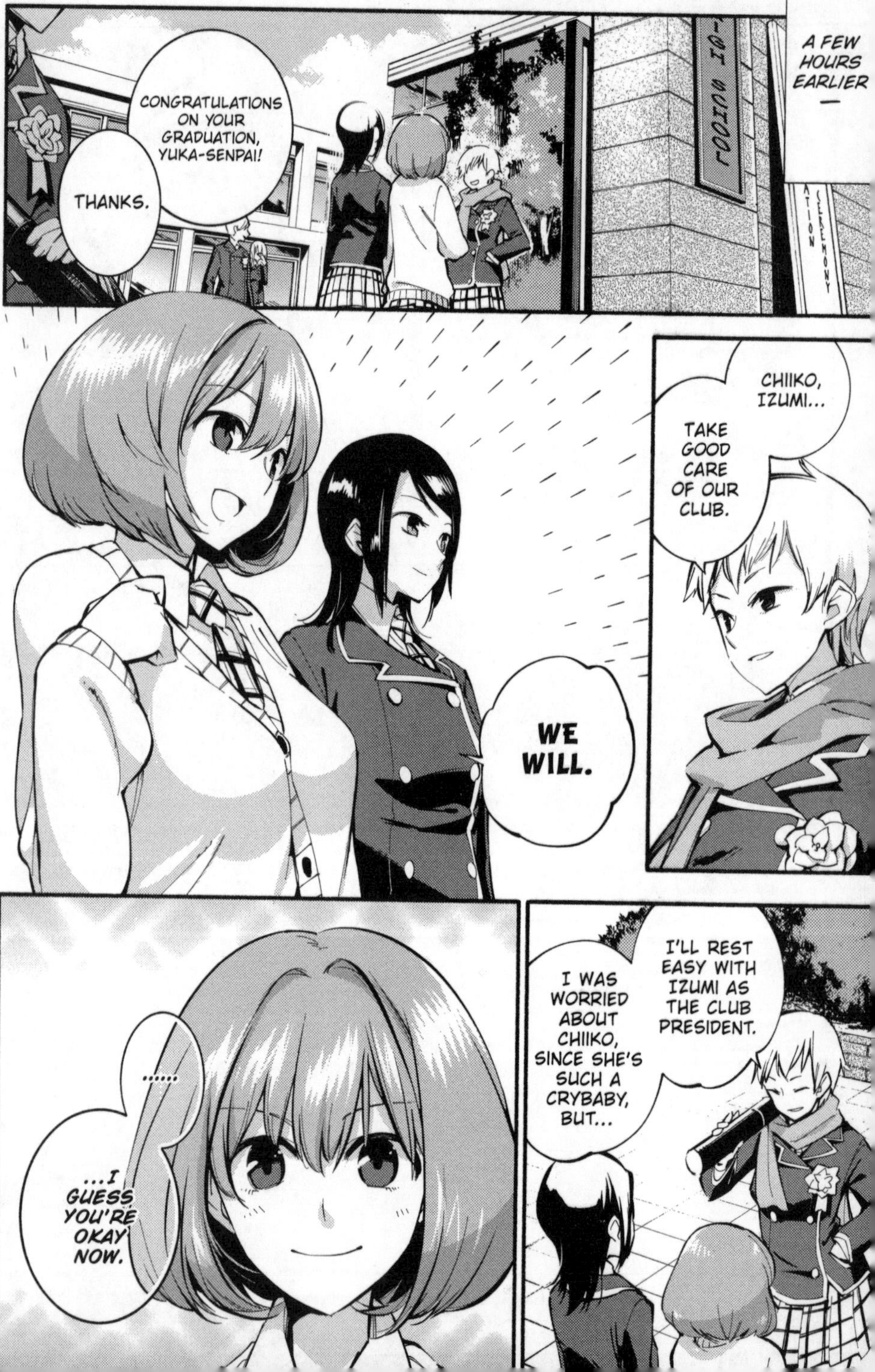
A FEW HOURS EARLIER —
CONGRATULATIONS ON YOUR GRADUATION, YUKA-SENPAI!
THANKS.
CHIIKO, IZUMI...
TAKE GOOD CARE OF OUR CLUB.
WE WILL.
I'LL REST EASY WITH IZUMI AS THE CLUB PRESIDENT.
I WAS WORRIED ABOUT CHIIKO, SINCE SHE'S SUCH A CRYBABY, BUT...
......
...I GUESS YOU'RE OKAY NOW.

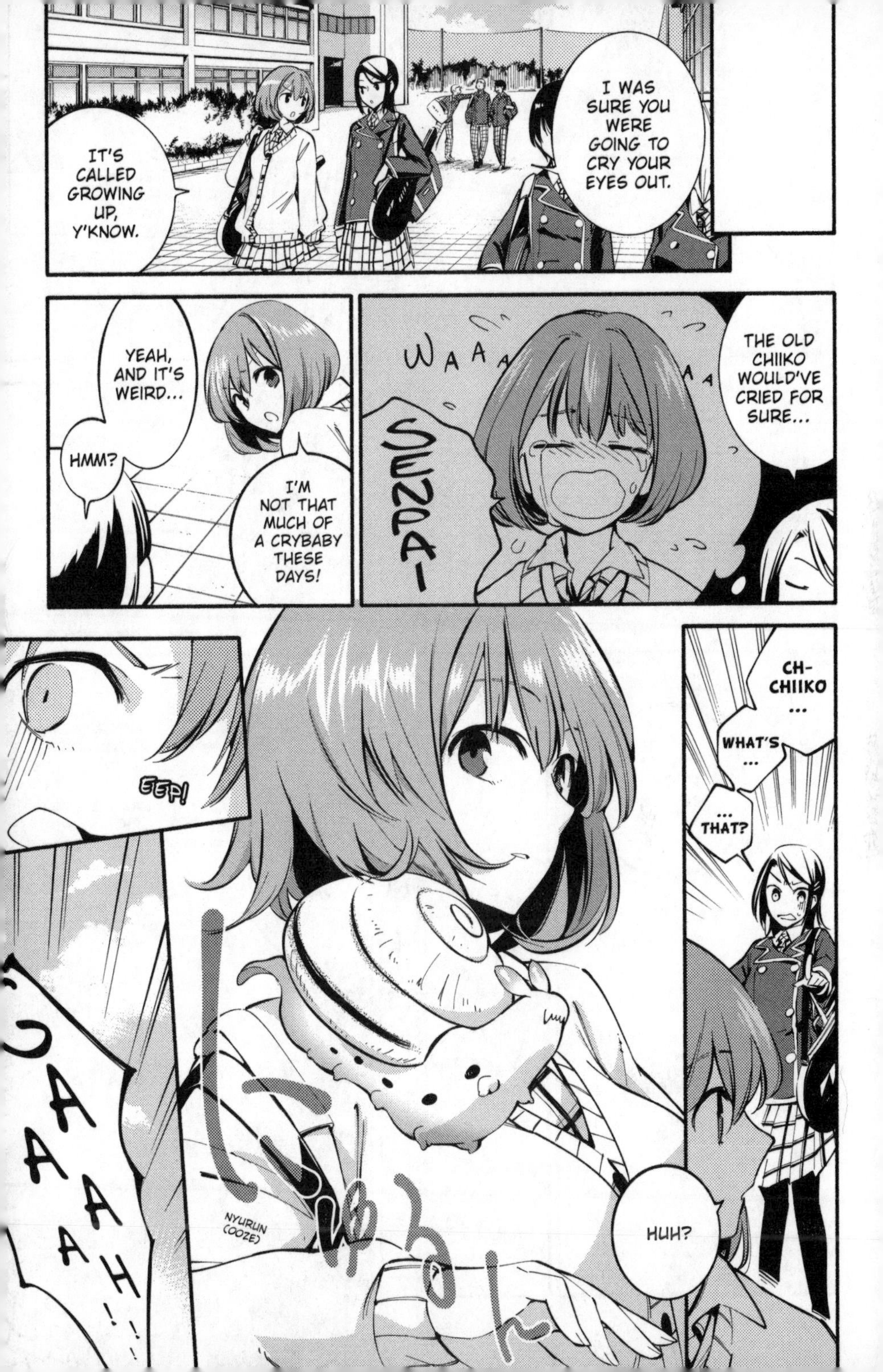
I WAS SURE YOU WERE GOING TO CRY YOUR EYES OUT.
IT'S CALLED GROWING UP, Y'KNOW.
THE OLD CHIIKO WOULD'VE CRIED FOR SURE...
WAAAA
SENPAI
YEAH, AND IT'S WEIRD...
HMM?
I'M NOT THAT MUCH OF A CRYBABY THESE DAYS!
CH-CHIIKO...
WHAT'S...
...THAT?
HUH?
EEP!
NYURUN (COOZE)
GAAAAAH!!!

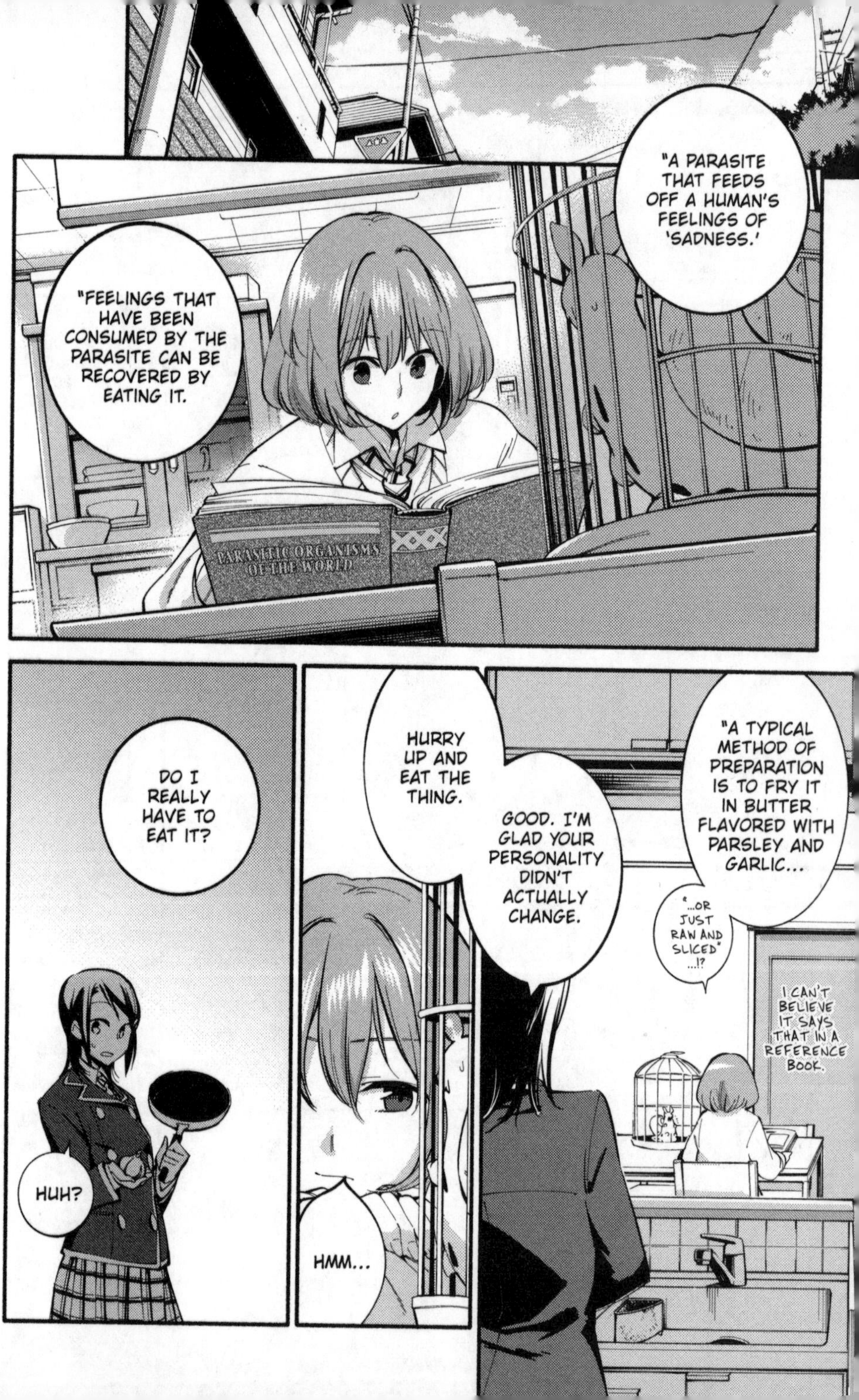
"A PARASITE THAT FEEDS OFF A HUMAN'S FEELINGS OF 'SADNESS.'
"FEELINGS THAT HAVE BEEN CONSUMED BY THE PARASITE CAN BE RECOVERED BY EATING IT.
PARASITIC ORGANISMS OF THE WORLD
"A TYPICAL METHOD OF PREPARATION IS TO FRY IT IN BUTTER FLAVORED WITH PARSLEY AND GARLIC...
"...OR JUST RAW AND SLICED" ...!?
I CAN'T BELIEVE IT SAYS THAT IN A REFERENCE BOOK.
GOOD. I'M GLAD YOUR PERSONALITY DIDN'T ACTUALLY CHANGE.
HURRY UP AND EAT THE THING.
HMM...
DO I REALLY HAVE TO EAT IT?
HUH?

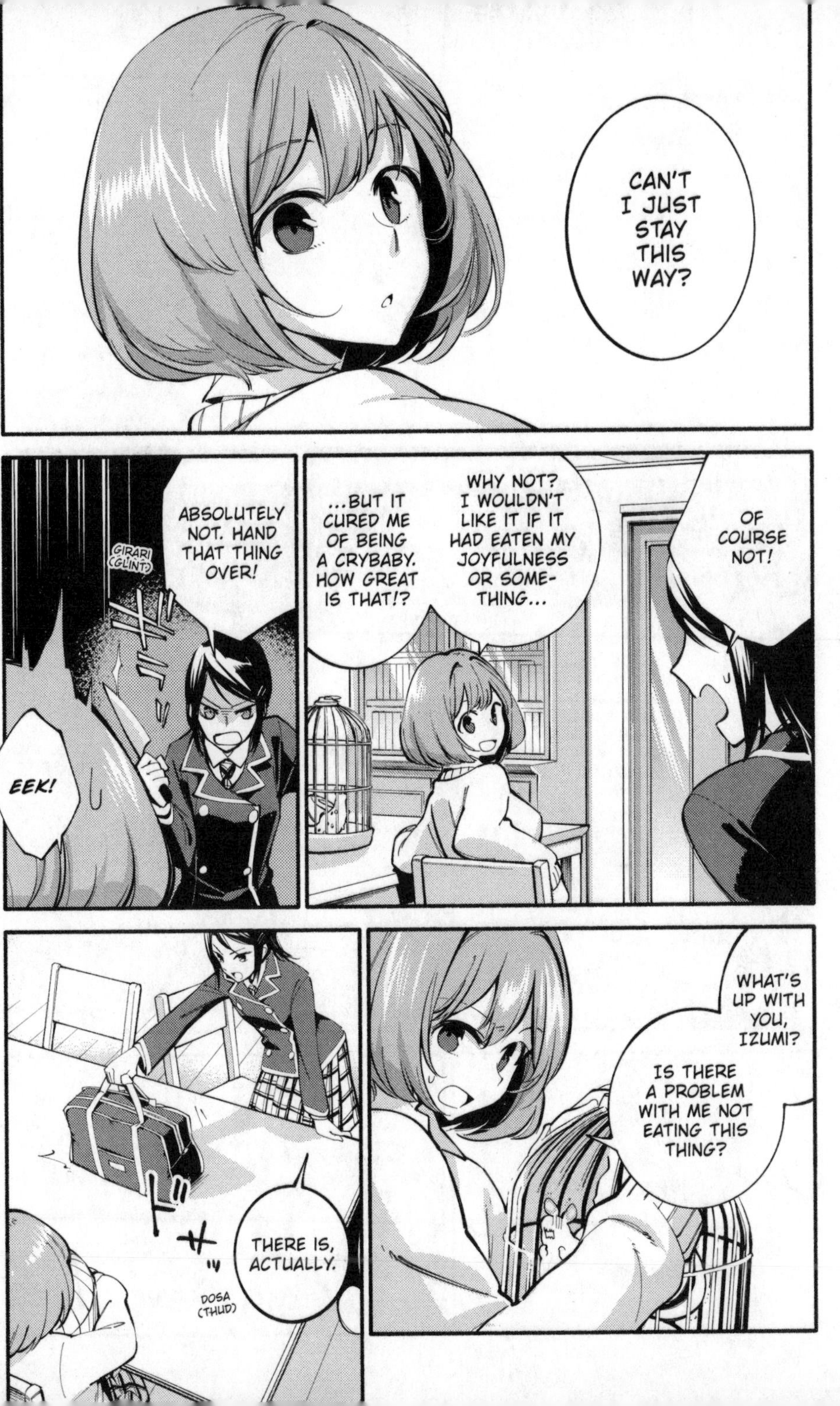
CAN'T I JUST STAY THIS WAY?
OF COURSE NOT!
WHY NOT? I WOULDN'T LIKE IT IF IT HAD EATEN MY JOYFULNESS OR SOME-THING...
...BUT IT CURED ME OF BEING A CRYBABY. HOW GREAT IS THAT!?
ABSOLUTELY NOT. HAND THAT THING OVER!
GIRARI (GLINT)
EEK!
WHAT'S UP WITH YOU, IZUMI?
IS THERE A PROBLEM WITH ME NOT EATING THIS THING?
THERE IS, ACTUALLY.
DOSA (THUD)

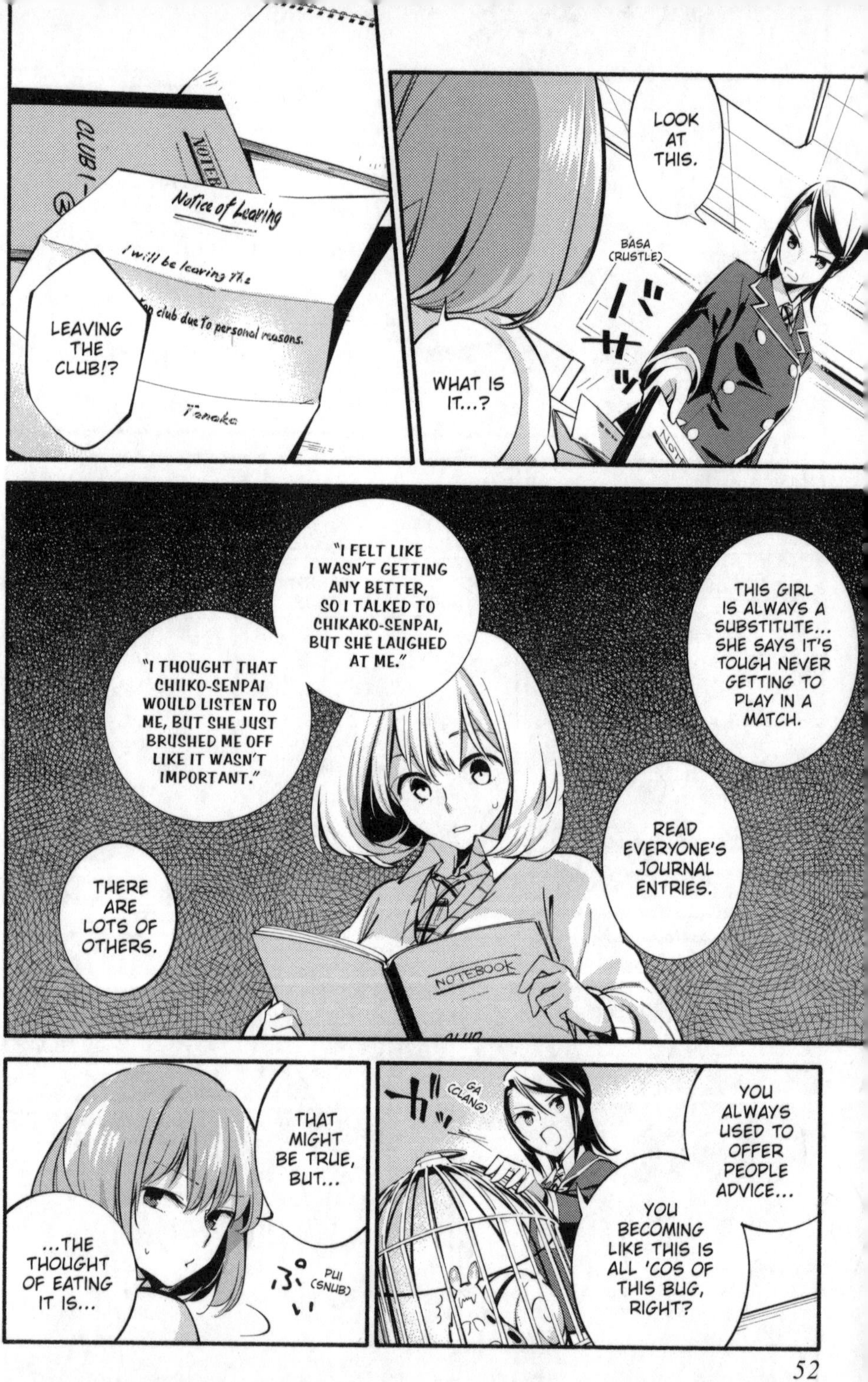
LOOK AT THIS.
BASA (RUSTLE)
WHAT IS IT...?
NOTEBOOK
CLUB
Notice of Leaving
I will be leaving the
club due to personal reasons.
Tanaka
LEAVING THE CLUB!?
THIS GIRL IS ALWAYS A SUBSTITUTE... SHE SAYS IT'S TOUGH NEVER GETTING TO PLAY IN A MATCH.
"I FELT LIKE I WASN'T GETTING ANY BETTER, SO I TALKED TO CHIKAKO-SENPAI, BUT SHE LAUGHED AT ME."
"I THOUGHT THAT CHIIKO-SENPAI WOULD LISTEN TO ME, BUT SHE JUST BRUSHED ME OFF LIKE IT WASN'T IMPORTANT."
READ EVERYONE'S JOURNAL ENTRIES.
THERE ARE LOTS OF OTHERS.
NOTEBOOK
GA (CLANG)
YOU ALWAYS USED TO OFFER PEOPLE ADVICE...
YOU BECOMING LIKE THIS IS ALL 'COS OF THIS BUG, RIGHT?
THAT MIGHT BE TRUE, BUT...
PUI (SNUB)
...THE THOUGHT OF EATING IT IS...

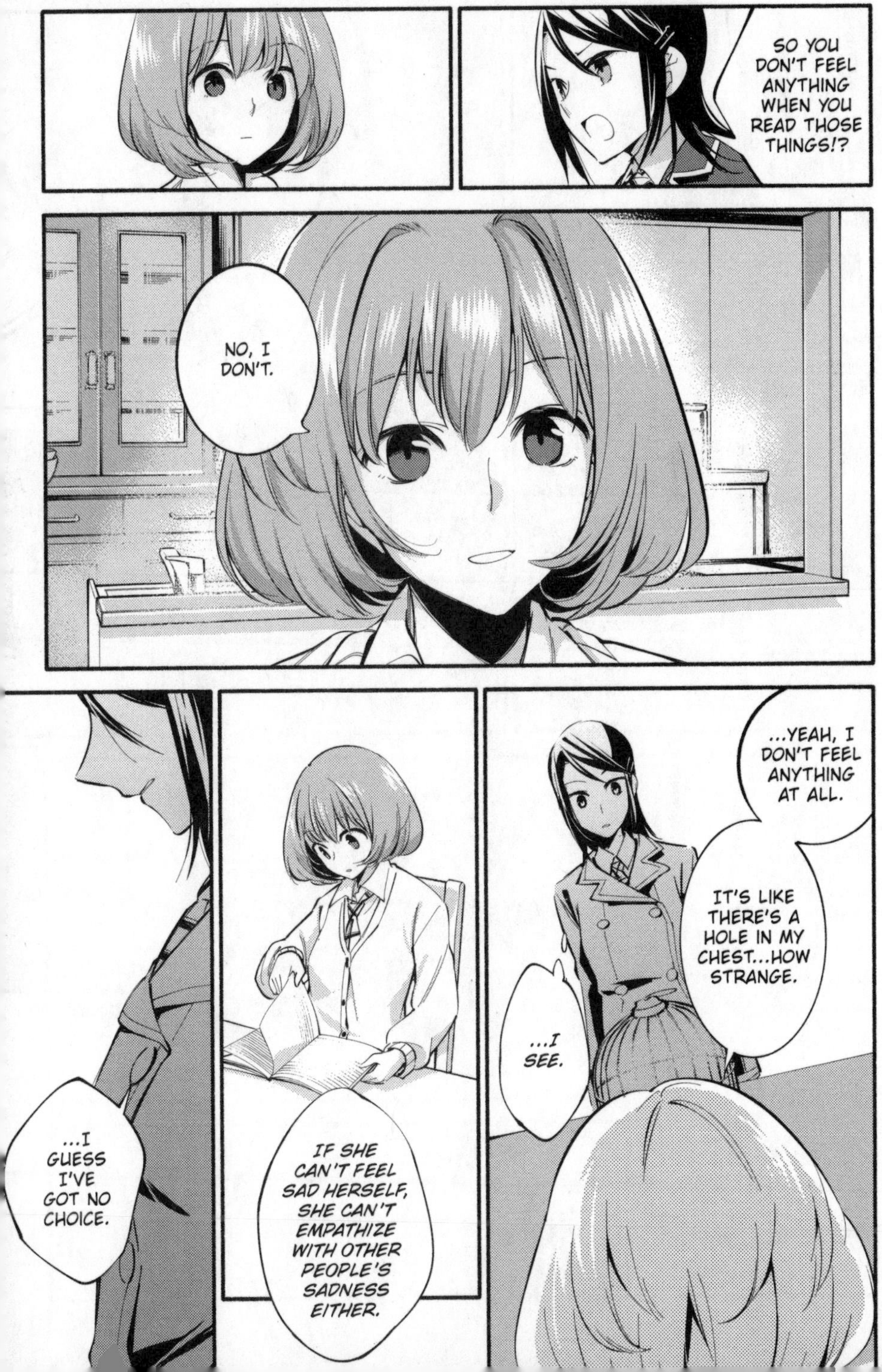
SO YOU DON'T FEEL ANYTHING WHEN YOU READ THOSE THINGS!?
NO, I DON'T.
...YEAH, I DON'T FEEL ANYTHING AT ALL.
IT'S LIKE THERE'S A HOLE IN MY CHEST...HOW STRANGE.
...I SEE.
IF SHE CAN'T FEEL SAD HERSELF, SHE CAN'T EMPATHIZE WITH OTHER PEOPLE'S SADNESS EITHER.
...I GUESS I'VE GOT NO CHOICE.

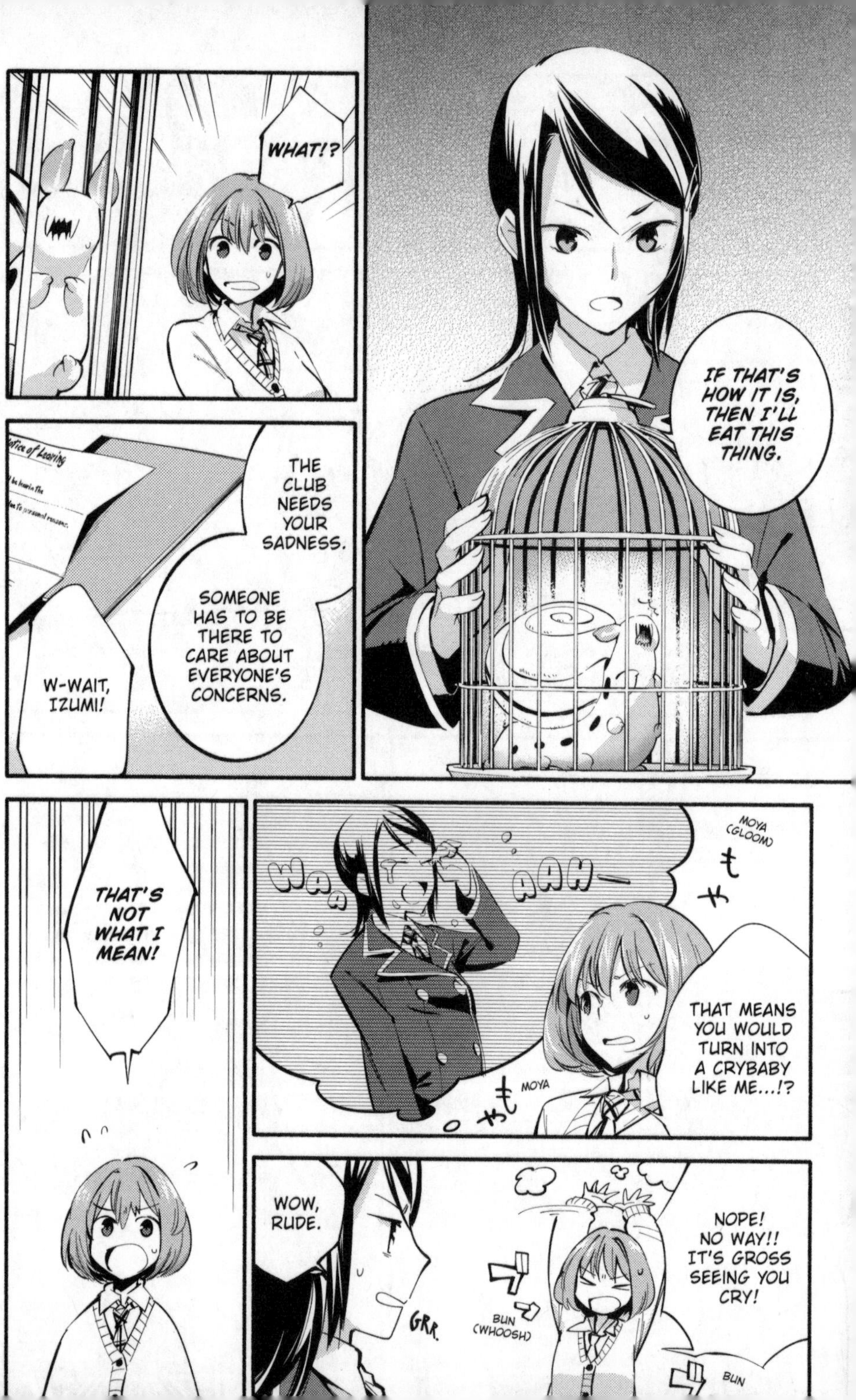
IF THAT'S HOW IT IS, THEN I'LL EAT THIS THING.
WHAT!?
THE CLUB NEEDS YOUR SADNESS.
SOMEONE HAS TO BE THERE TO CARE ABOUT EVERYONE'S CONCERNS.
W-WAIT, IZUMI!
MOYA (GLOOM)
WAAAAH—
THAT MEANS YOU WOULD TURN INTO A CRYBABY LIKE ME...!?
MOYA
NOPE! NO WAY!! IT'S GROSS SEEING YOU CRY!
BUN (WHOOSH)
BUN
WOW, RUDE.
GRR.
THAT'S NOT WHAT I MEAN!

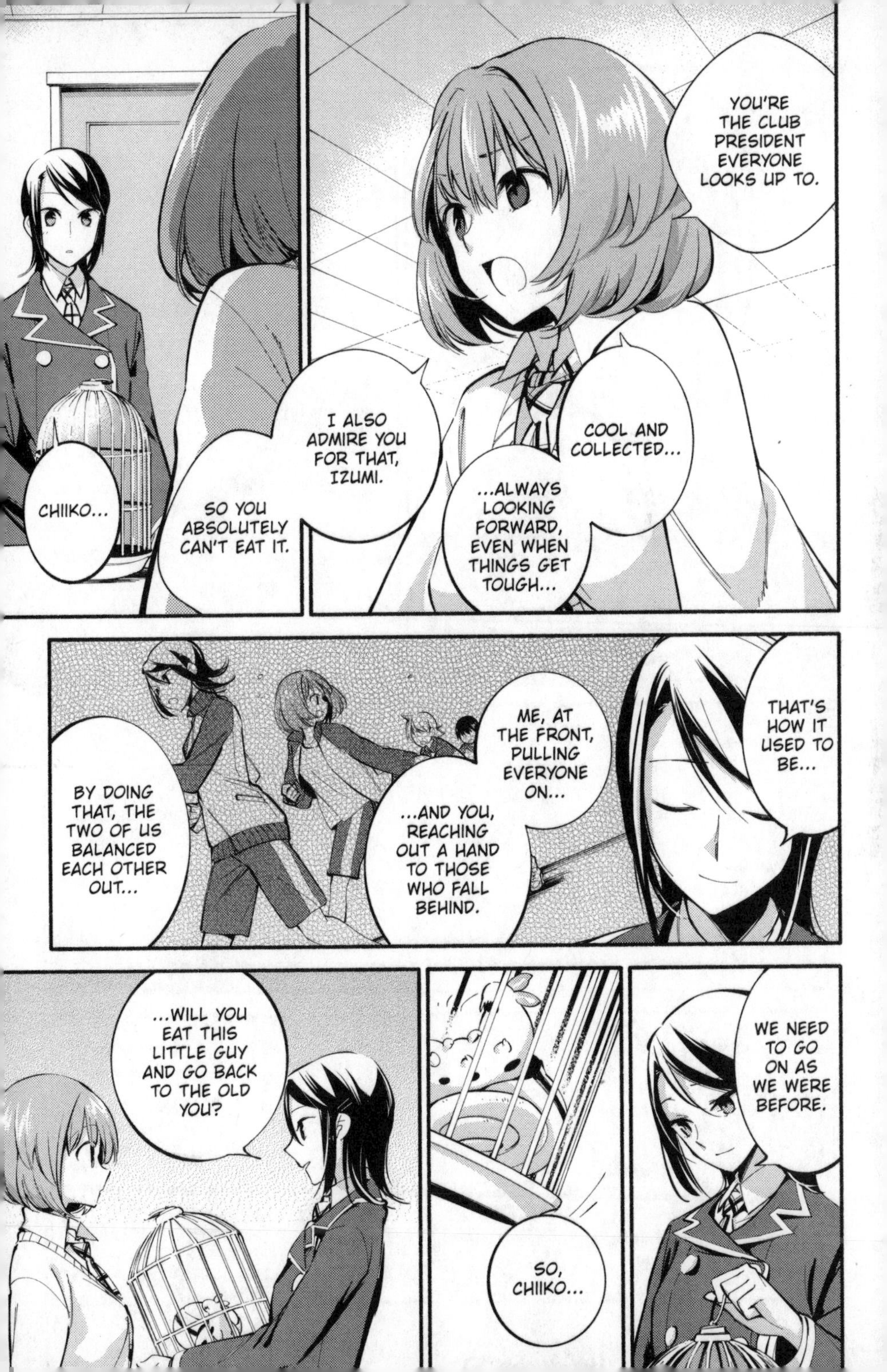
YOU'RE THE CLUB PRESIDENT EVERYONE LOOKS UP TO.
COOL AND COLLECTED...
...ALWAYS LOOKING FORWARD, EVEN WHEN THINGS GET TOUGH...
I ALSO ADMIRE YOU FOR THAT, IZUMI.
SO YOU ABSOLUTELY CAN'T EAT IT.
CHIIKO...
THAT'S HOW IT USED TO BE...
ME, AT THE FRONT, PULLING EVERYONE ON...
...AND YOU, REACHING OUT A HAND TO THOSE WHO FALL BEHIND.
BY DOING THAT, THE TWO OF US BALANCED EACH OTHER OUT...
WE NEED TO GO ON AS WE WERE BEFORE.
SO, CHIIKO...
...WILL YOU EAT THIS LITTLE GUY AND GO BACK TO THE OLD YOU?

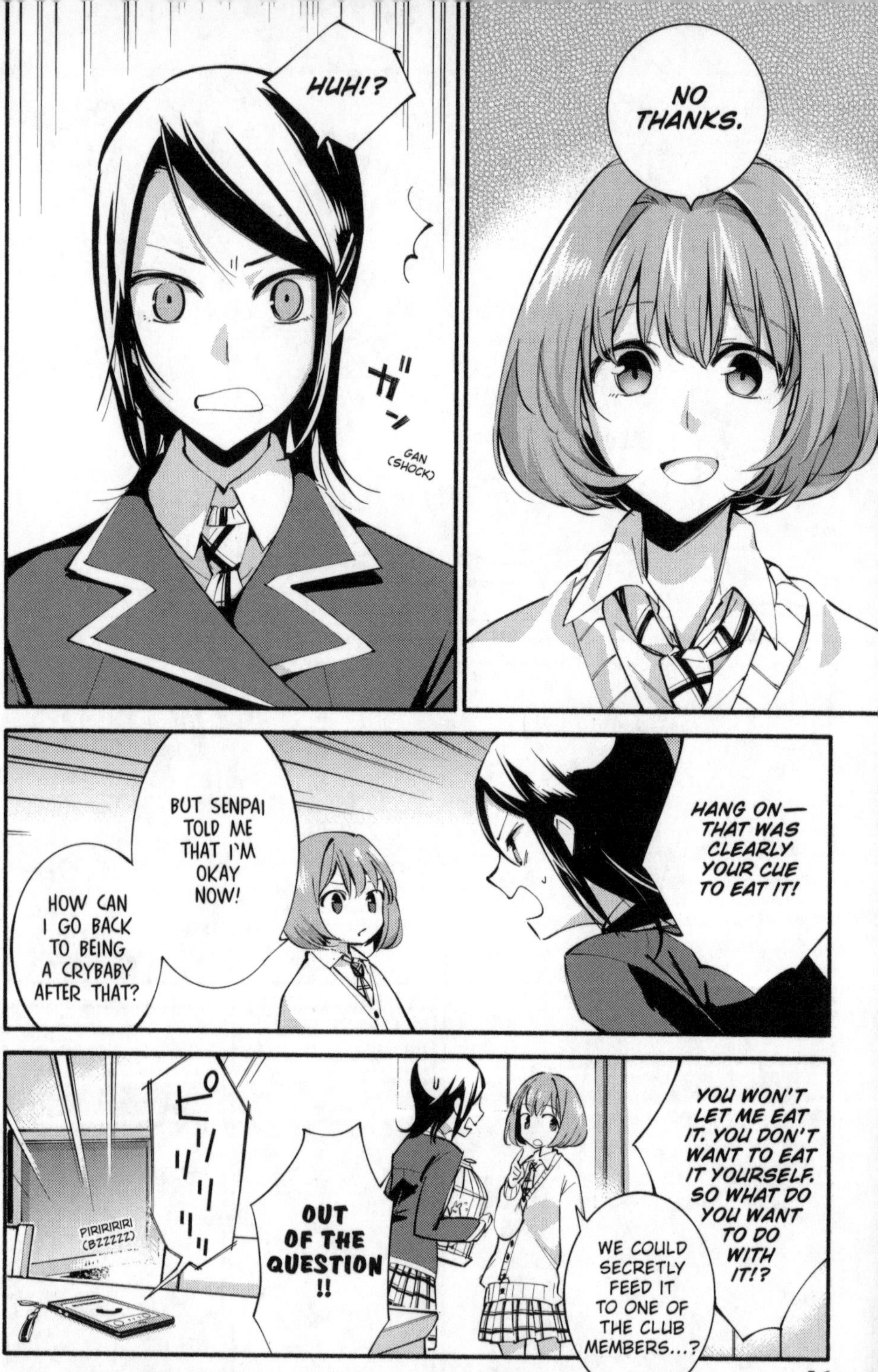
NO THANKS.
HUH!?
ガーン
GAN (SHOCK)
HANG ON—THAT WAS CLEARLY YOUR CUE TO EAT IT!
BUT SENPAI TOLD ME THAT I'M OKAY NOW!
HOW CAN I GO BACK TO BEING A CRYBABY AFTER THAT?
YOU WON'T LET ME EAT IT. YOU DON'T WANT TO EAT IT YOURSELF. SO WHAT DO YOU WANT TO DO WITH IT!?
WE COULD SECRETLY FEED IT TO ONE OF THE CLUB MEMBERS...?
OUT OF THE QUESTION !!
ピリリリリ
PIRIRIRIRI (BZZZZZ)

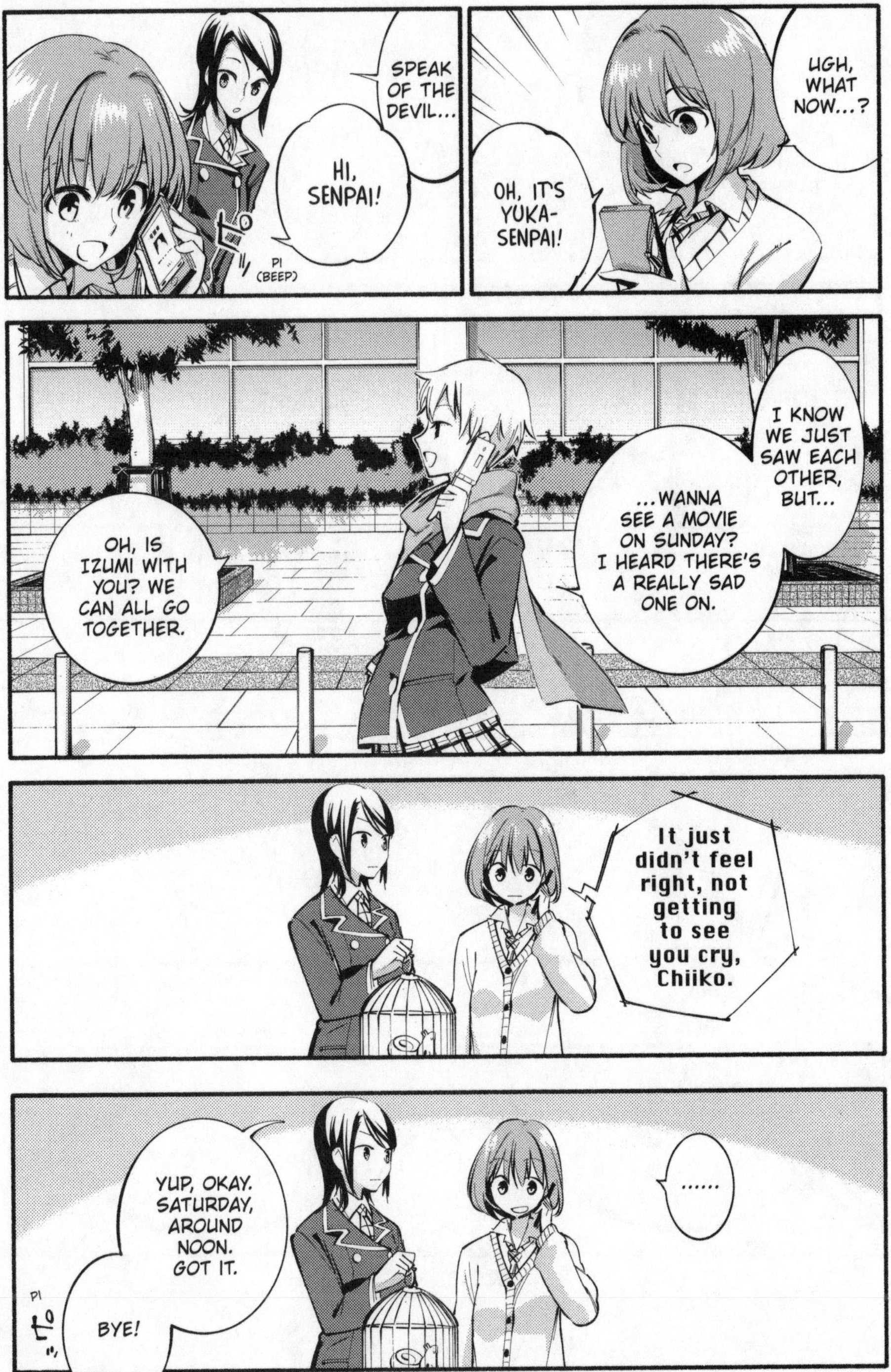
UGH, WHAT NOW...?
OH, IT'S YUKA-SENPAI!
SPEAK OF THE DEVIL...
HI, SENPAI!
PI (BEEP)
I KNOW WE JUST SAW EACH OTHER, BUT...
...WANNA SEE A MOVIE ON SUNDAY? I HEARD THERE'S A REALLY SAD ONE ON.
OH, IS IZUMI WITH YOU? WE CAN ALL GO TOGETHER.
It just didn't feel right, not getting to see you cry, Chiiko.
......
YUP, OKAY. SATURDAY, AROUND NOON. GOT IT.
BYE!
PI

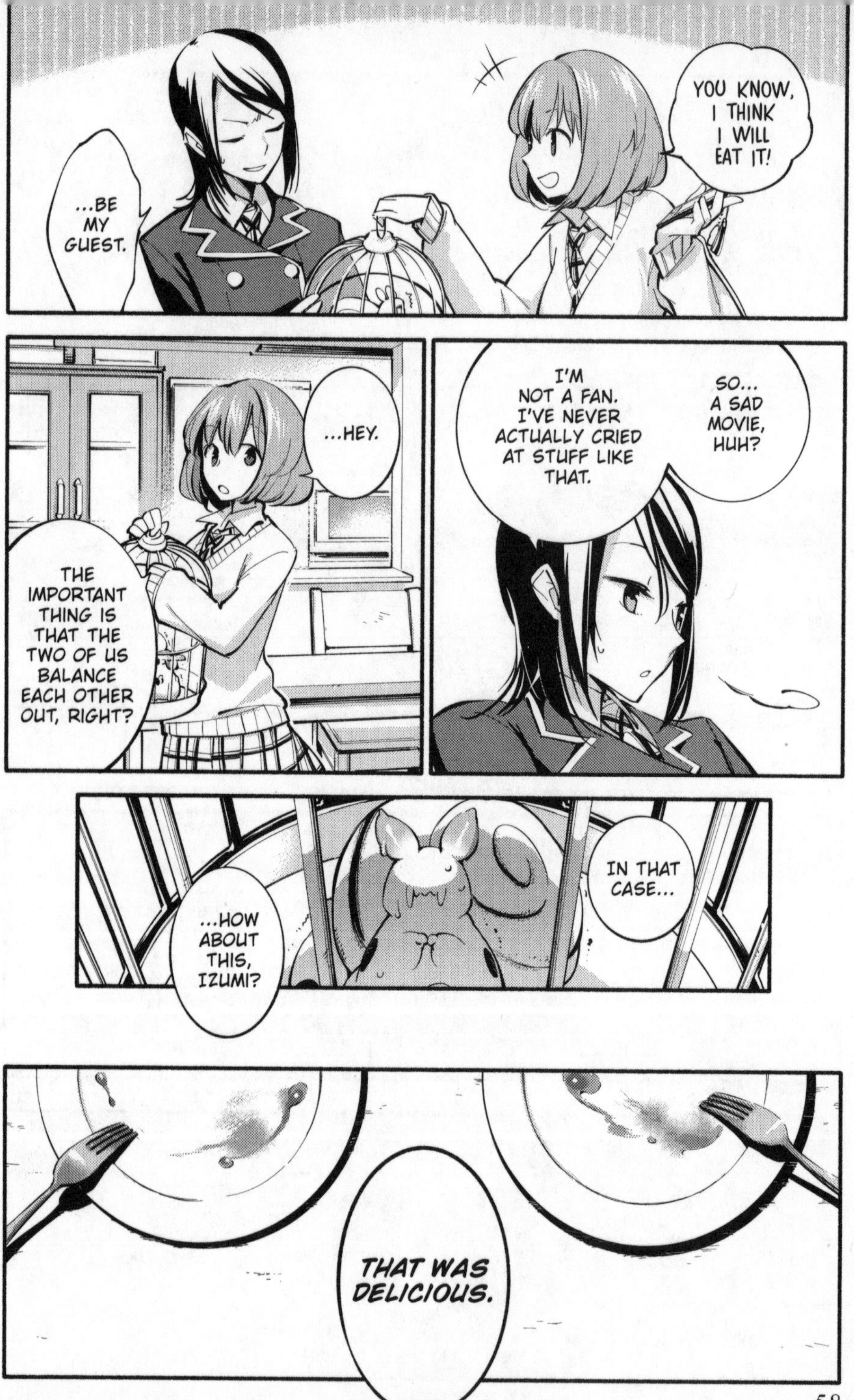
YOU KNOW, I THINK I WILL EAT IT!
...BE MY GUEST.
SO... A SAD MOVIE, HUH?
I'M NOT A FAN. I'VE NEVER ACTUALLY CRIED AT STUFF LIKE THAT.
...HEY.
THE IMPORTANT THING IS THAT THE TWO OF US BALANCE EACH OTHER OUT, RIGHT?
IN THAT CASE...
...HOW ABOUT THIS, IZUMI?
THAT WAS DELICIOUS.

【Tear-Flavored Escargot】

This is a one-shot that I wrote before I started doing serial stories. The idea was for me to get used to meeting with an editor while creating a manga. I was actually supposed to create a story eight pages long, but making things short is difficult.

Initial release: *Dengeki Daioh*, December 2014 issue

Farewell to My Alter

NIO NAKATANI SHORT STORY COLLECTION

Happiness in the Shape of a Scar

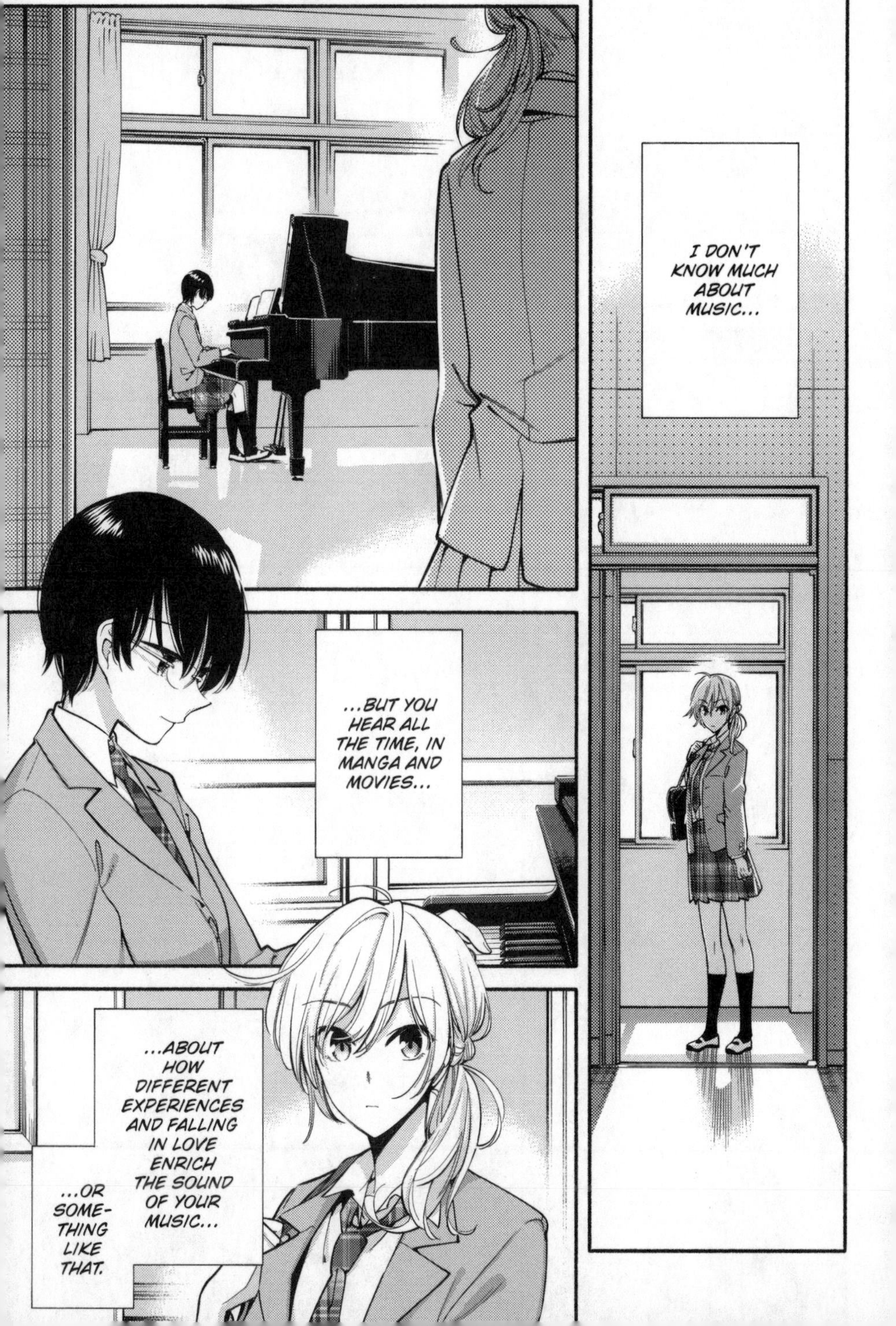
I DON'T KNOW MUCH ABOUT MUSIC...
...BUT YOU HEAR ALL THE TIME, IN MANGA AND MOVIES...
...ABOUT HOW DIFFERENT EXPERIENCES AND FALLING IN LOVE ENRICH THE SOUND OF YOUR MUSIC...
...OR SOME-THING LIKE THAT.

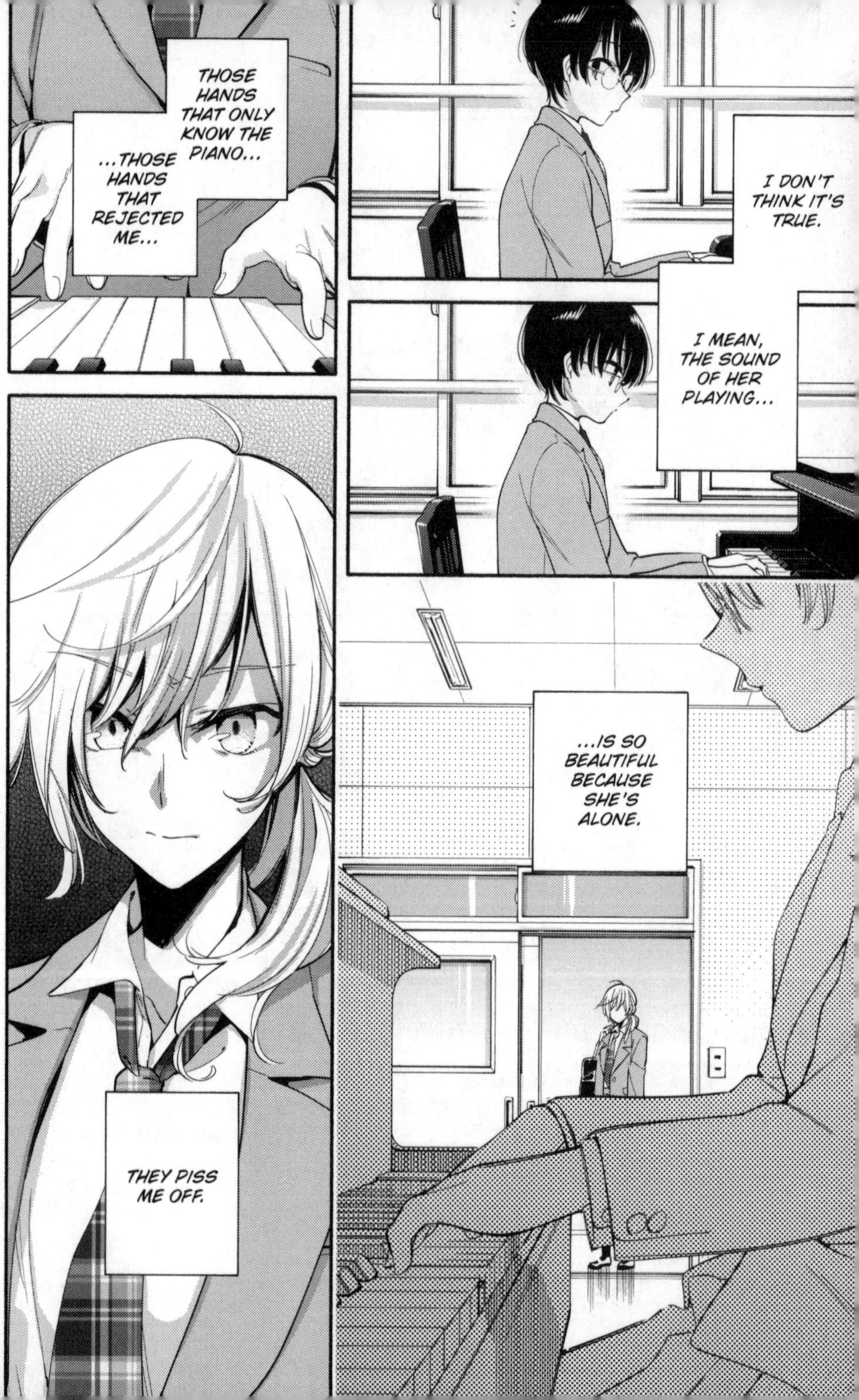
I DON'T THINK IT'S TRUE.
I MEAN, THE SOUND OF HER PLAYING...
THOSE HANDS THAT ONLY KNOW THE PIANO...
...THOSE HANDS THAT REJECTED ME...
...IS SO BEAUTIFUL BECAUSE SHE'S ALONE.
THEY PISS ME OFF.

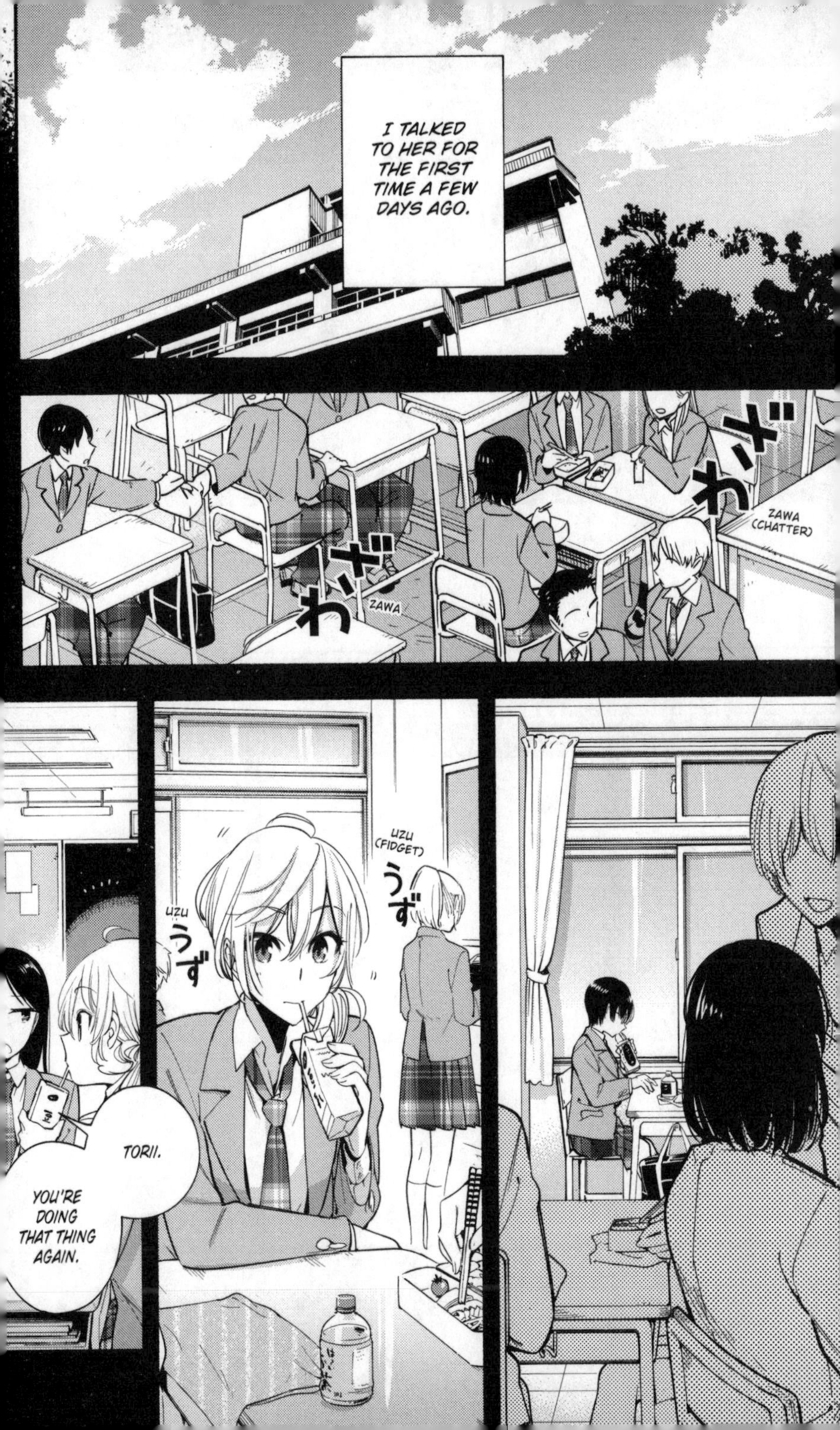
I TALKED TO HER FOR THE FIRST TIME A FEW DAYS AGO.
ざわ
ZAWA (CHATTER)
ざわ
ZAWA
うず
UZU (FIDGET)
うず
UZU
TORII.
YOU'RE DOING THAT THING AGAIN.

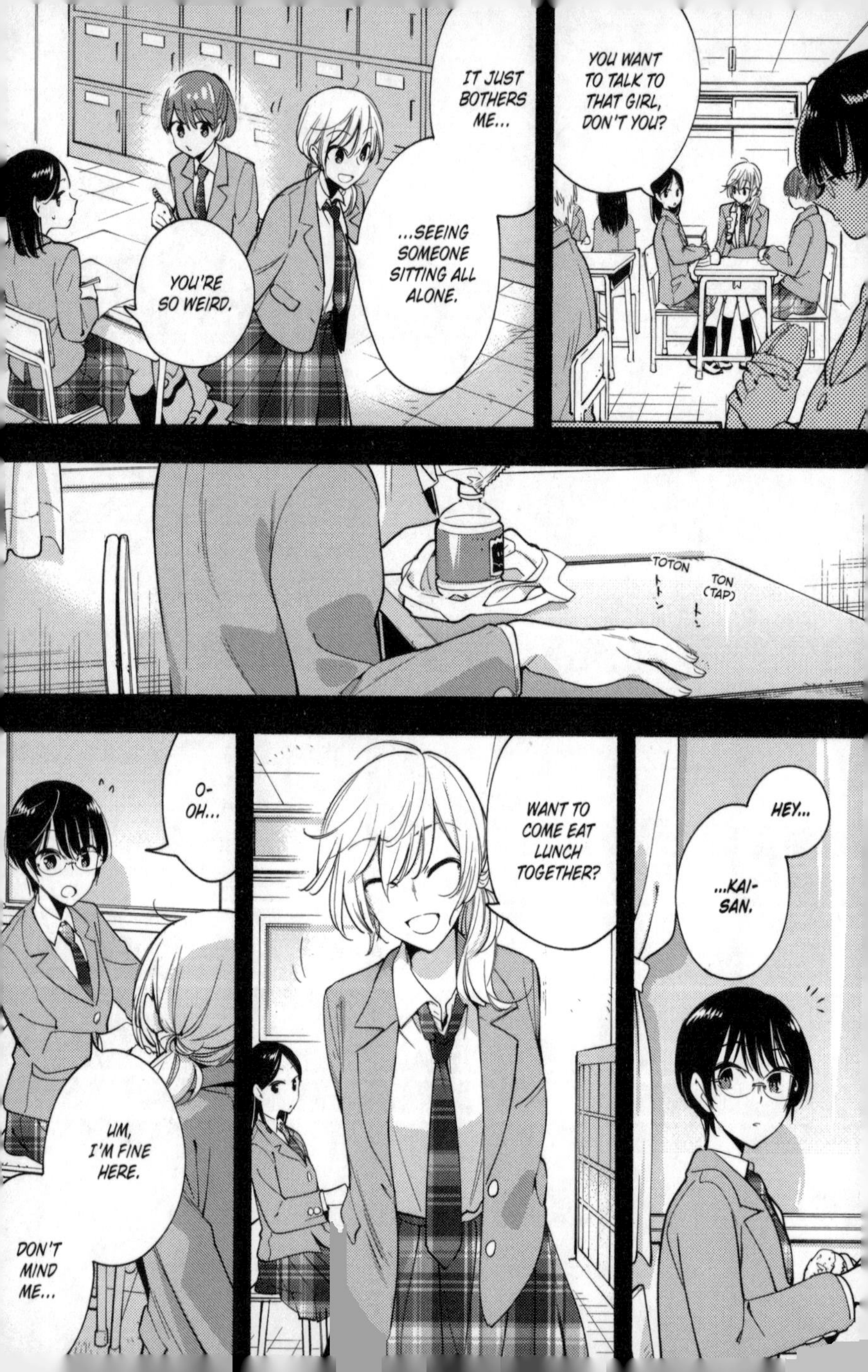
YOU WANT TO TALK TO THAT GIRL, DON'T YOU?
IT JUST BOTHERS ME...
...SEEING SOMEONE SITTING ALL ALONE.
YOU'RE SO WEIRD.
TOTON
TON (TAP)
HEY...
...KAI-SAN.
WANT TO COME EAT LUNCH TOGETHER?
O-OH...
UM, I'M FINE HERE.
DON'T MIND ME...

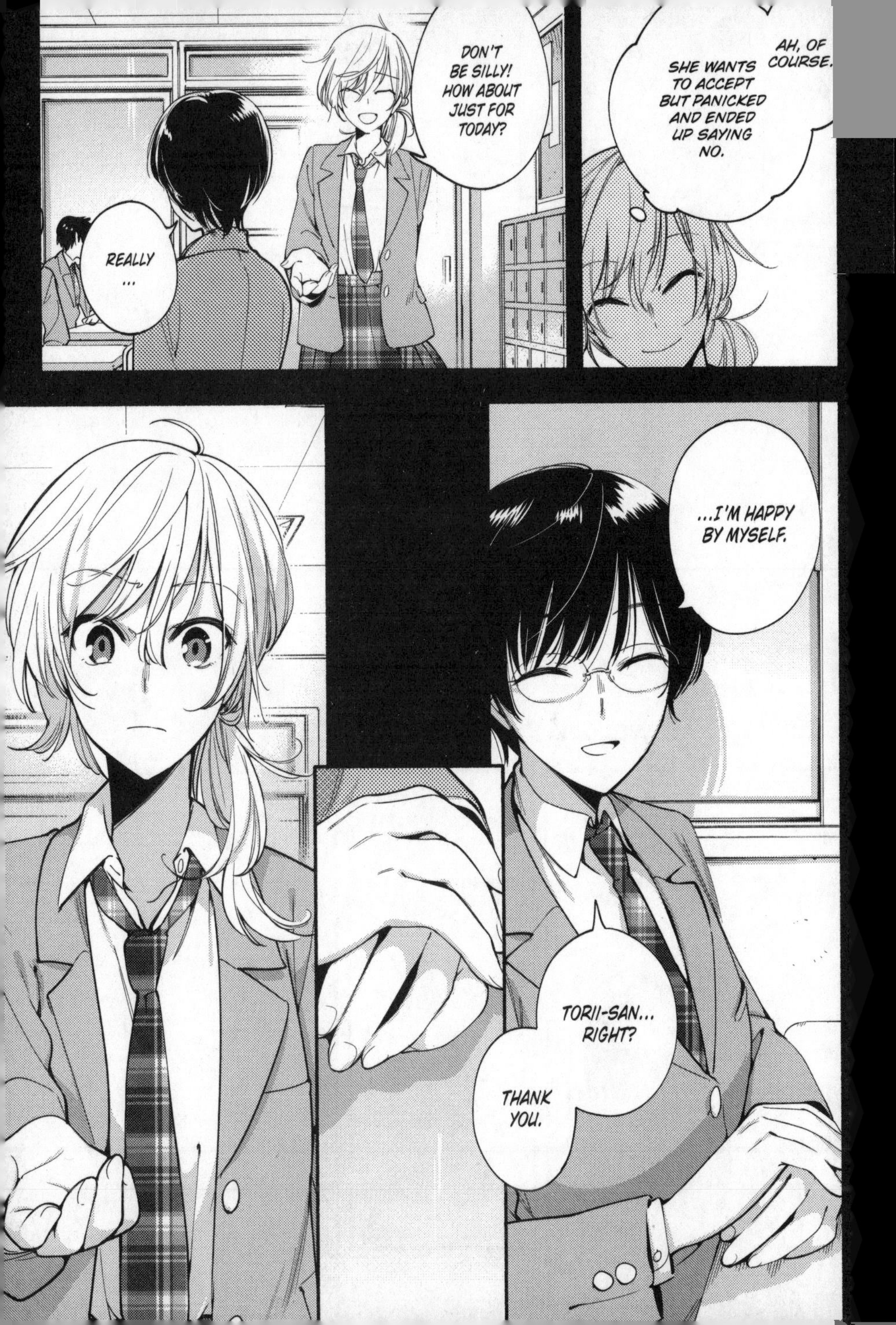
AH, OF COURSE.
SHE WANTS TO ACCEPT BUT PANICKED AND ENDED UP SAYING NO.
DON'T BE SILLY! HOW ABOUT JUST FOR TODAY?
REALLY ...
...I'M HAPPY BY MYSELF.
TORII-SAN... RIGHT?
THANK YOU.

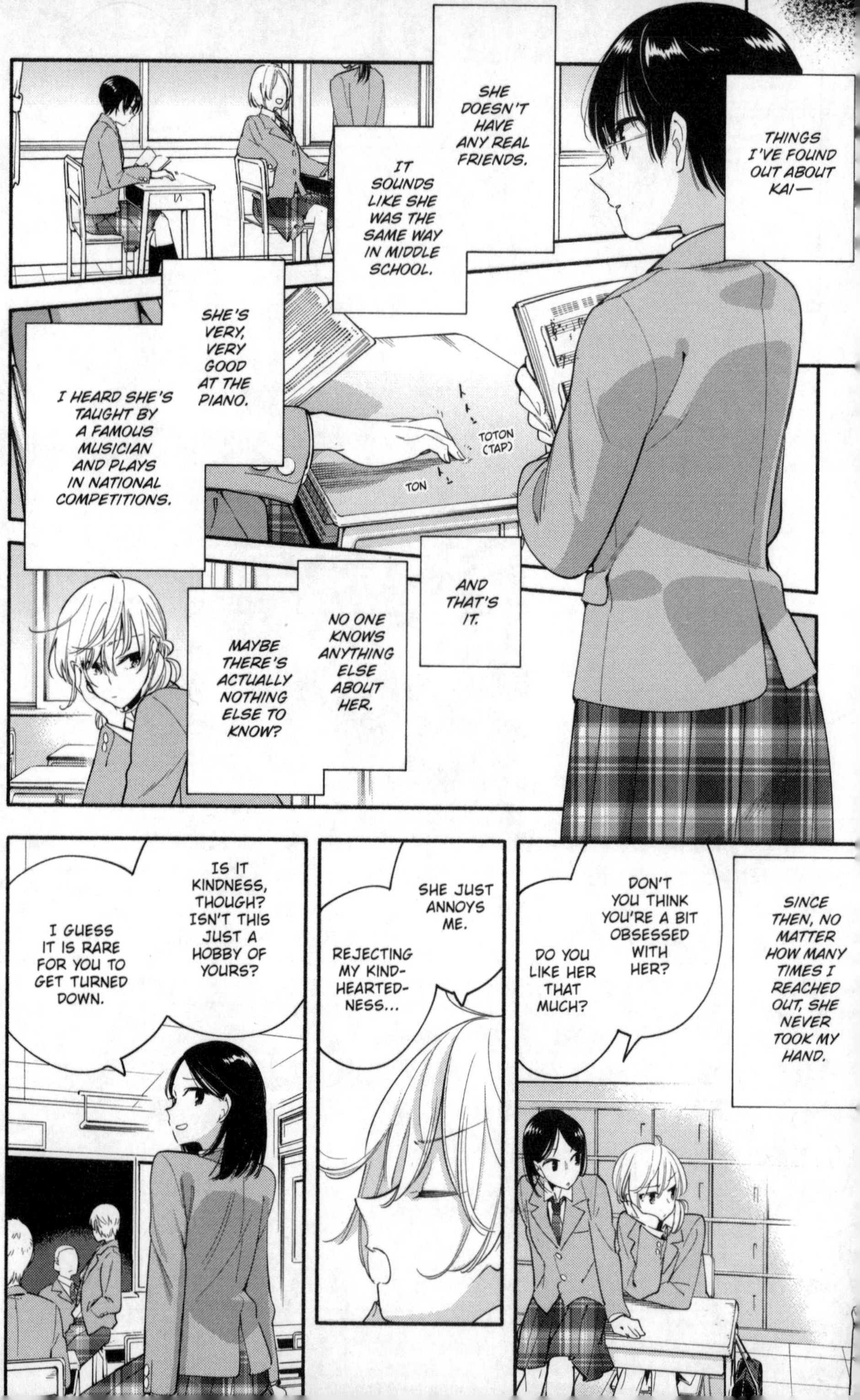
THINGS I'VE FOUND OUT ABOUT KAI—
SHE DOESN'T HAVE ANY REAL FRIENDS.
IT SOUNDS LIKE SHE WAS THE SAME WAY IN MIDDLE SCHOOL.
SHE'S VERY, VERY GOOD AT THE PIANO.
I HEARD SHE'S TAUGHT BY A FAMOUS MUSICIAN AND PLAYS IN NATIONAL COMPETITIONS.
TOTON (TAP)
TON
AND THAT'S IT.
NO ONE KNOWS ANYTHING ELSE ABOUT HER.
MAYBE THERE'S ACTUALLY NOTHING ELSE TO KNOW?
SINCE THEN, NO MATTER HOW MANY TIMES I REACHED OUT, SHE NEVER TOOK MY HAND.
DON'T YOU THINK YOU'RE A BIT OBSESSED WITH HER?
DO YOU LIKE HER THAT MUCH?
SHE JUST ANNOYS ME.
REJECTING MY KIND-HEARTED-NESS...
IS IT KINDNESS, THOUGH? ISN'T THIS JUST A HOBBY OF YOURS?
I GUESS IT IS RARE FOR YOU TO GET TURNED DOWN.

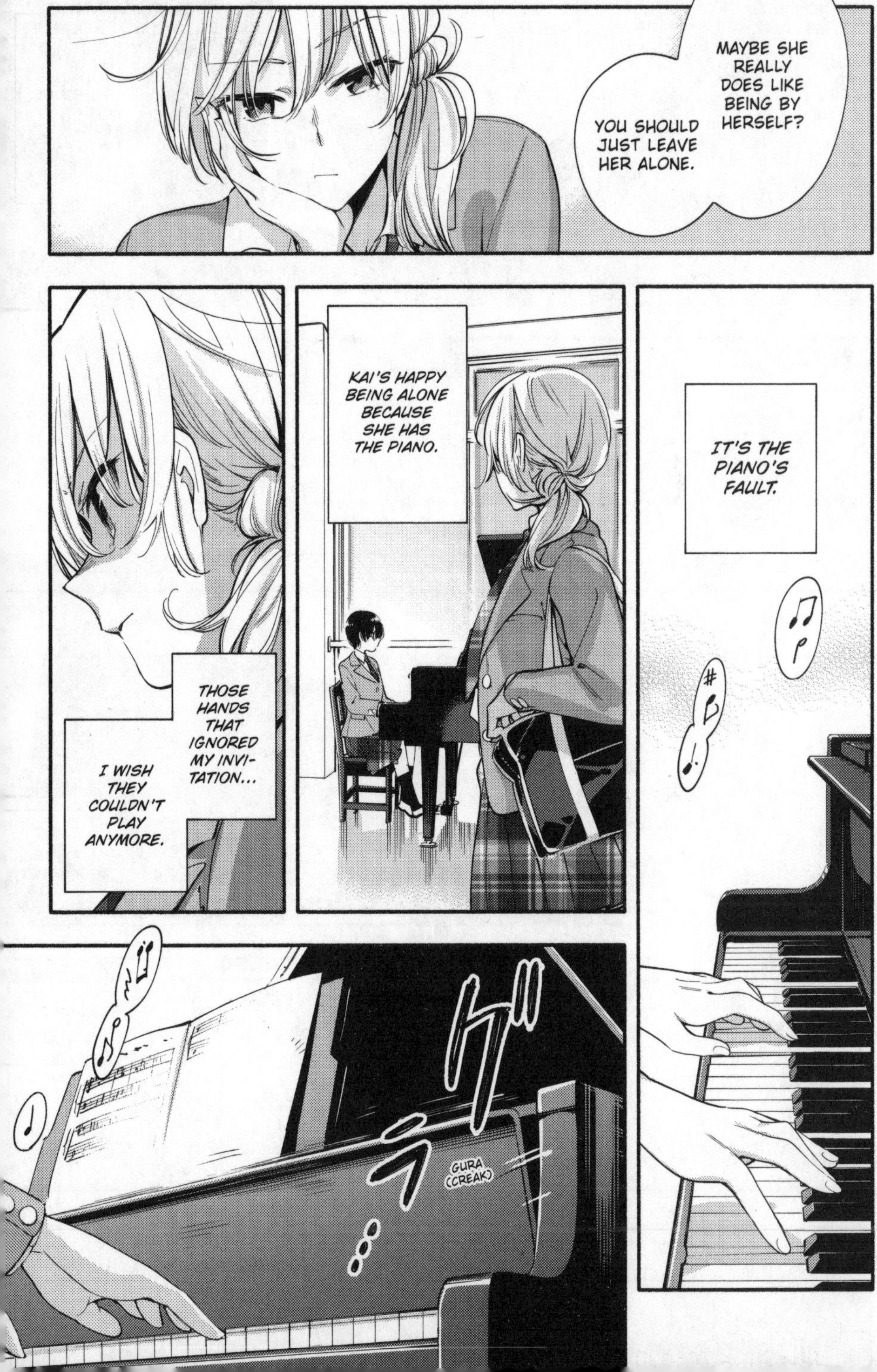
MAYBE SHE REALLY DOES LIKE BEING BY HERSELF?
YOU SHOULD JUST LEAVE HER ALONE.
IT'S THE PIANO'S FAULT.
KAI'S HAPPY BEING ALONE BECAUSE SHE HAS THE PIANO.
THOSE HANDS THAT IGNORED MY INVI-TATION...
I WISH THEY COULDN'T PLAY ANYMORE.
GURA (CREAK)

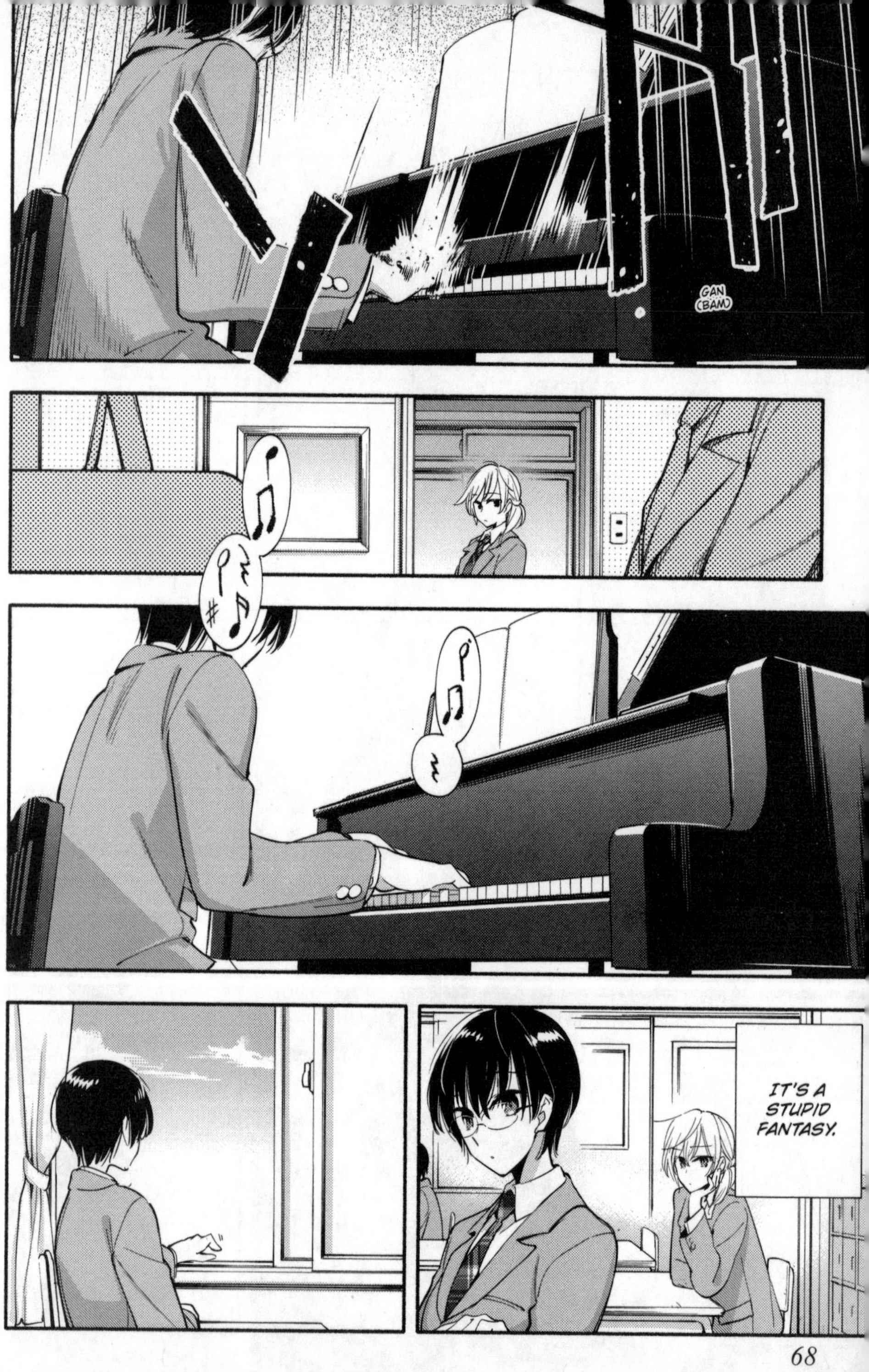
GAN
(BAM)
IT'S A STUPID FANTASY.

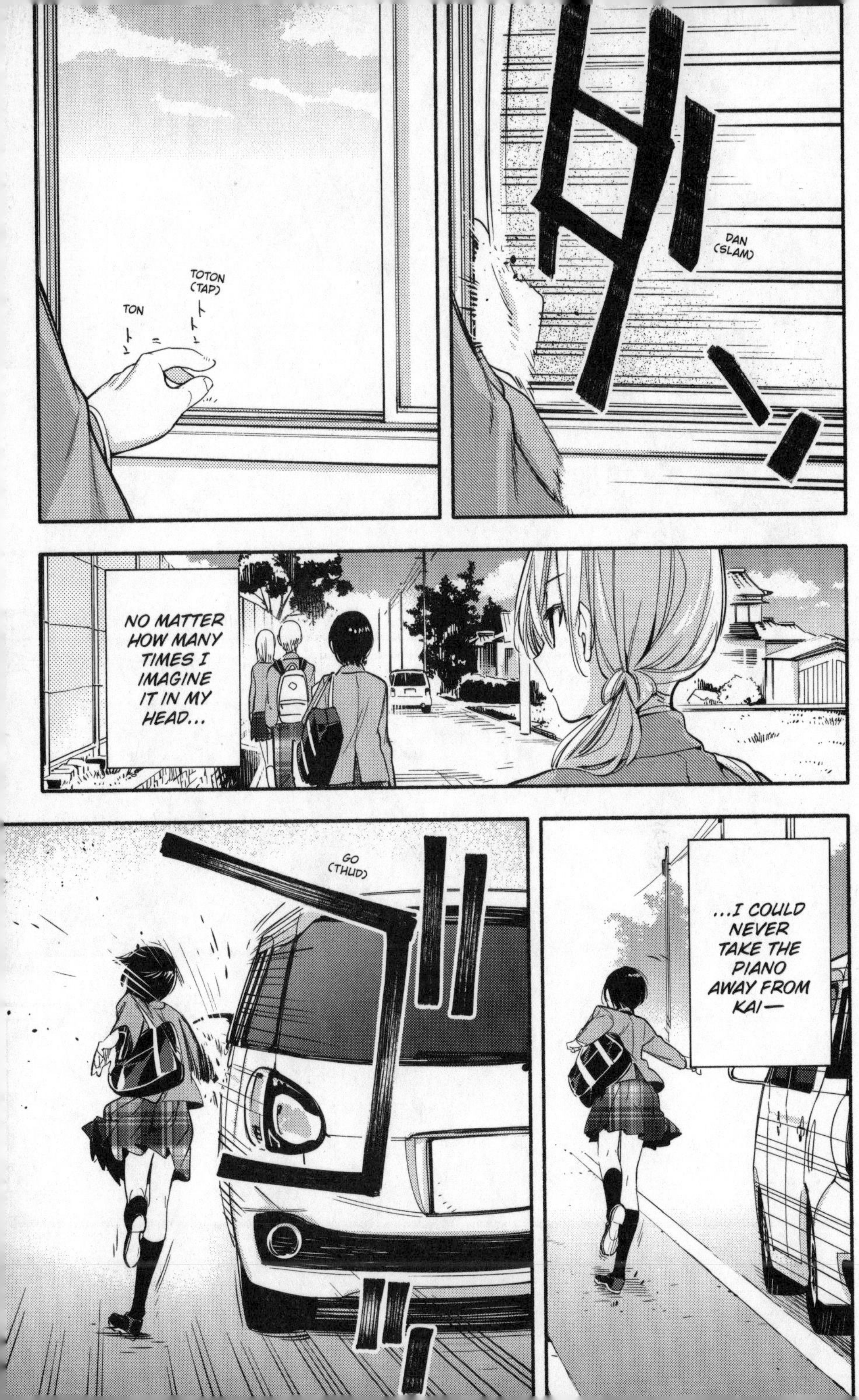
DAN
(SLAM)
TOTON
(TAP)
TON
NO MATTER HOW MANY TIMES I IMAGINE IT IN MY HEAD...
...I COULD NEVER TAKE THE PIANO AWAY FROM KAI—
GO
(THUD)

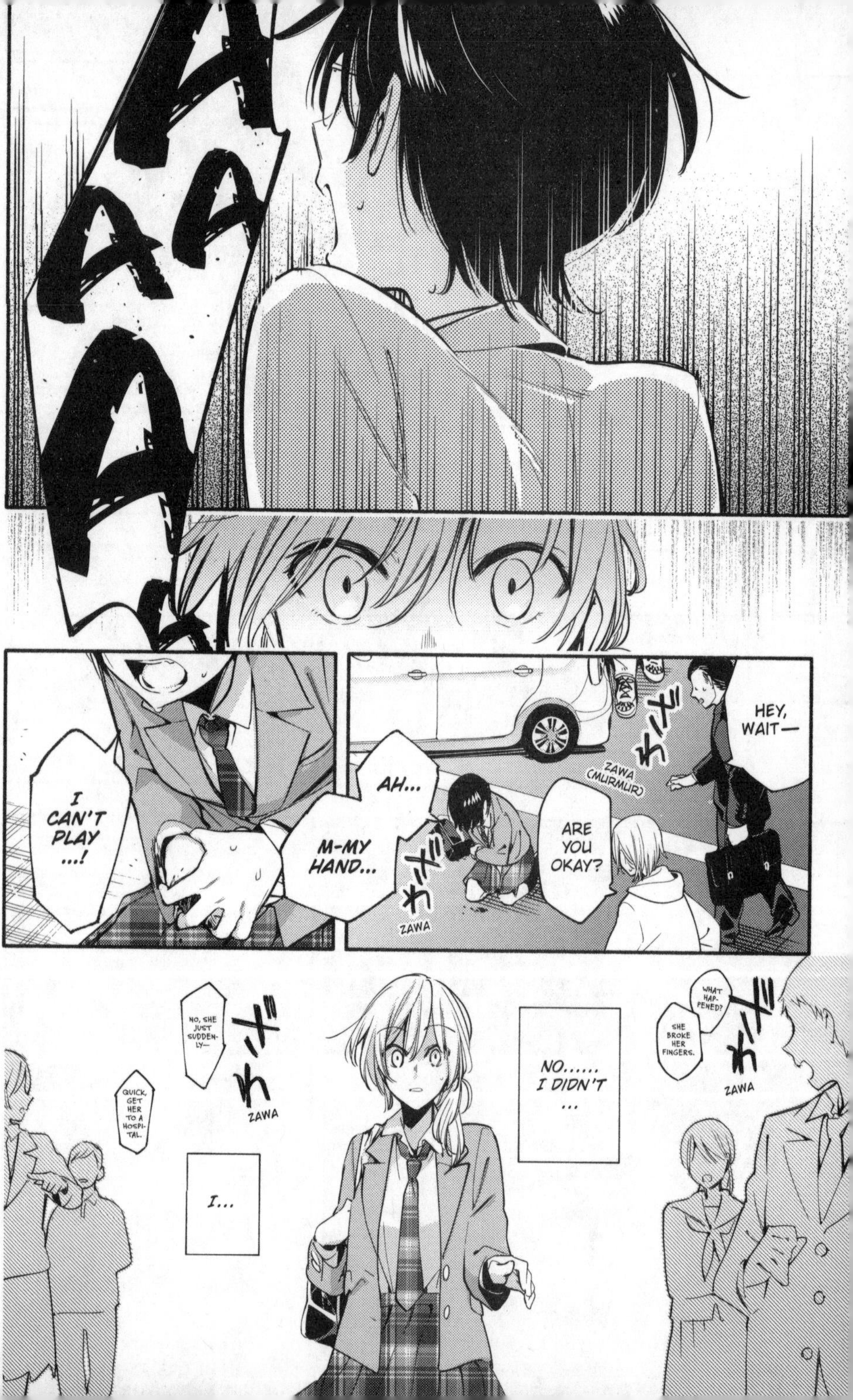
AAAAAA
HEY, WAIT—
ざわ
ZAWA (MURMUR)
ARE YOU OKAY?
AH...
M-MY HAND...
ざわ
ZAWA
I CAN'T PLAY ...!
WHAT HAPPENED?
SHE BROKE HER FINGERS.
ざわ
ZAWA
NO...... I DIDN'T ...
NO, SHE JUST SUDDENLY—
ざわ
ZAWA
QUICK, GET HER TO A HOSPITAL.
I...

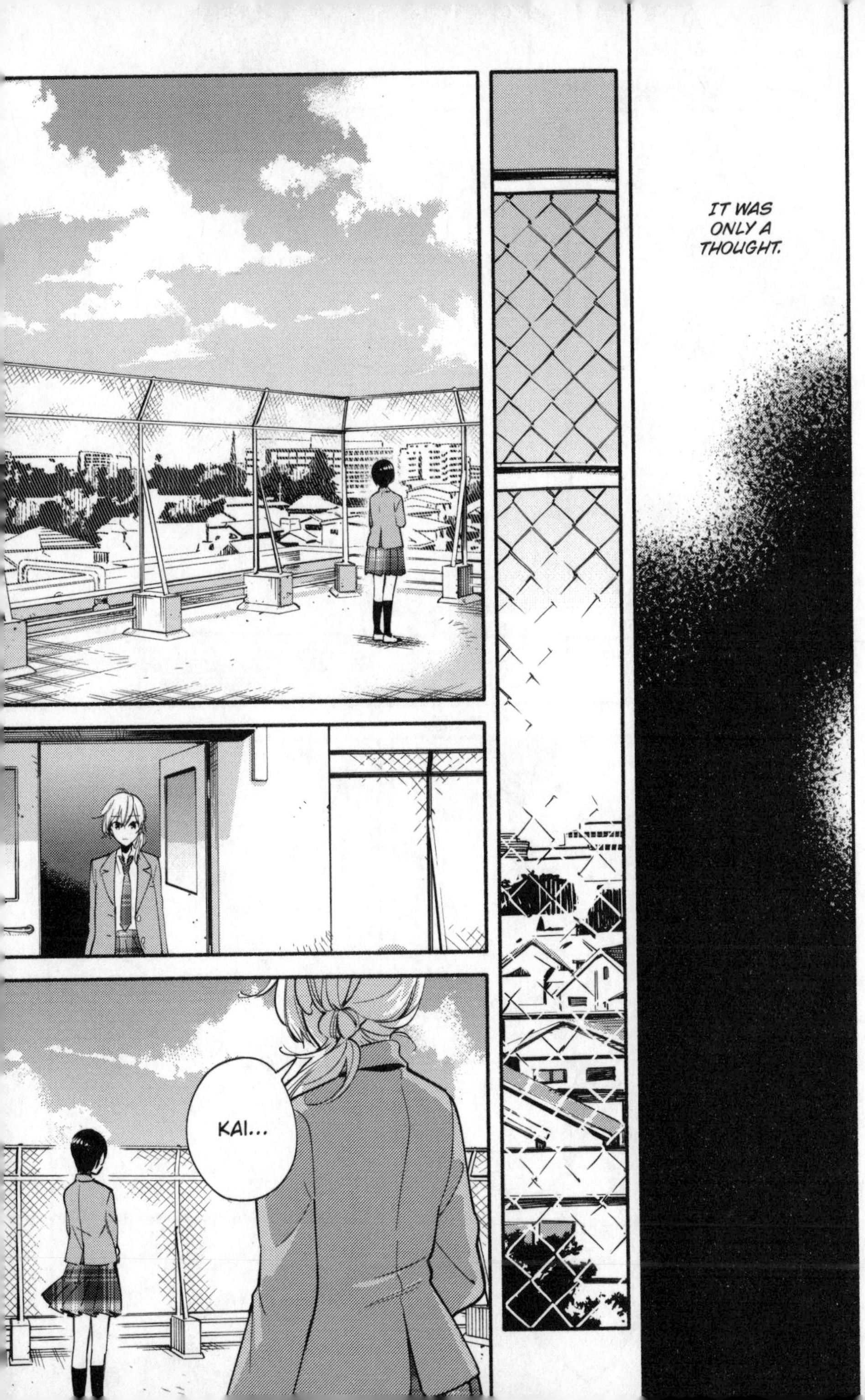
IT WAS ONLY A THOUGHT.
KAI...

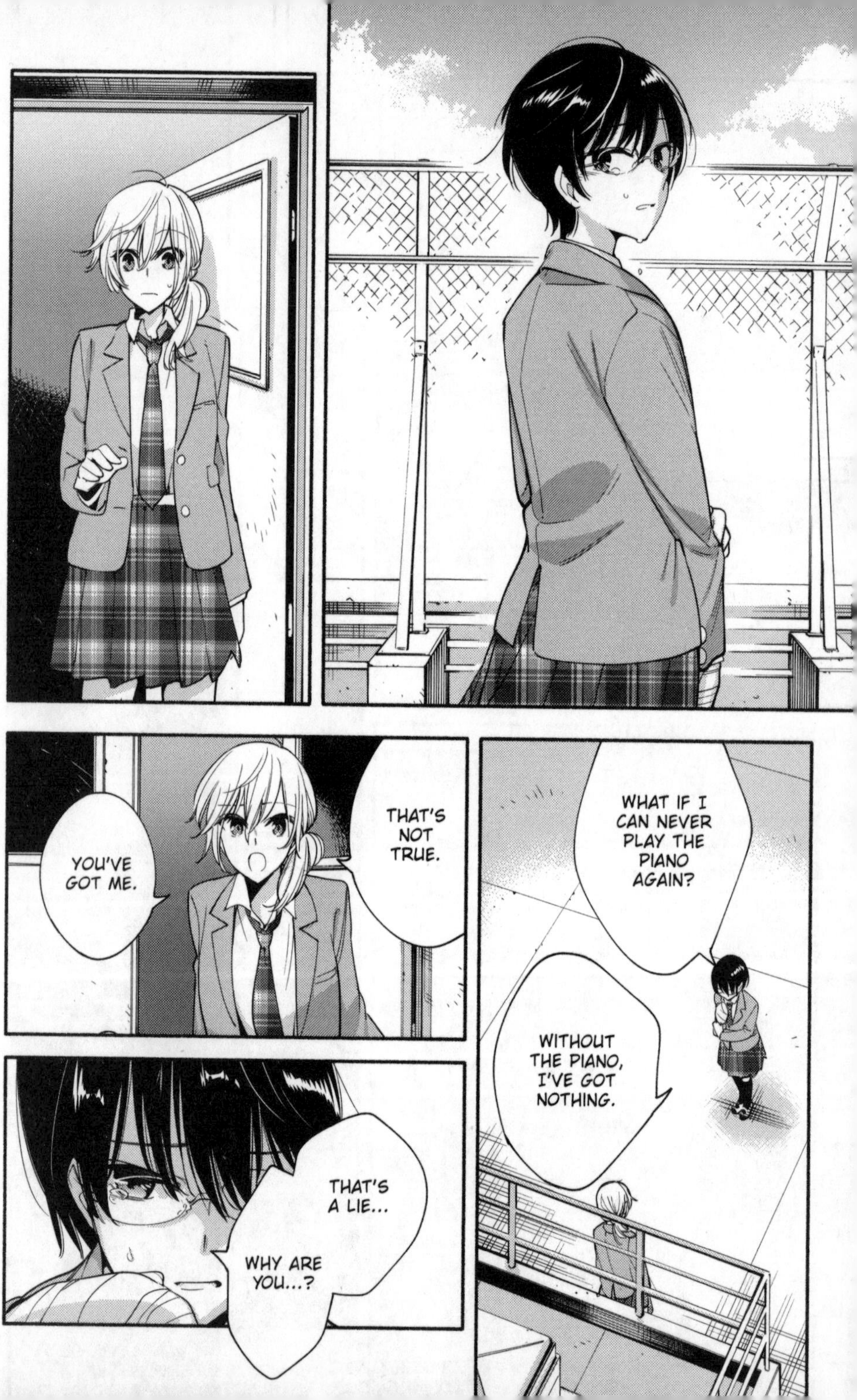
WHAT IF I CAN NEVER PLAY THE PIANO AGAIN?
WITHOUT THE PIANO, I'VE GOT NOTHING.
THAT'S NOT TRUE.
YOU'VE GOT ME.
THAT'S A LIE...
WHY ARE YOU...?

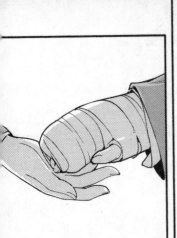

I WANT TO BE HERE FOR YOU.

I'M GOING TO DEVOTE MYSELF TO THIS GIRL...

...TO MAKE UP FOR WHAT I WISHED UPON HER.

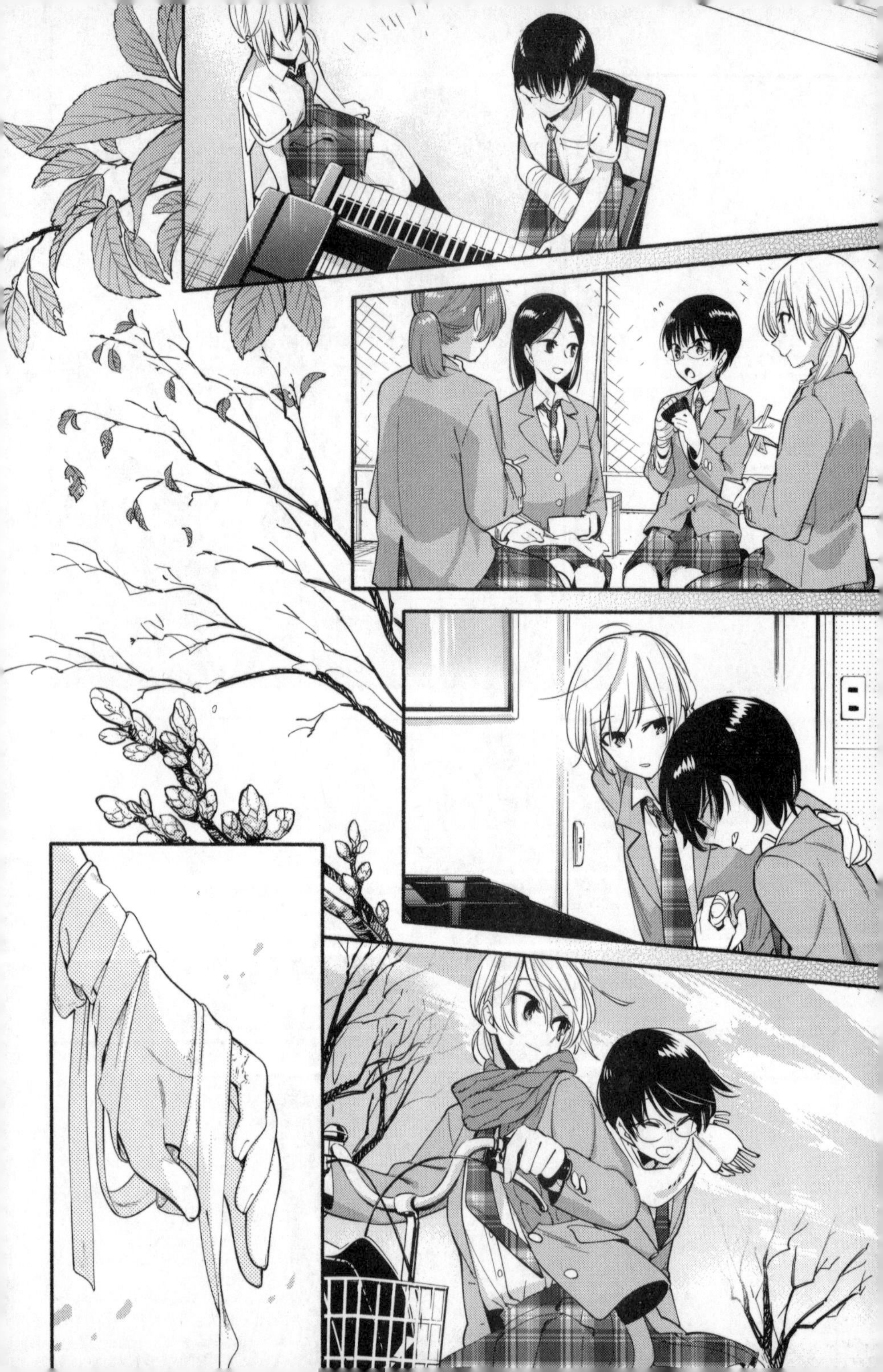

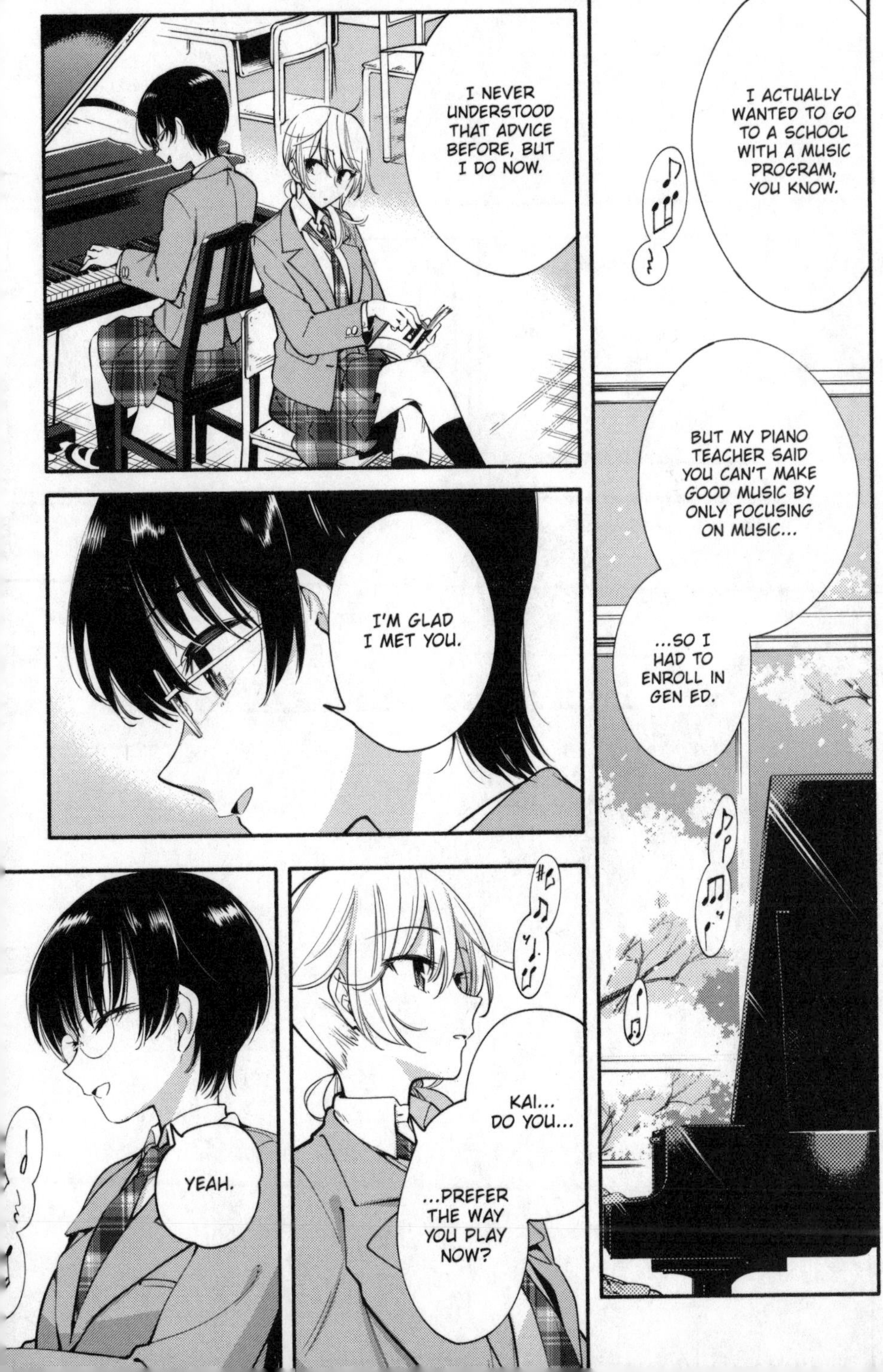
I ACTUALLY WANTED TO GO TO A SCHOOL WITH A MUSIC PROGRAM, YOU KNOW.
BUT MY PIANO TEACHER SAID YOU CAN'T MAKE GOOD MUSIC BY ONLY FOCUSING ON MUSIC...
...SO I HAD TO ENROLL IN GEN ED.
I NEVER UNDERSTOOD THAT ADVICE BEFORE, BUT I DO NOW.
I'M GLAD I MET YOU.
KAI... DO YOU...
...PREFER THE WAY YOU PLAY NOW?
YEAH.

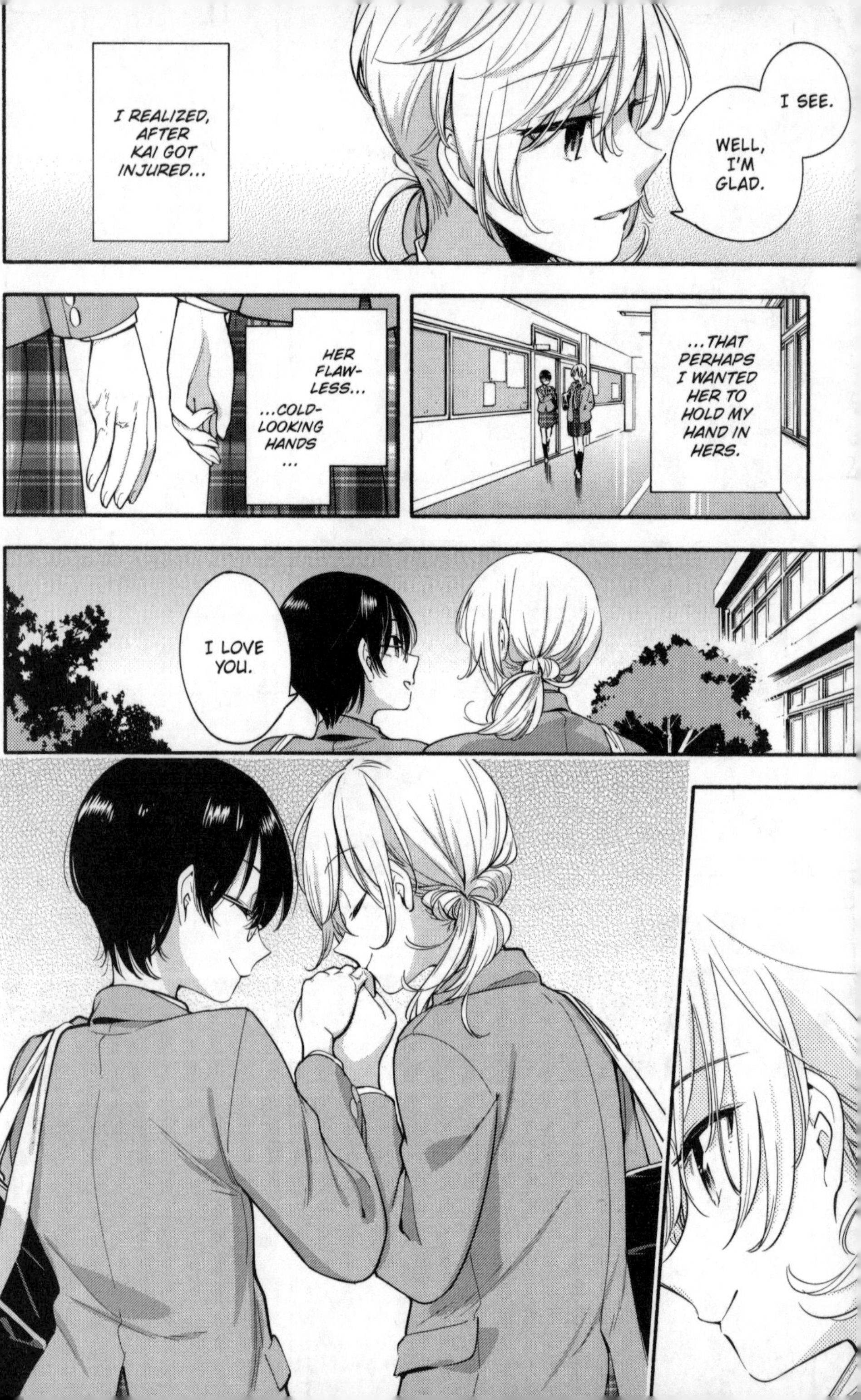
I SEE.
WELL, I'M GLAD.
I REALIZED, AFTER KAI GOT INJURED...
...THAT PERHAPS I WANTED HER TO HOLD MY HAND IN HERS.
HER FLAW-LESS...
...COLD-LOOKING HANDS...
I LOVE YOU.

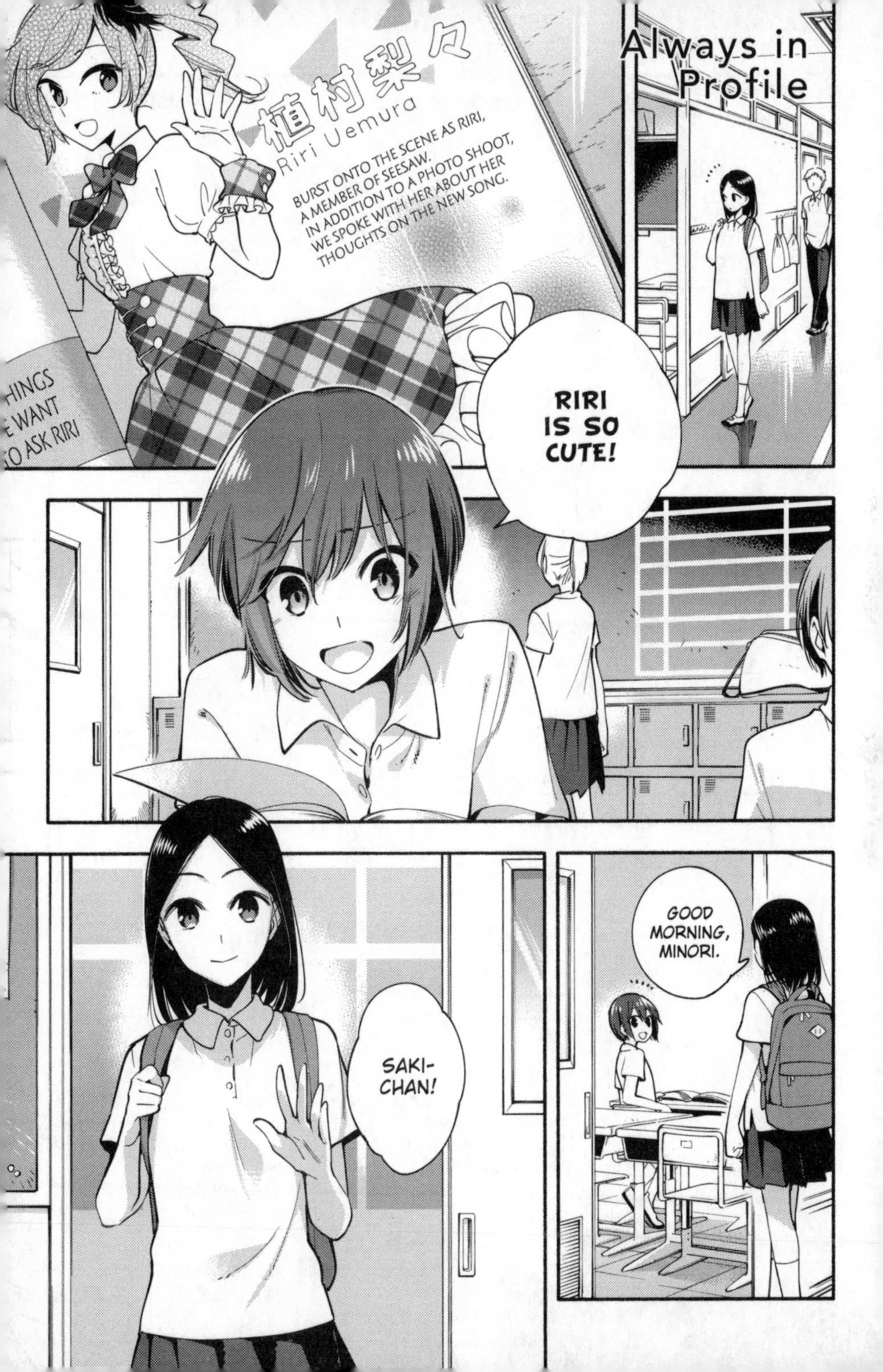
Always in Profile
植村梨々
Riri Uemura
BURST ONTO THE SCENE AS RIRI, A MEMBER OF SEESAW. IN ADDITION TO A PHOTO SHOOT, WE SPOKE WITH HER ABOUT HER THOUGHTS ON THE NEW SONG.
RIRI IS SO CUTE!
GOOD MORNING, MINORI.
SAKI-CHAN!

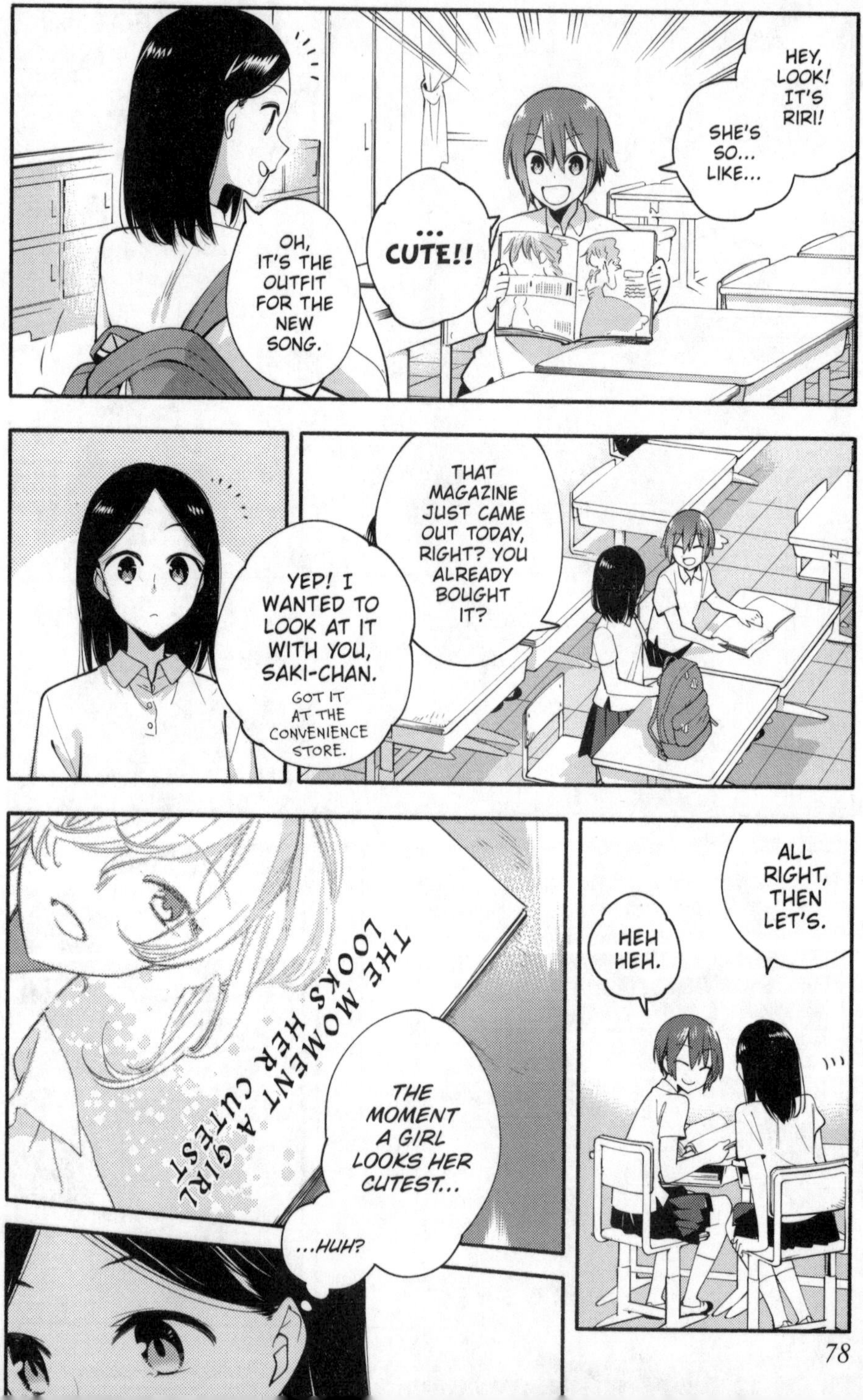
HEY, LOOK! IT'S RIRI!
SHE'S SO... LIKE...
... CUTE!!
OH, IT'S THE OUTFIT FOR THE NEW SONG.
THAT MAGAZINE JUST CAME OUT TODAY, RIGHT? YOU ALREADY BOUGHT IT?
YEP! I WANTED TO LOOK AT IT WITH YOU, SAKI-CHAN.
GOT IT AT THE CONVENIENCE STORE.
ALL RIGHT, THEN LET'S.
HEH HEH.
THE MOMENT A GIRL LOOKS HER CUTEST
THE MOMENT A GIRL LOOKS HER CUTEST...
...HUH?

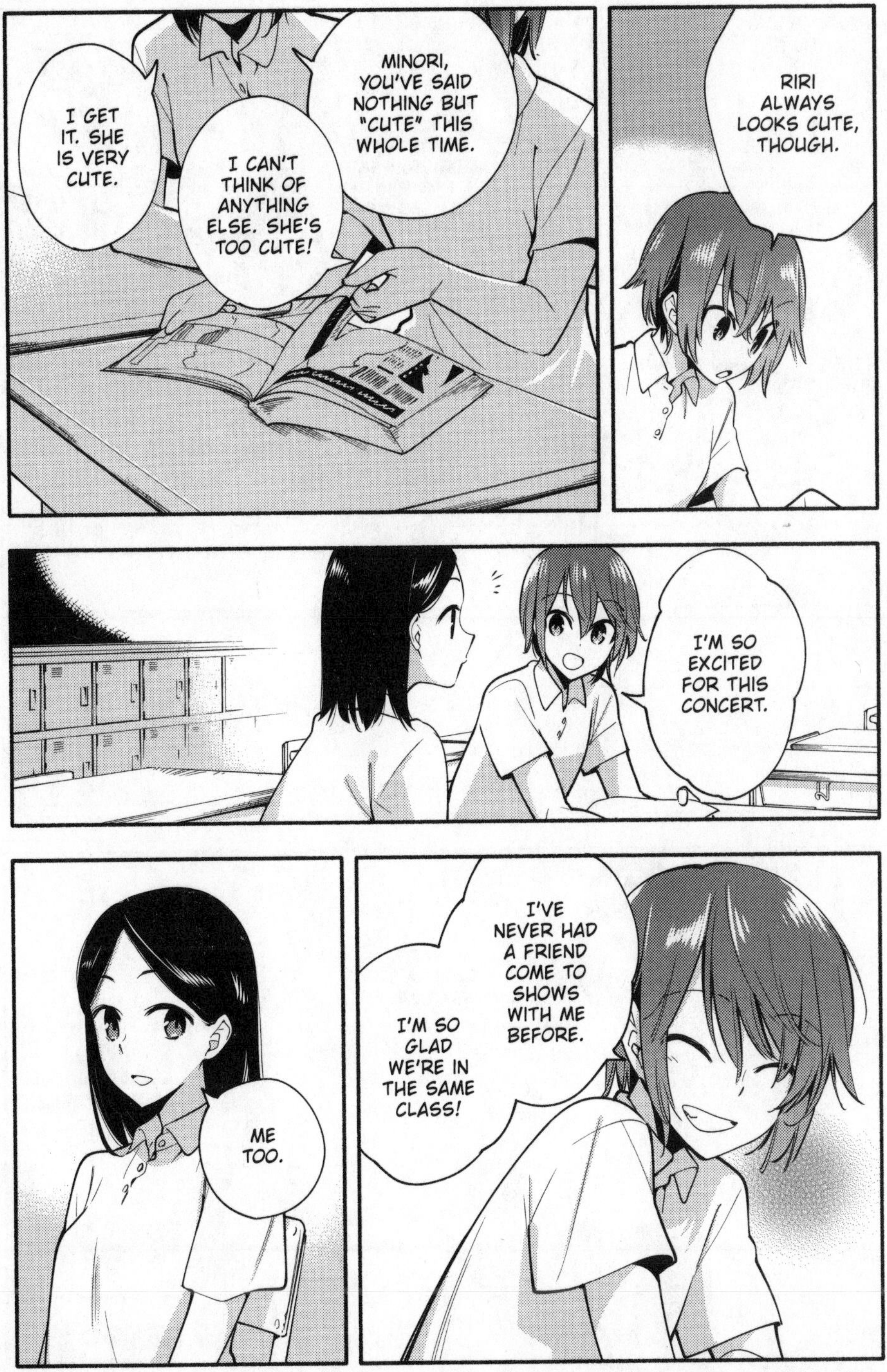
RIRI ALWAYS LOOKS CUTE, THOUGH.
MINORI, YOU'VE SAID NOTHING BUT "CUTE" THIS WHOLE TIME.
I CAN'T THINK OF ANYTHING ELSE. SHE'S TOO CUTE!
I GET IT. SHE IS VERY CUTE.
I'M SO EXCITED FOR THIS CONCERT.
I'VE NEVER HAD A FRIEND COME TO SHOWS WITH ME BEFORE.
I'M SO GLAD WE'RE IN THE SAME CLASS!
ME TOO.

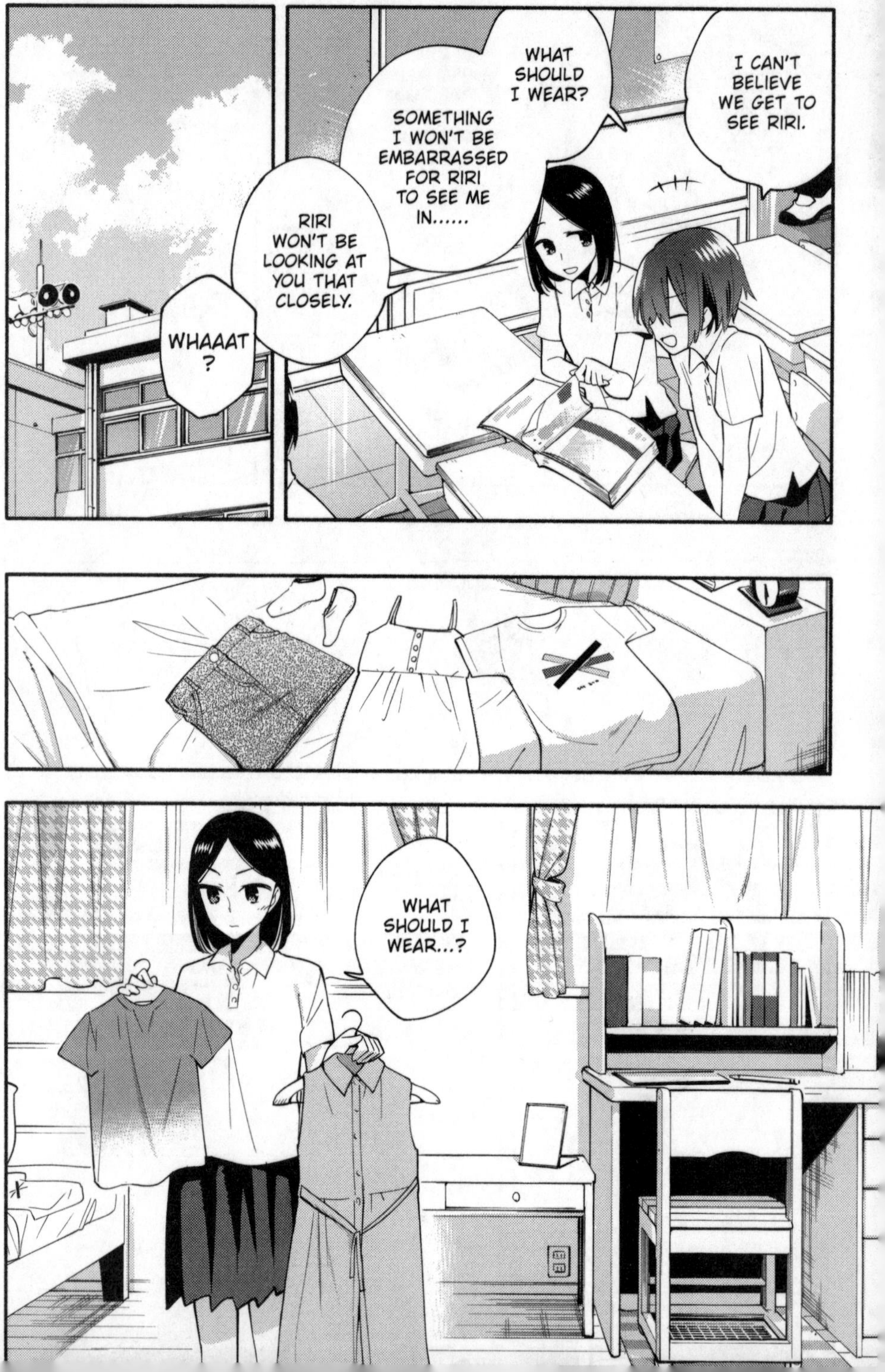
I CAN'T BELIEVE WE GET TO SEE RIRI.
WHAT SHOULD I WEAR?
SOMETHING I WON'T BE EMBARRASSED FOR RIRI TO SEE ME IN......
RIRI WON'T BE LOOKING AT YOU THAT CLOSELY.
WHAAAT?
WHAT SHOULD I WEAR...?

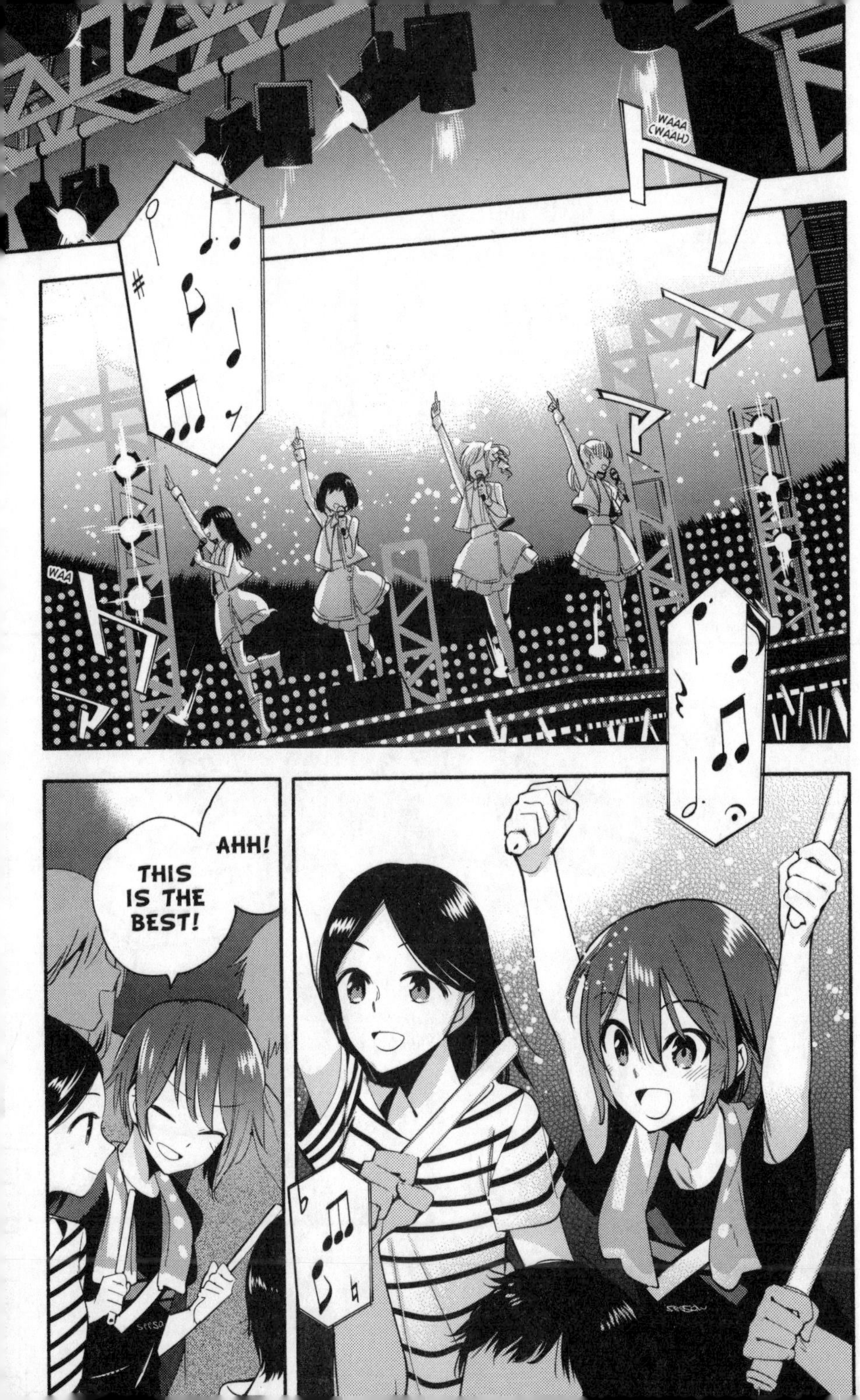
WAAA (WAAH)
WAA
AHH!
THIS IS THE BEST!

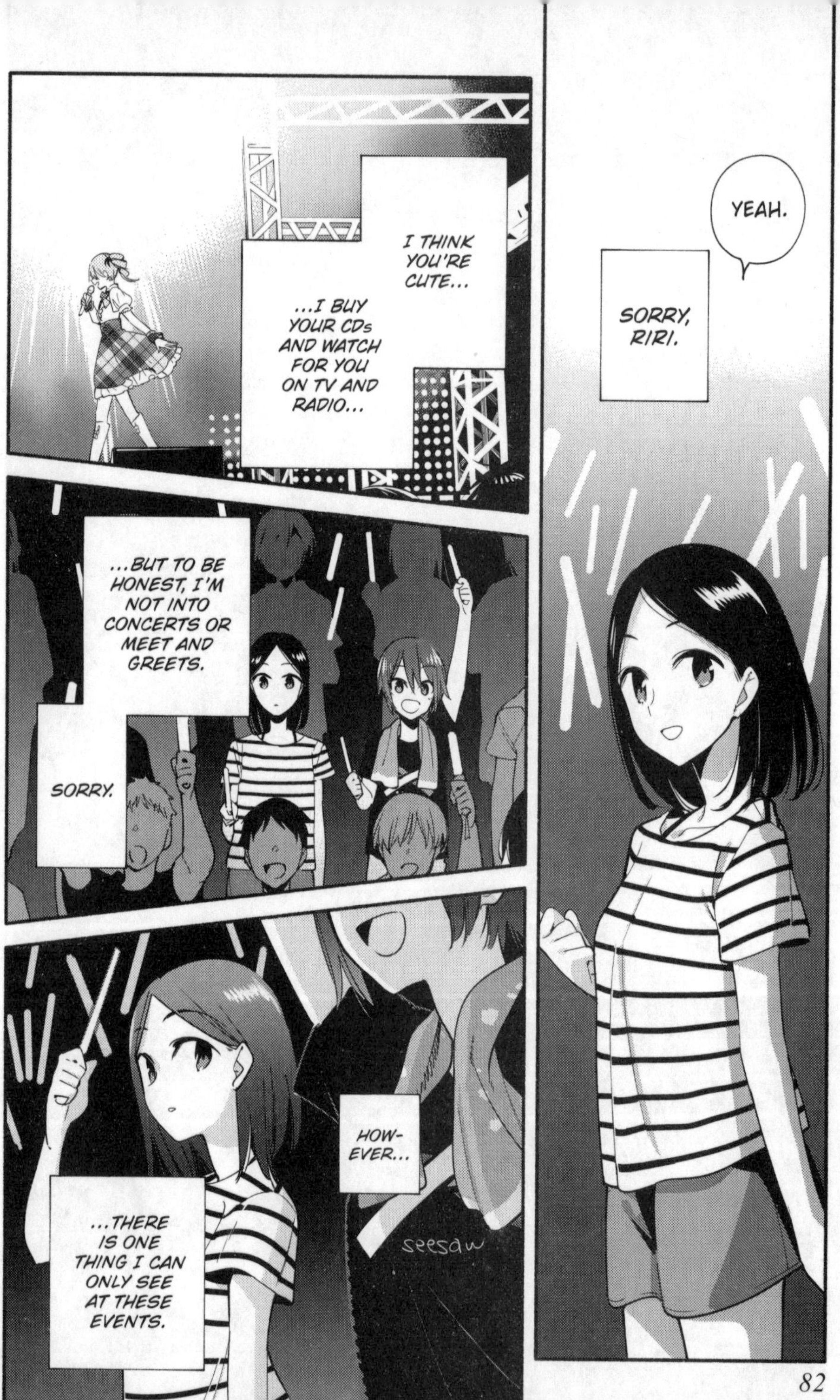
YEAH.
SORRY, RIRI.
I THINK YOU'RE CUTE...
...I BUY YOUR CDs AND WATCH FOR YOU ON TV AND RADIO...
...BUT TO BE HONEST, I'M NOT INTO CONCERTS OR MEET AND GREETS.
SORRY.
HOW-EVER...
...THERE IS ONE THING I CAN ONLY SEE AT THESE EVENTS.
seesaw

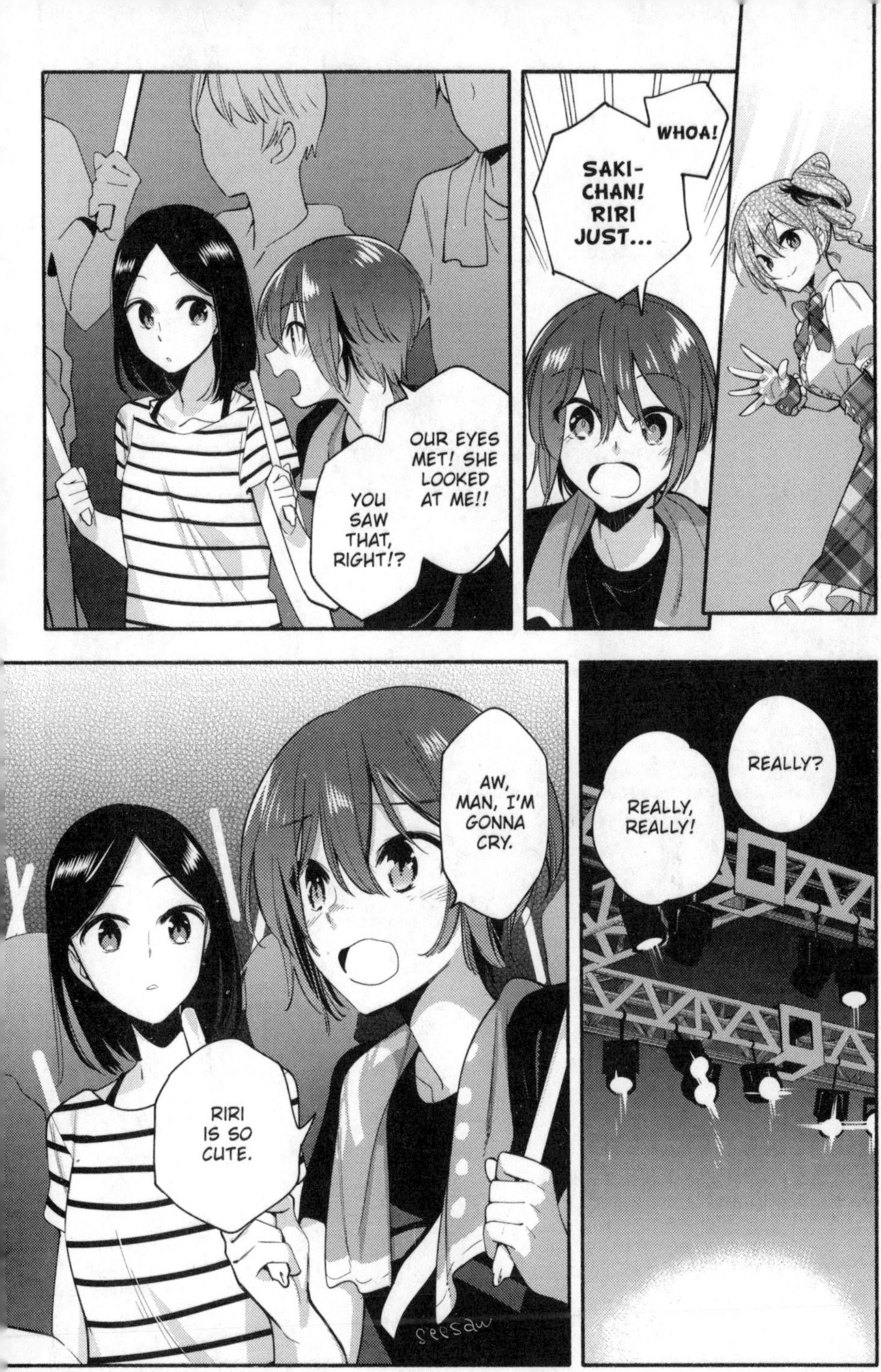
WHOA!
SAKI-CHAN! RIRI JUST...
OUR EYES MET! SHE LOOKED AT ME!!
YOU SAW THAT, RIGHT!?
REALLY?
REALLY, REALLY!
AW, MAN, I'M GONNA CRY.
RIRI IS SO CUTE.

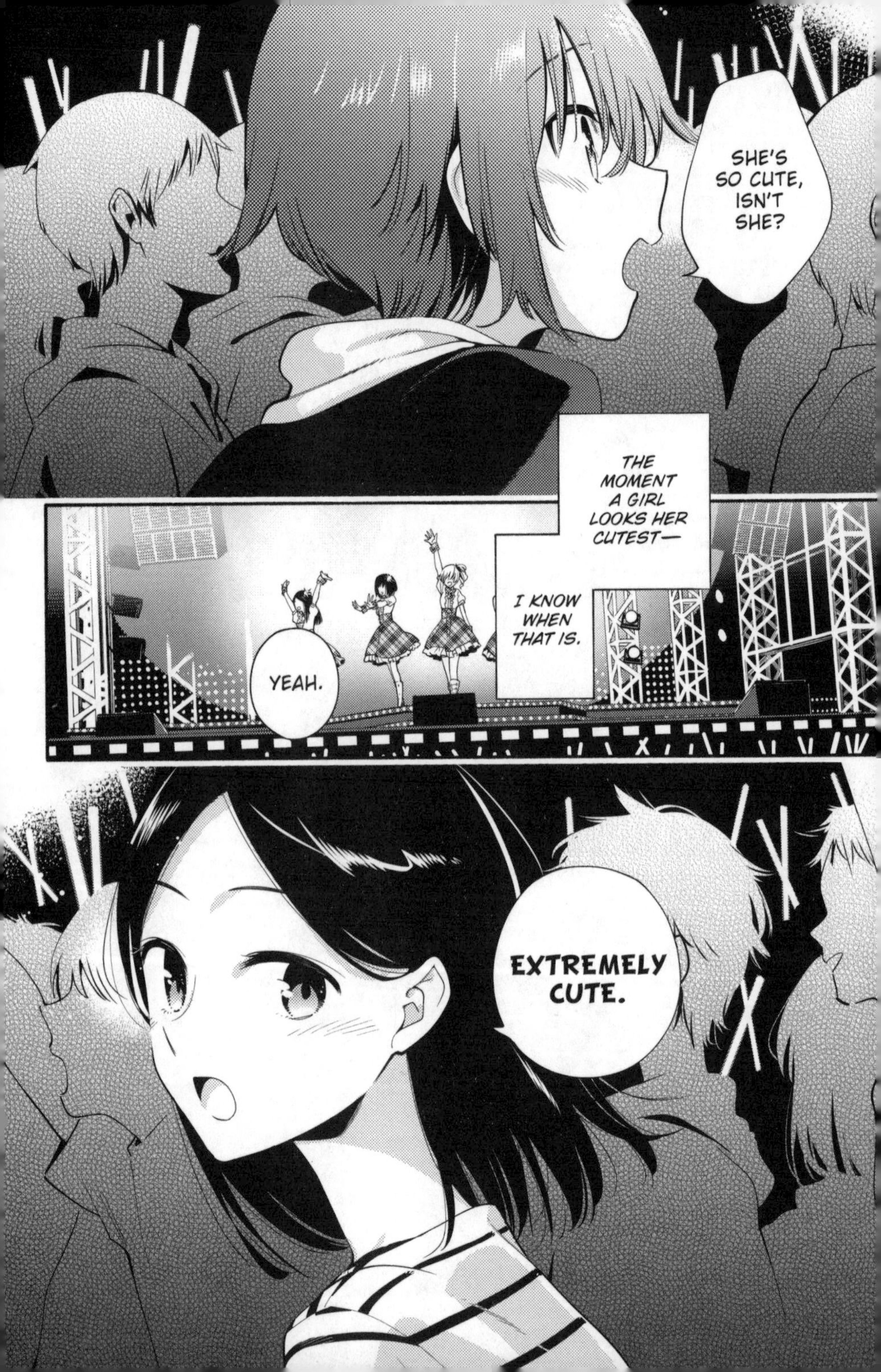
SHE'S SO CUTE, ISN'T SHE?
THE MOMENT A GIRL LOOKS HER CUTEST—
I KNOW WHEN THAT IS.
YEAH.
EXTREMELY CUTE.

Comm-ear-ication

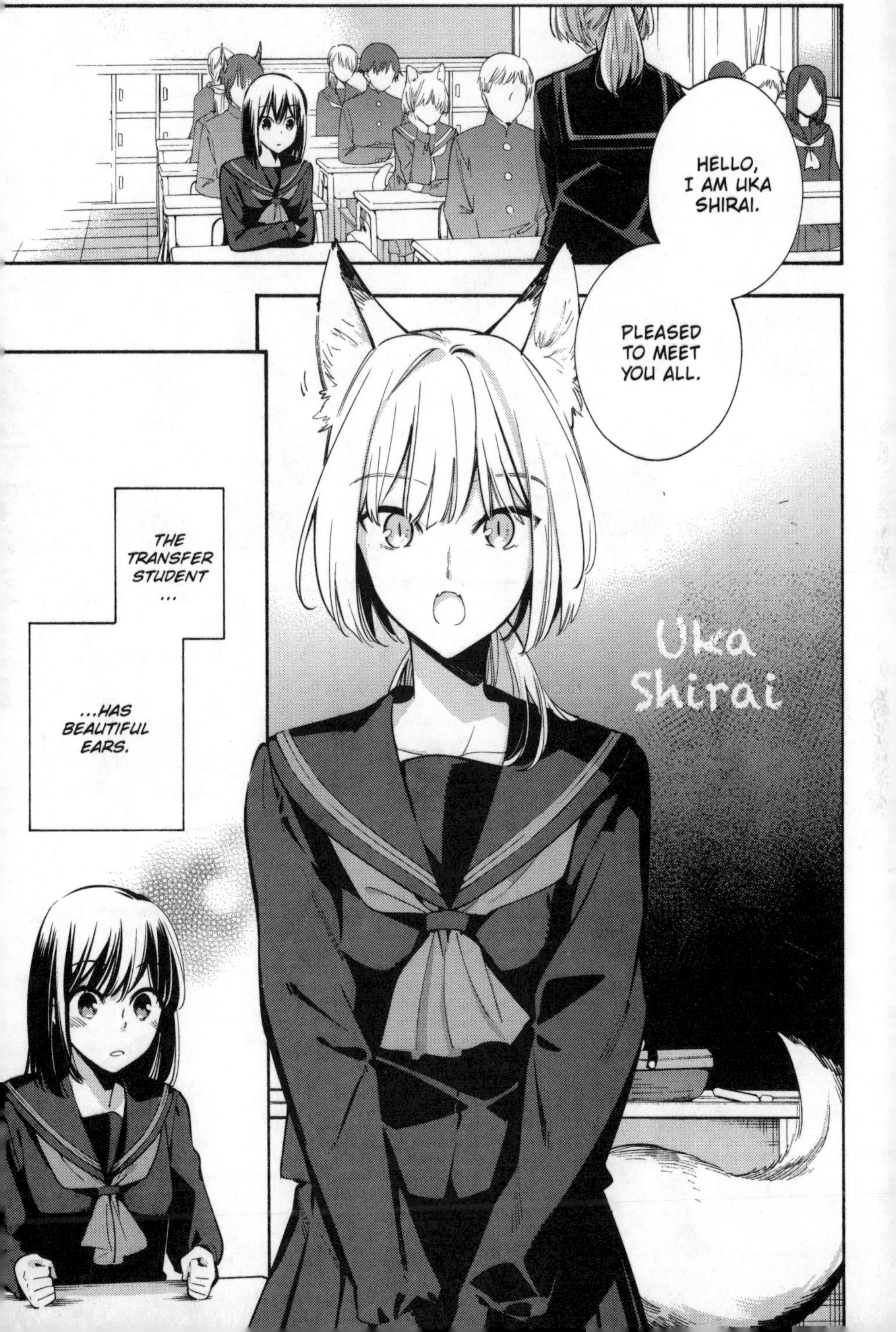
HELLO, I AM UKA SHIRAI.
PLEASED TO MEET YOU ALL.
Uka Shirai
THE TRANSFER STUDENT ...
...HAS BEAUTIFUL EARS.

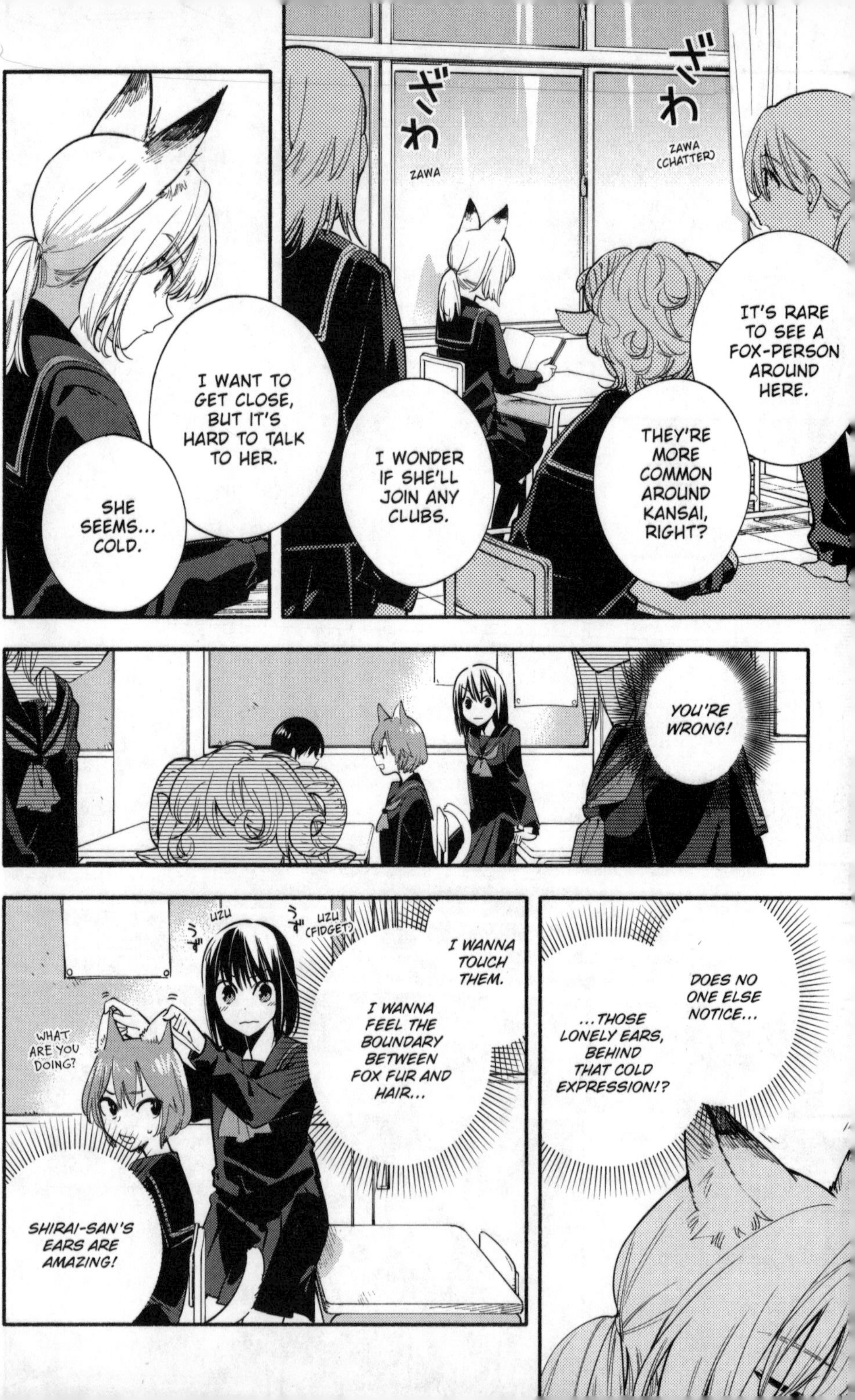
ざわ
ZAWA (CHATTER)
ざわ
ZAWA
IT'S RARE TO SEE A FOX-PERSON AROUND HERE.
THEY'RE MORE COMMON AROUND KANSAI, RIGHT?
I WONDER IF SHE'LL JOIN ANY CLUBS.
I WANT TO GET CLOSE, BUT IT'S HARD TO TALK TO HER.
SHE SEEMS... COLD.
YOU'RE WRONG!
DOES NO ONE ELSE NOTICE...
...THOSE LONELY EARS, BEHIND THAT COLD EXPRESSION!?
I WANNA TOUCH THEM.
I WANNA FEEL THE BOUNDARY BETWEEN FOX FUR AND HAIR...
うず
UZU
うず
UZU (FIDGET)
WHAT ARE YOU DOING?
SHIRAI-SAN'S EARS ARE AMAZING!

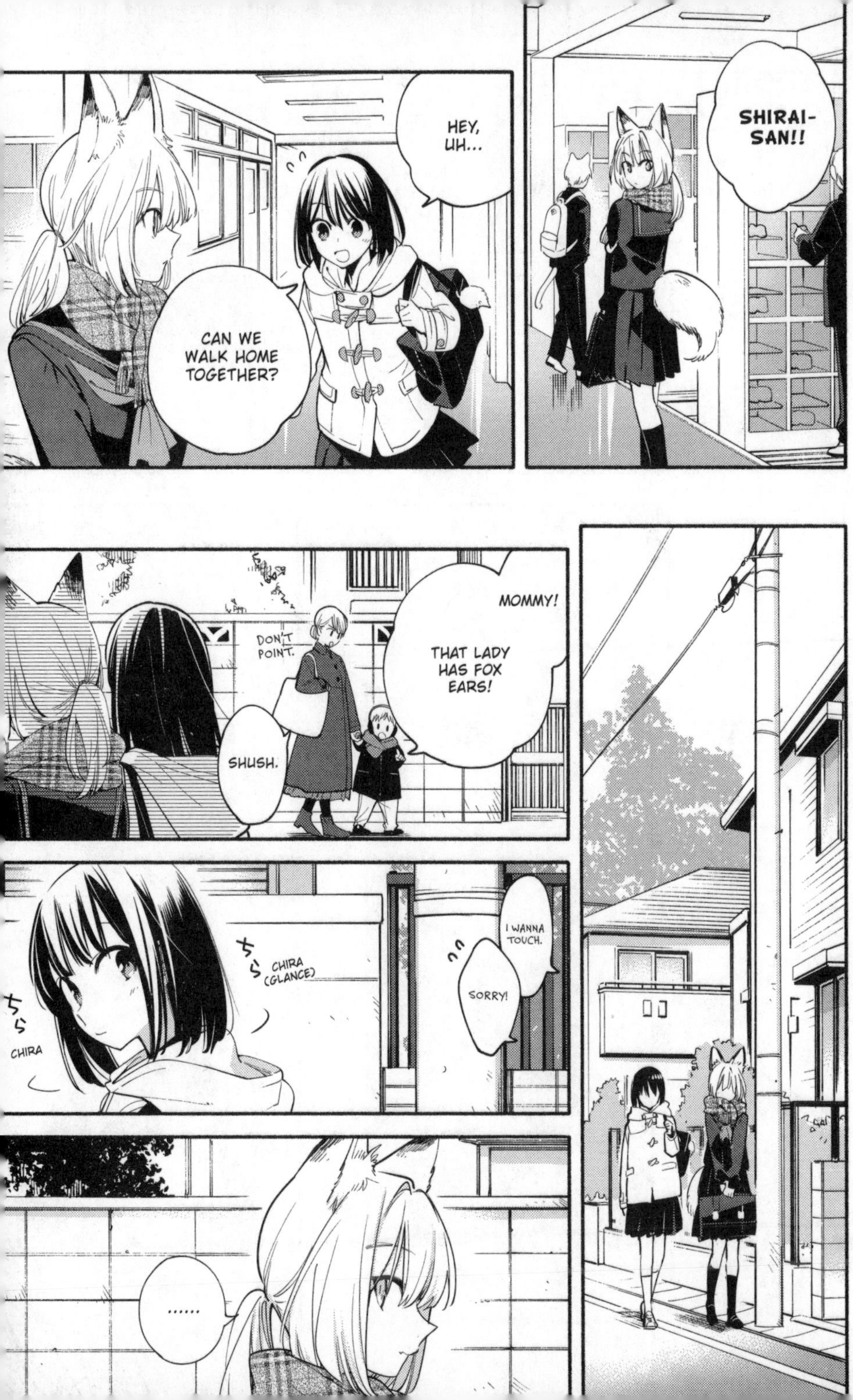

SHIRAI-SAN!!
HEY, UH...
CAN WE WALK HOME TOGETHER?
MOMMY!
THAT LADY HAS FOX EARS!
DON'T POINT.
SHUSH.
I WANNA TOUCH.
SORRY!
CHIRA (GLANCE)
CHIRA
......

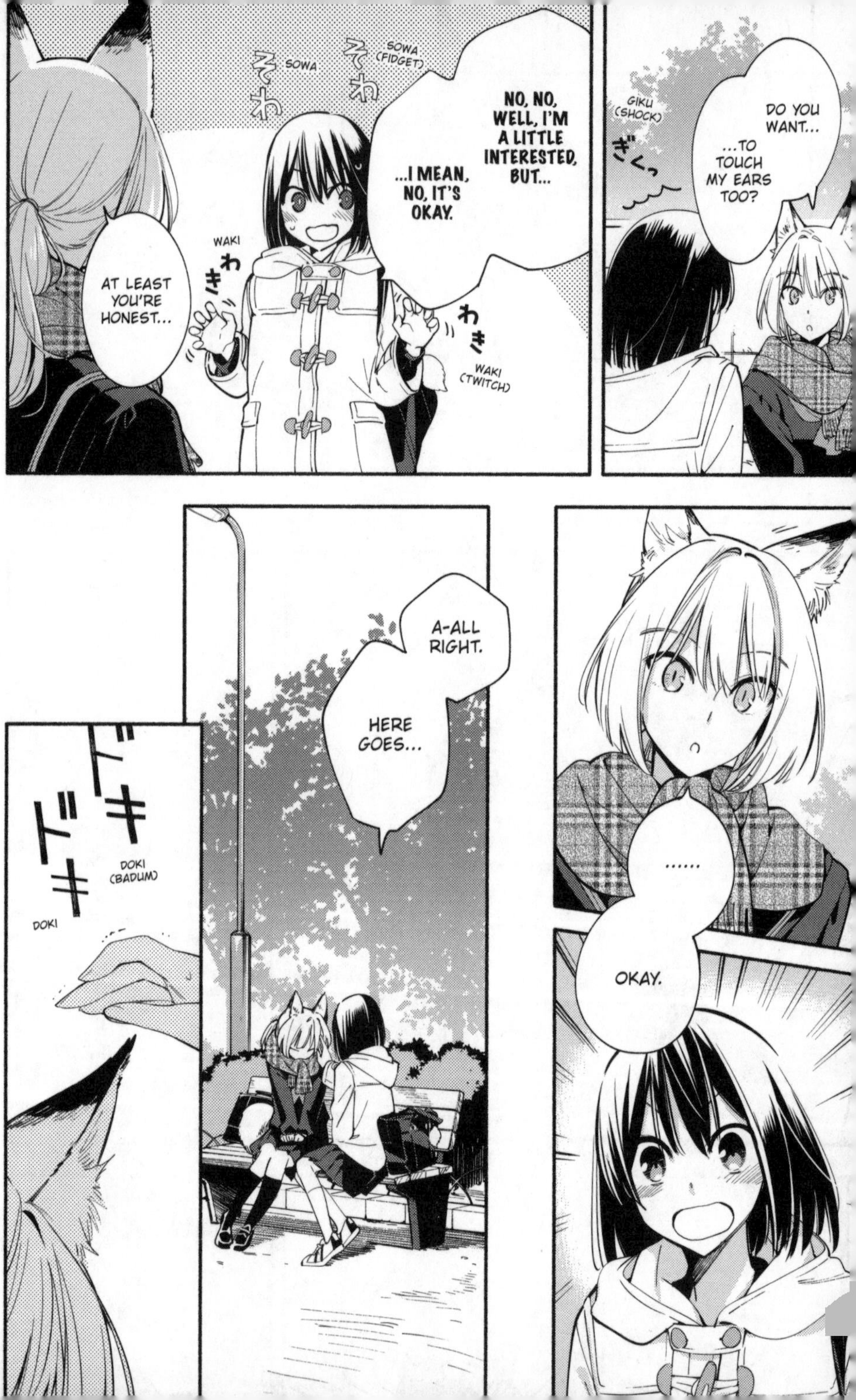
DO YOU WANT...
...TO TOUCH MY EARS TOO?
ぎくっ
GIKU (SHOCK)
NO, NO, WELL, I'M A LITTLE INTERESTED, BUT...
...I MEAN, NO, IT'S OKAY.
そわ
SOWA (FIDGET)
そわ
SOWA
わき
WAKI (TWITCH)
わき
WAKI
AT LEAST YOU'RE HONEST...
......
OKAY.
A-ALL RIGHT.
HERE GOES...
ドキ
DOKI (BADUM)
ドキ
DOKI

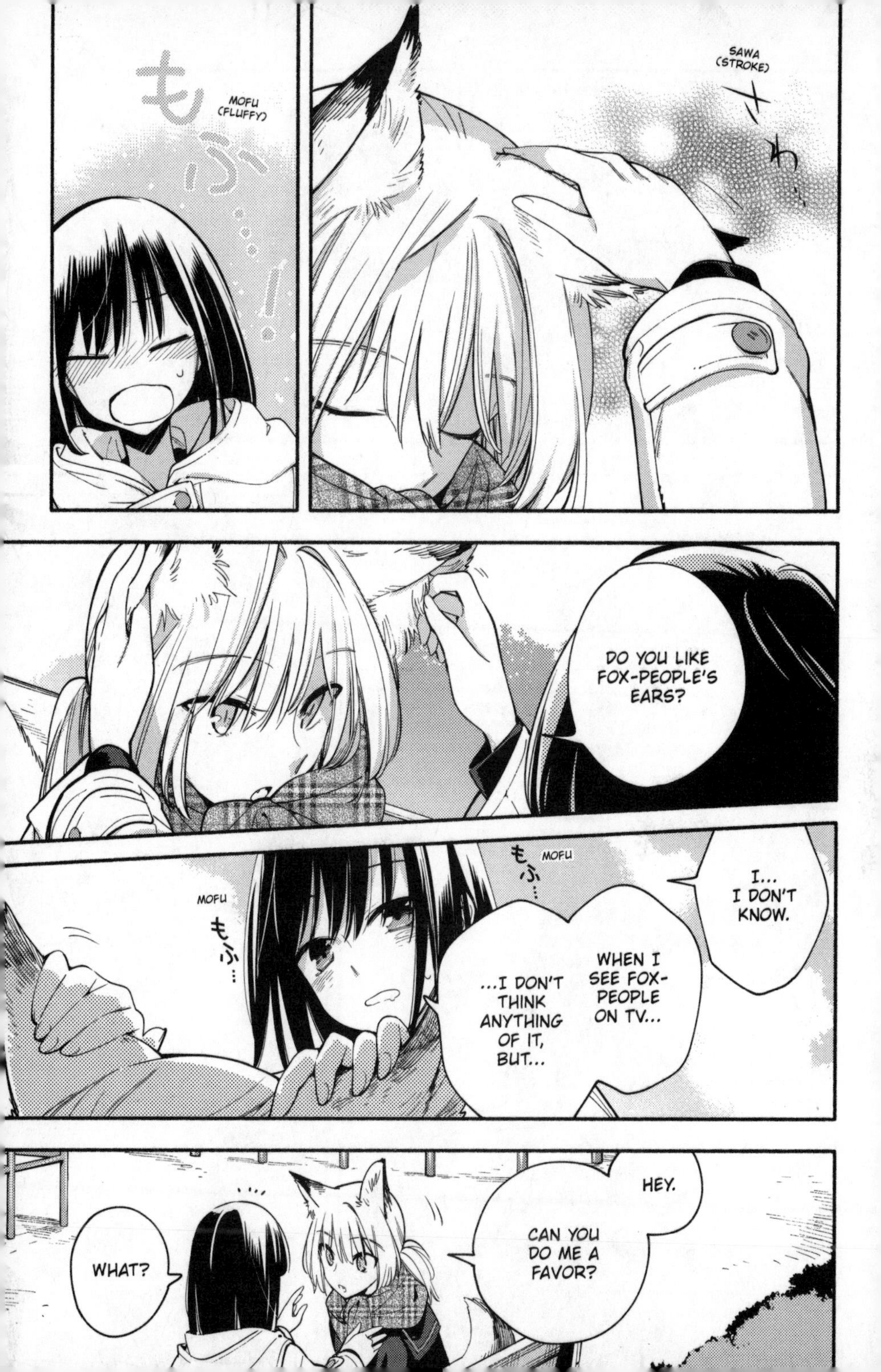
SAWA (STROKE)
さわ…
MOFU (FLUFFY)
もふ…!
DO YOU LIKE FOX-PEOPLE'S EARS?
MOFU
もふ…
I… I DON'T KNOW.
WHEN I SEE FOX-PEOPLE ON TV…
…I DON'T THINK ANYTHING OF IT, BUT…
MOFU
もふ…
HEY.
CAN YOU DO ME A FAVOR?
…
WHAT?

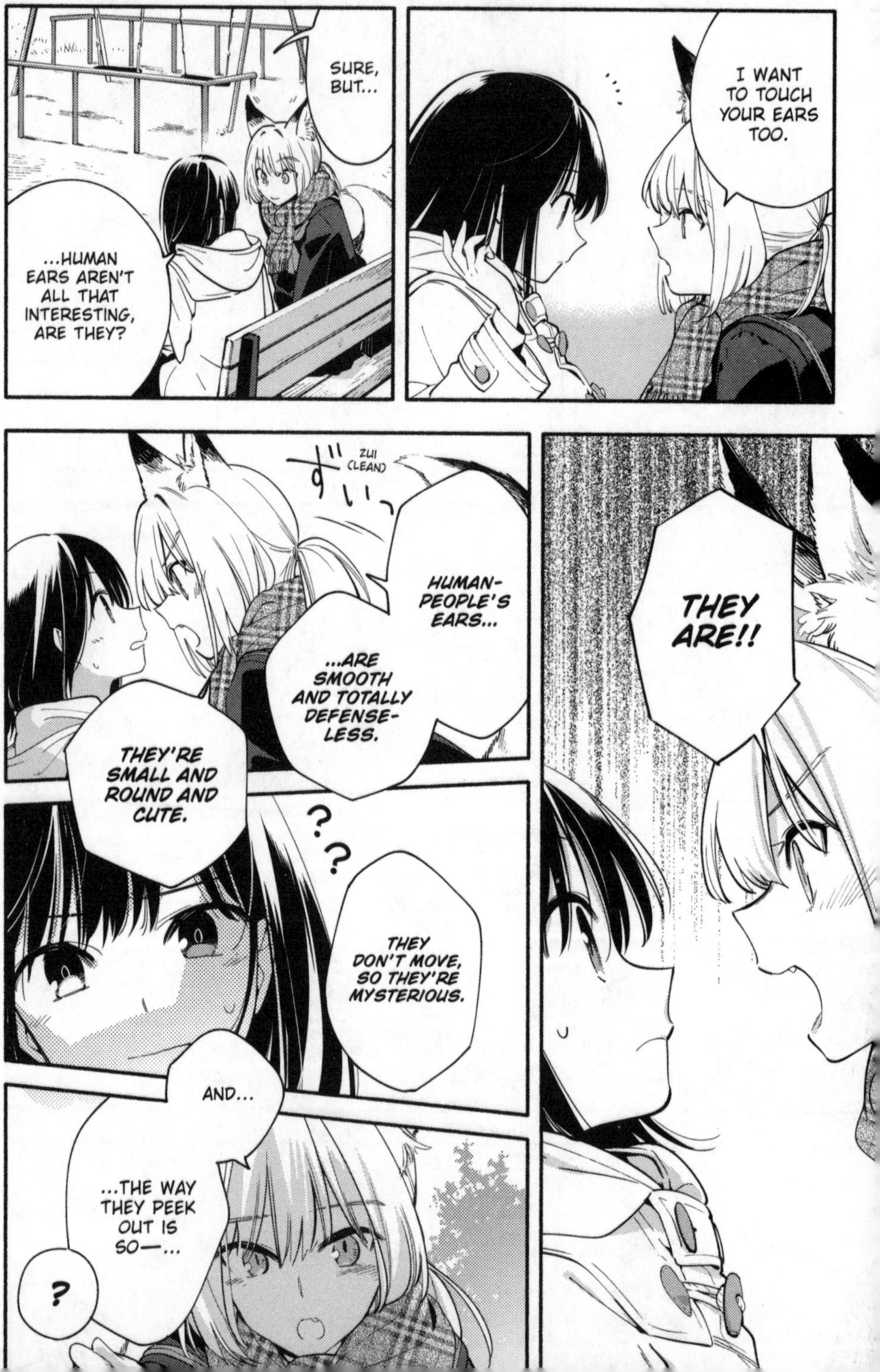
I WANT TO TOUCH YOUR EARS TOO.
SURE, BUT...
...HUMAN EARS AREN'T ALL THAT INTERESTING, ARE THEY?
THEY ARE!!
ずいー
ZUI (LEAN)
HUMAN-PEOPLE'S EARS...
...ARE SMOOTH AND TOTALLY DEFENSE-LESS.
THEY'RE SMALL AND ROUND AND CUTE.
? ?
THEY DON'T MOVE, SO THEY'RE MYSTERIOUS.
AND...
...THE WAY THEY PEEK OUT IS SO—...
?

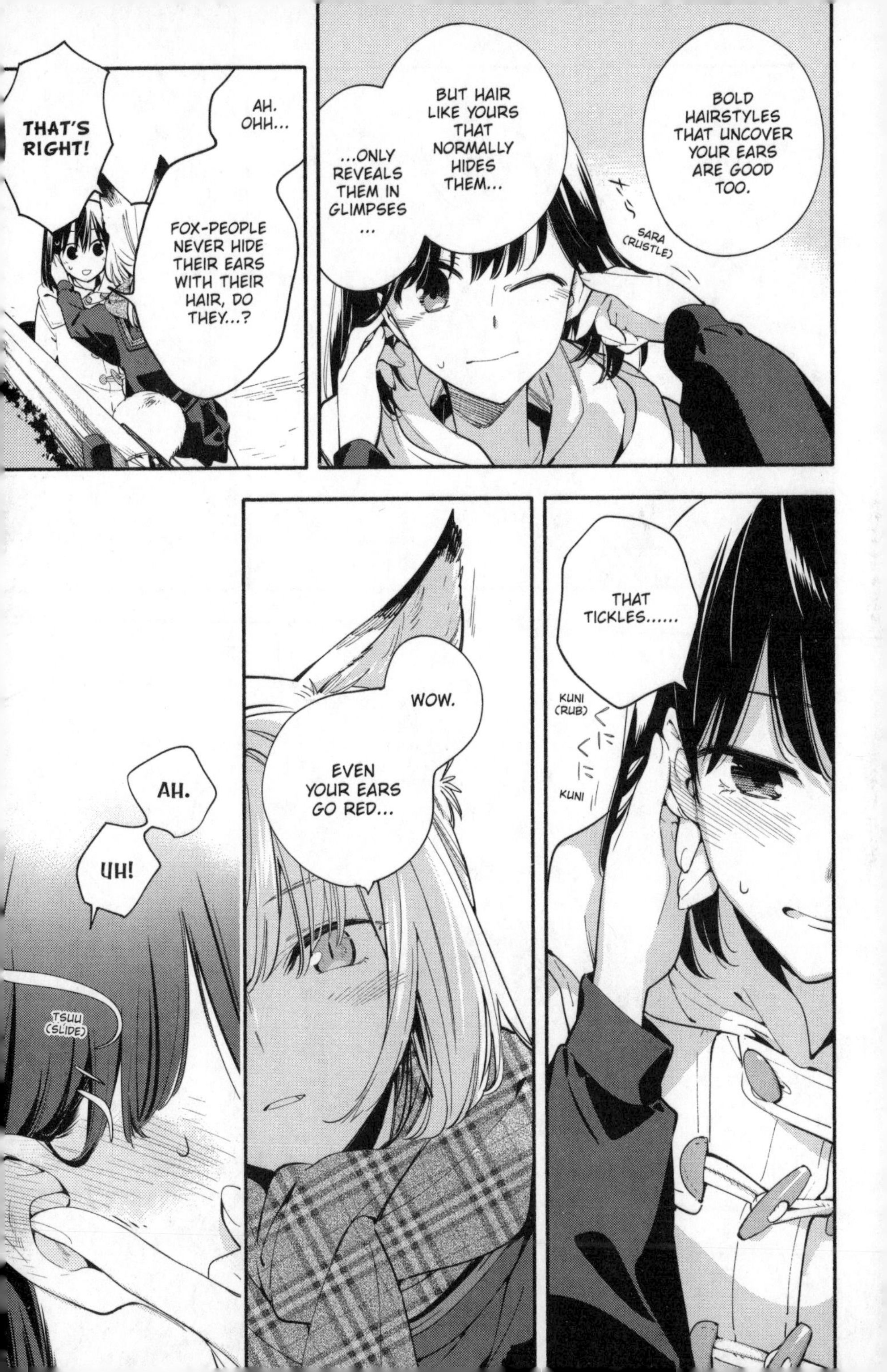
BOLD HAIRSTYLES THAT UNCOVER YOUR EARS ARE GOOD TOO.
SARA (RUSTLE)
BUT HAIR LIKE YOURS THAT NORMALLY HIDES THEM...
...ONLY REVEALS THEM IN GLIMPSES...
AH. OHH...
FOX-PEOPLE NEVER HIDE THEIR EARS WITH THEIR HAIR, DO THEY...?
THAT'S RIGHT!
THAT TICKLES......
KUNI (RUB)
KUNI
WOW.
EVEN YOUR EARS GO RED...
AH.
UH!
TSUU (SLIDE)

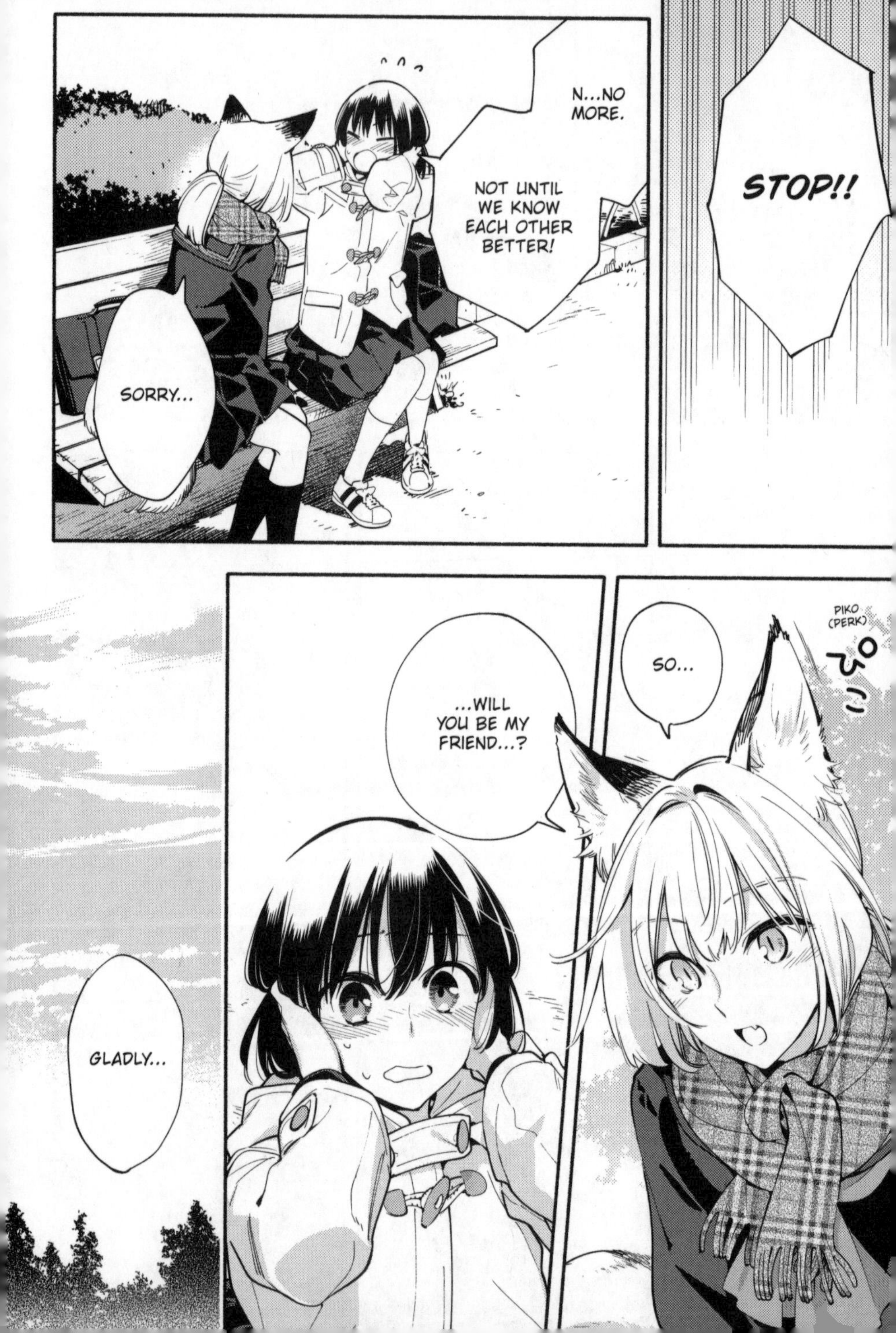
STOP!!
N...NO MORE.
NOT UNTIL WE KNOW EACH OTHER BETTER!
SORRY...
PIKO (PERK)
SO...
...WILL YOU BE MY FRIEND...?
GLADLY...

【Happiness in the Shape of a Scar】

I can't believe I thought I could tell this story in sixteen pages...
It seems that I like to depict people's less charming feelings, such
as obsession and guilt, and polish them up into something that
appears attractive, especially for short stories.

Initial release: *Éclair: A Girls' Love Anthology That Resonates in Your Heart*

【Always in Profile】

This story is about loving a girl who is obsessed with her favorite
female idol. Possibly as a reaction to the heavy themes of the
previous story, the next few make for lighter reading.

Initial release: *Éclair Blanche: A Girls' Love Anthology That Resonates in Your Heart*

【Comm-ear-ication】

This story started out with me just wanting to draw a girl with
fox ears, but I think it marries cuteness with a fair amount of
perversity, and I quite like it.

Initial release: *Éclair Bleue: A Girls' Love Anthology That Resonates in Your Heart*

Farewell to My Alter

NIO NAKATANI SHORT STORY COLLECTION

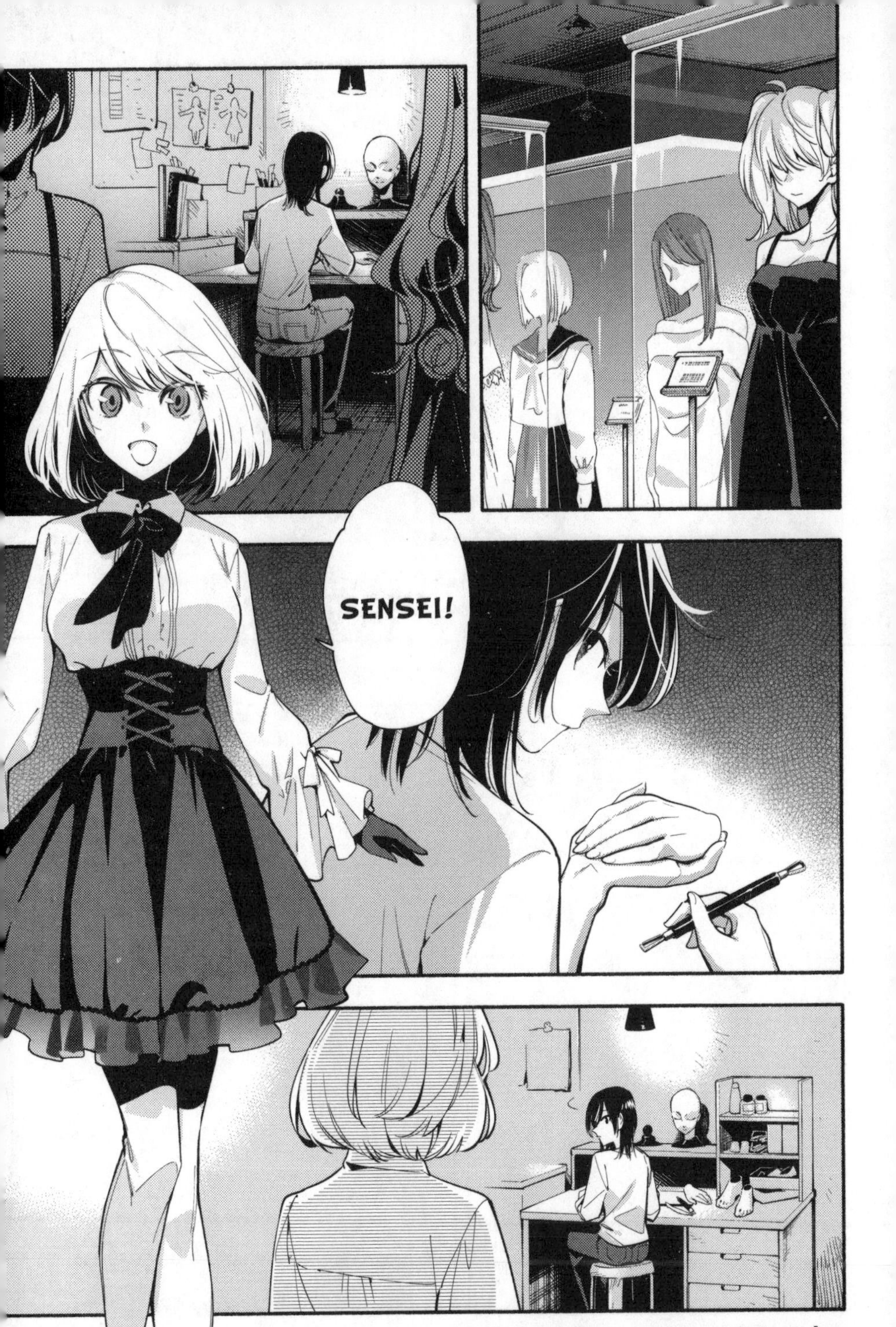
SENSEI!

I Am Custom-Made

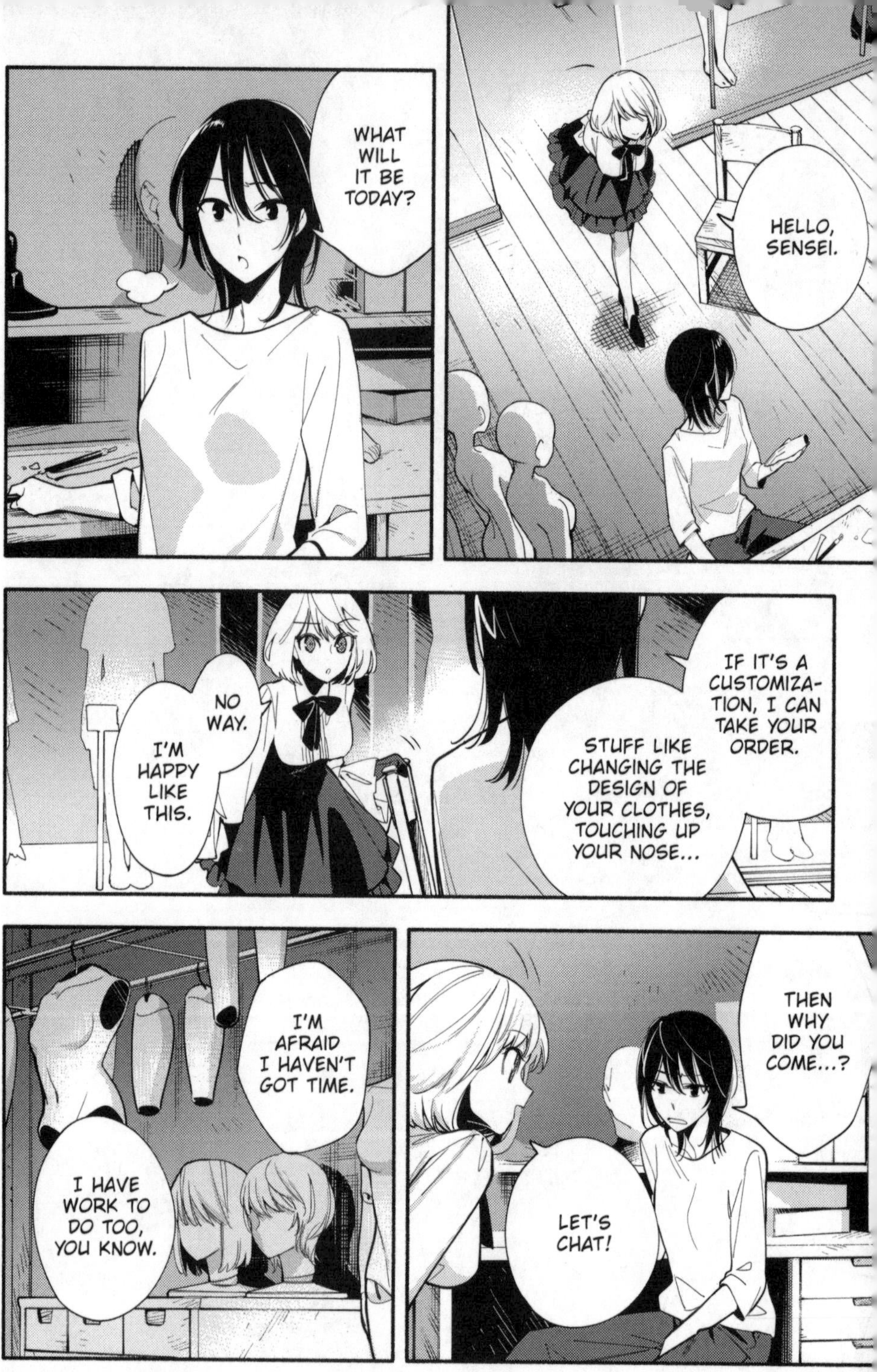
HELLO, SENSEI.
WHAT WILL IT BE TODAY?
IF IT'S A CUSTOMIZATION, I CAN TAKE YOUR ORDER.
STUFF LIKE CHANGING THE DESIGN OF YOUR CLOTHES, TOUCHING UP YOUR NOSE...
NO WAY.
I'M HAPPY LIKE THIS.
THEN WHY DID YOU COME...?
LET'S CHAT!
I'M AFRAID I HAVEN'T GOT TIME.
I HAVE WORK TO DO TOO, YOU KNOW.

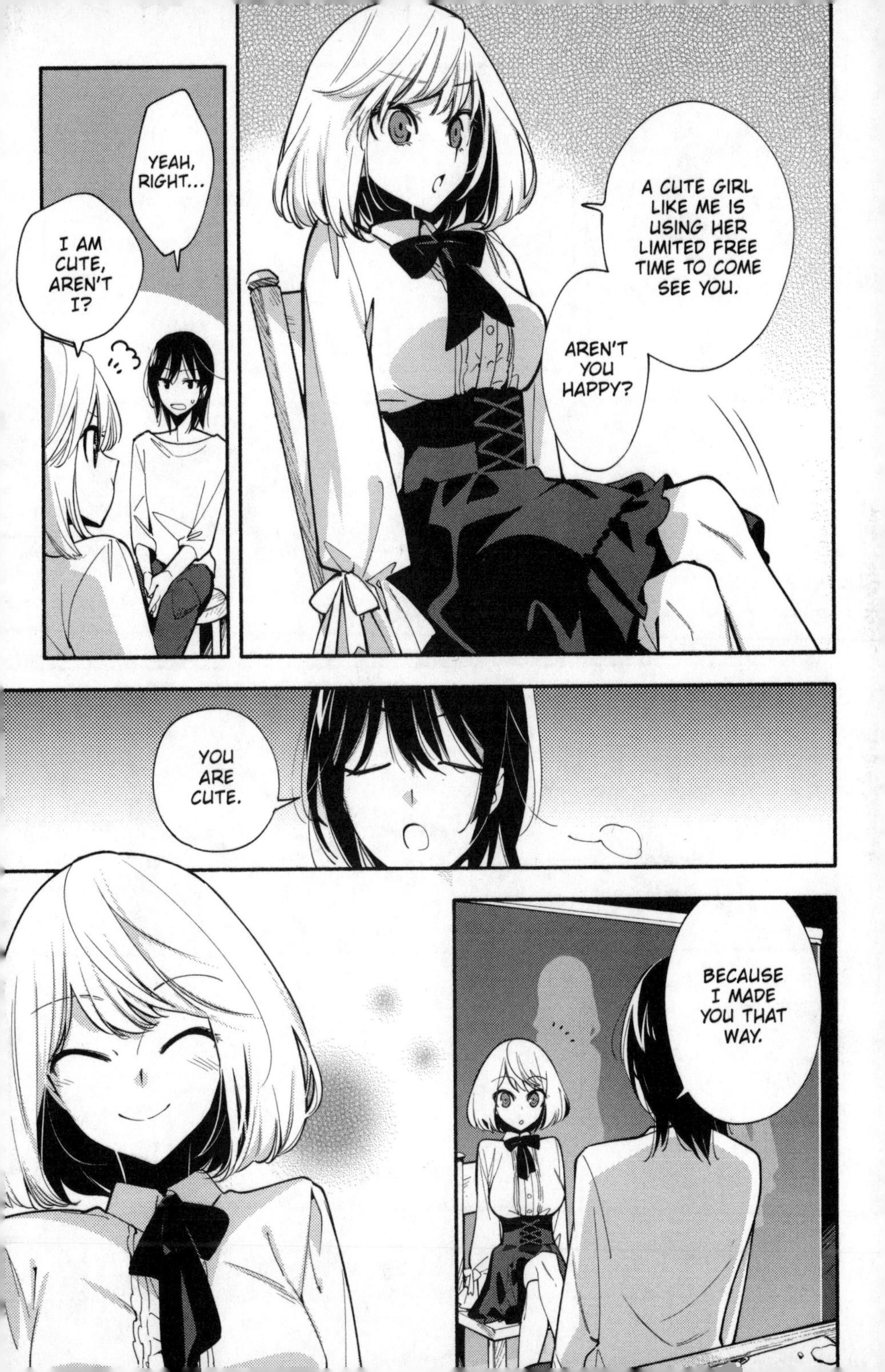
A CUTE GIRL LIKE ME IS USING HER LIMITED FREE TIME TO COME SEE YOU.
AREN'T YOU HAPPY?
YEAH, RIGHT...
I AM CUTE, AREN'T I?
YOU ARE CUTE.
BECAUSE I MADE YOU THAT WAY.

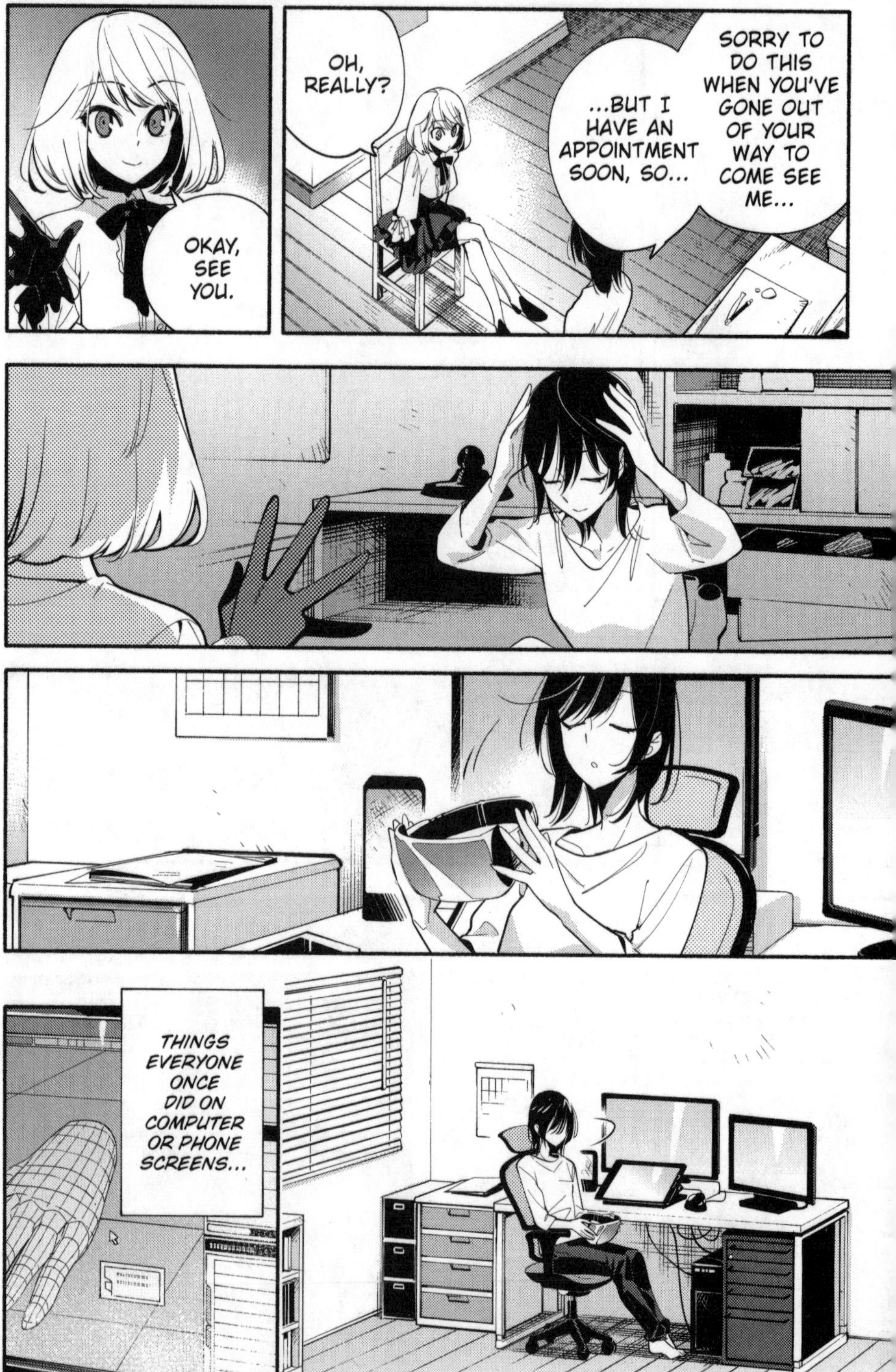
SORRY TO DO THIS WHEN YOU'VE GONE OUT OF YOUR WAY TO COME SEE ME...
...BUT I HAVE AN APPOINTMENT SOON, SO...
OH, REALLY?
OKAY, SEE YOU.
THINGS EVERYONE ONCE DID ON COMPUTER OR PHONE SCREENS...

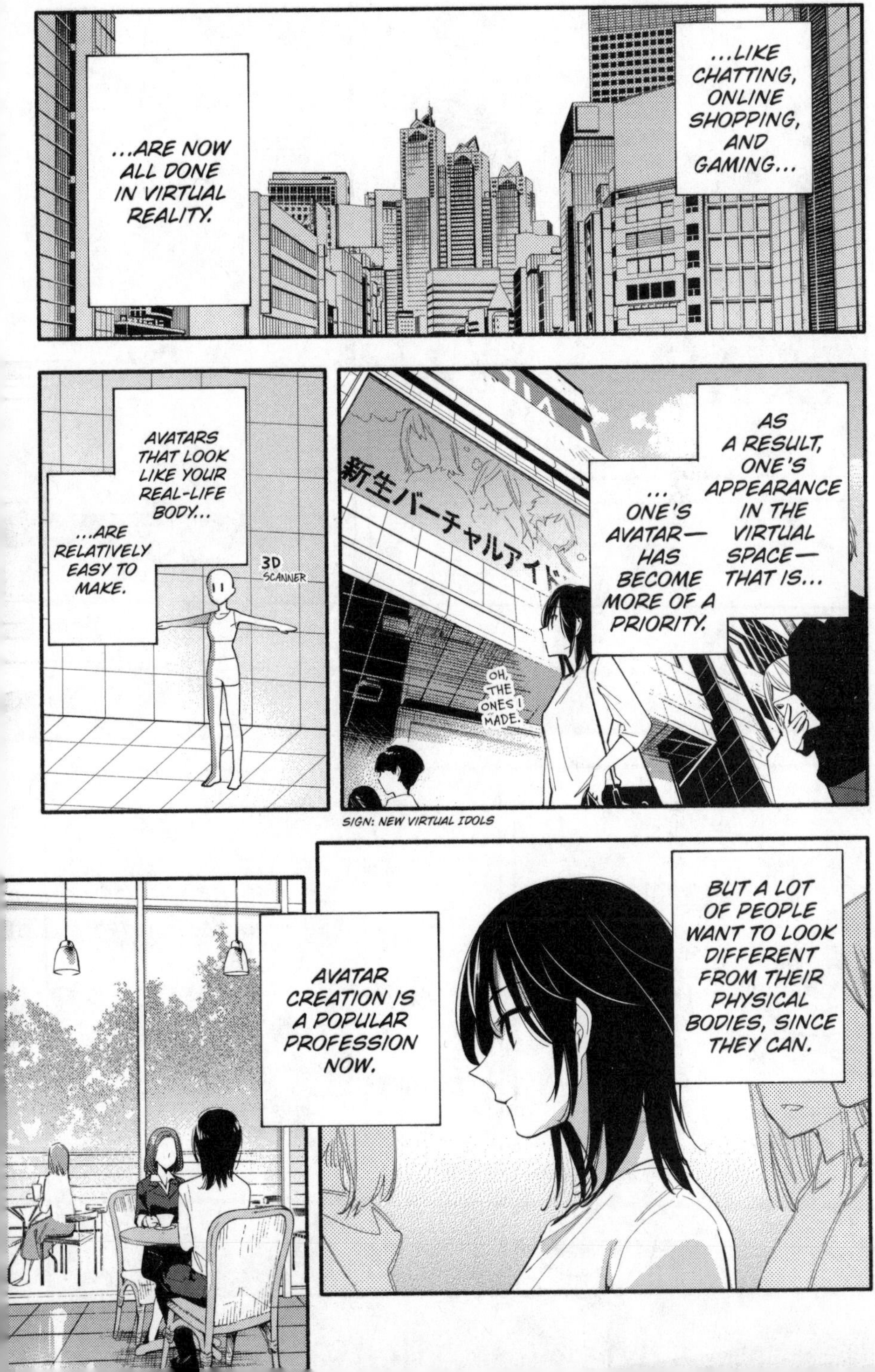
...LIKE CHATTING, ONLINE SHOPPING, AND GAMING...
...ARE NOW ALL DONE IN VIRTUAL REALITY.
AS A RESULT, ONE'S APPEARANCE IN THE VIRTUAL SPACE—THAT IS...
... ONE'S AVATAR—HAS BECOME MORE OF A PRIORITY.
新生バーチャルアイド
OH, THE ONES I MADE.
AVATARS THAT LOOK LIKE YOUR REAL-LIFE BODY...
...ARE RELATIVELY EASY TO MAKE.
3D SCANNER
SIGN: NEW VIRTUAL IDOLS
BUT A LOT OF PEOPLE WANT TO LOOK DIFFERENT FROM THEIR PHYSICAL BODIES, SINCE THEY CAN.
AVATAR CREATION IS A POPULAR PROFESSION NOW.

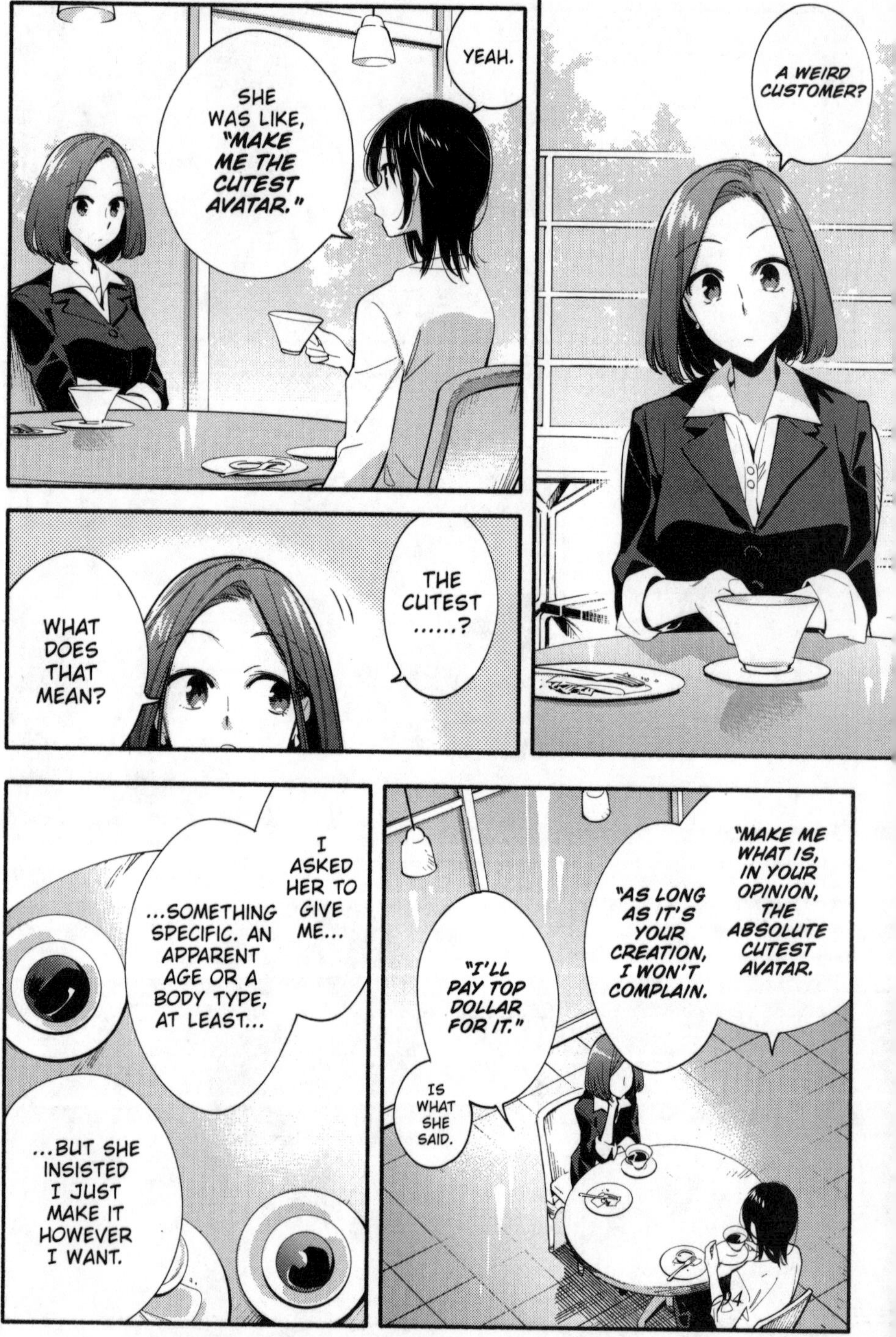
A WEIRD CUSTOMER?
YEAH.
SHE WAS LIKE, "MAKE ME THE CUTEST AVATAR."
THE CUTEST ......?
WHAT DOES THAT MEAN?
"MAKE ME WHAT IS, IN YOUR OPINION, THE ABSOLUTE CUTEST AVATAR.
"AS LONG AS IT'S YOUR CREATION, I WON'T COMPLAIN.
"I'LL PAY TOP DOLLAR FOR IT."
IS WHAT SHE SAID.
I ASKED HER TO GIVE ME...
...SOMETHING SPECIFIC. AN APPARENT AGE OR A BODY TYPE, AT LEAST...
...BUT SHE INSISTED I JUST MAKE IT HOWEVER I WANT.

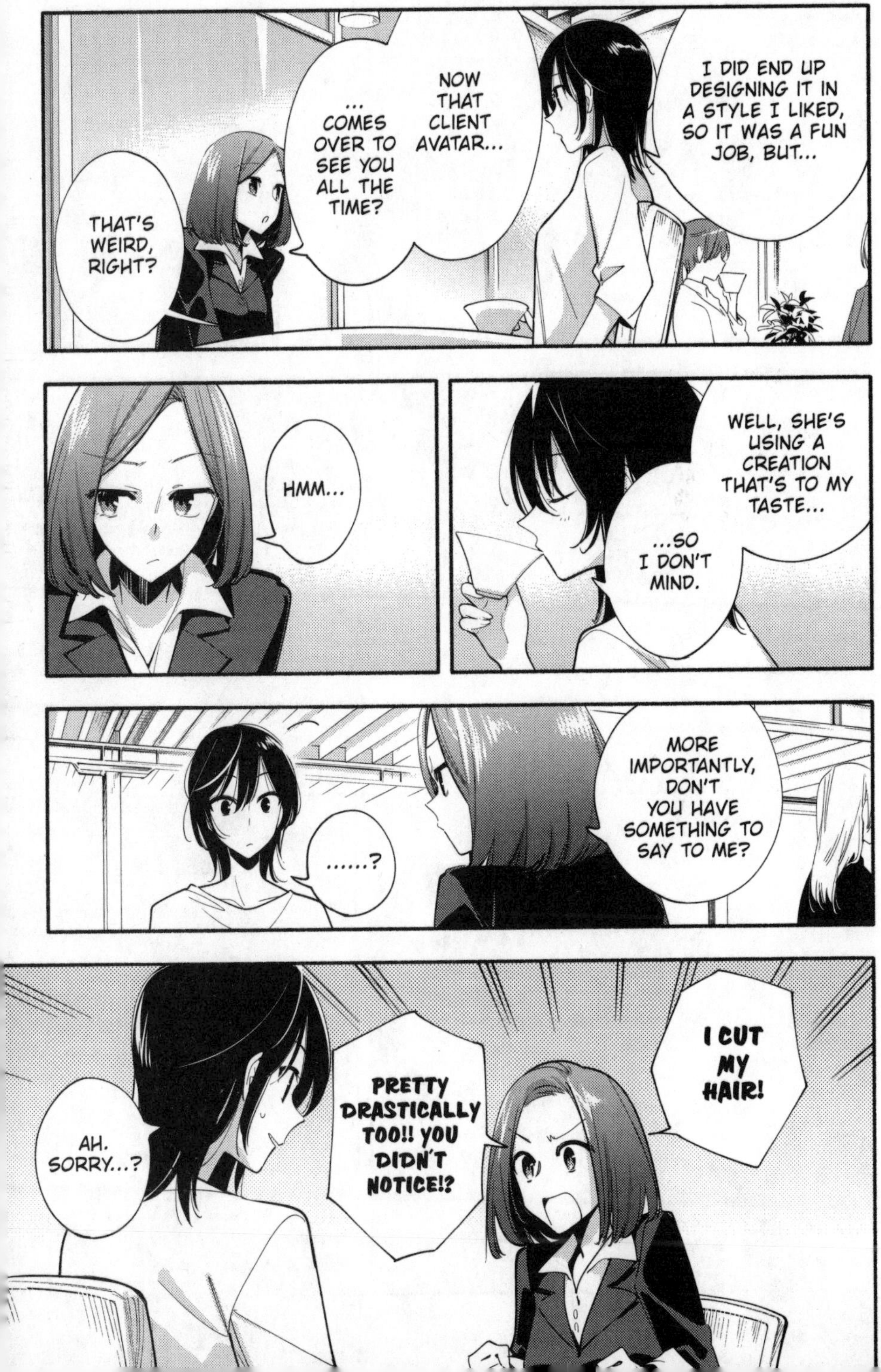
I DID END UP DESIGNING IT IN A STYLE I LIKED, SO IT WAS A FUN JOB, BUT...
NOW THAT CLIENT AVATAR...
...COMES OVER TO SEE YOU ALL THE TIME?
THAT'S WEIRD, RIGHT?
WELL, SHE'S USING A CREATION THAT'S TO MY TASTE...
...SO I DON'T MIND.
HMM...
MORE IMPORTANTLY, DON'T YOU HAVE SOMETHING TO SAY TO ME?
......?
I CUT MY HAIR!
PRETTY DRASTICALLY TOO!! YOU DIDN'T NOTICE!?
AH. SORRY...?

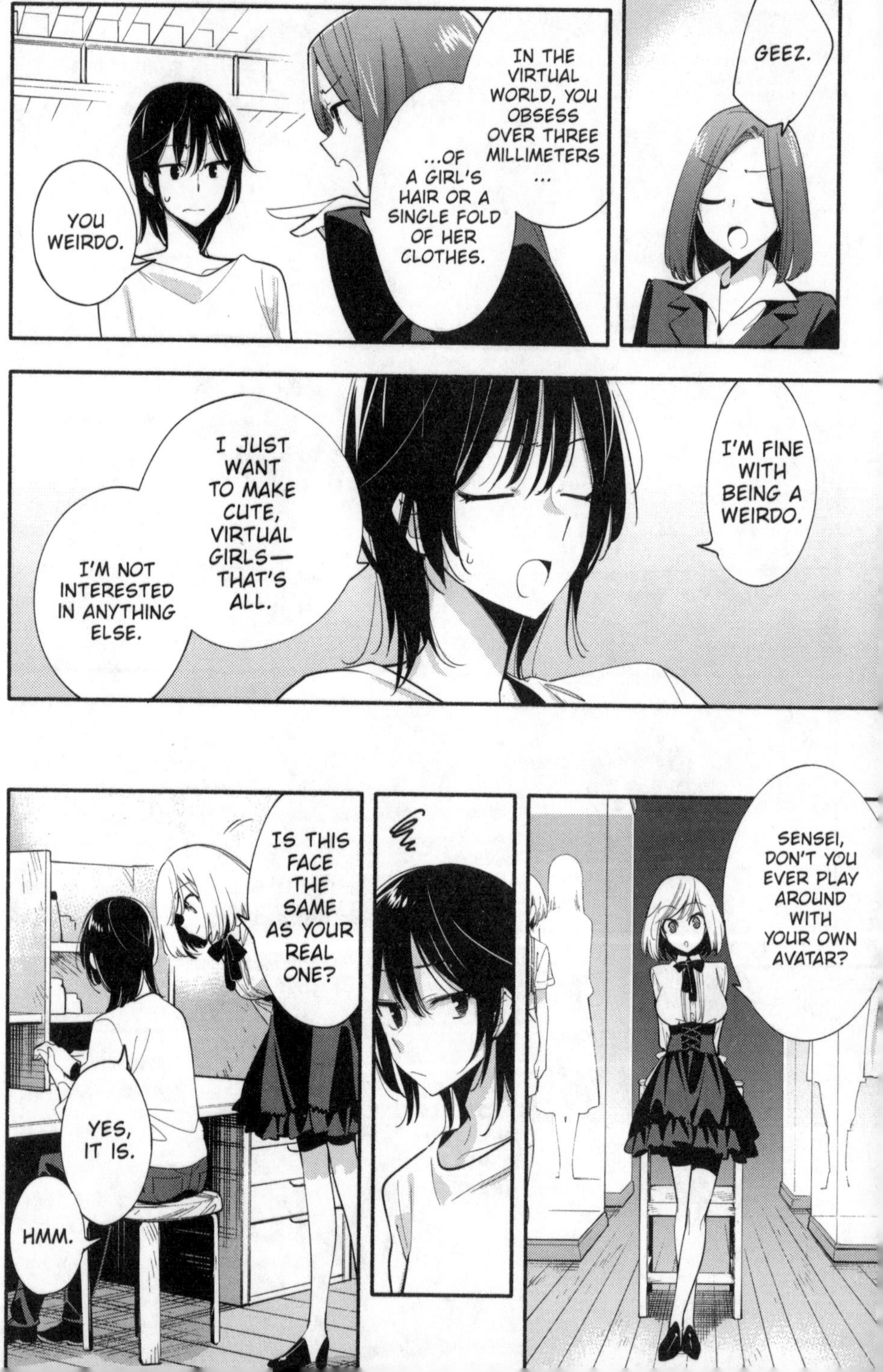
GEEZ.
IN THE VIRTUAL WORLD, YOU OBSESS OVER THREE MILLIMETERS...
...OF A GIRL'S HAIR OR A SINGLE FOLD OF HER CLOTHES.
YOU WEIRDO.
I'M FINE WITH BEING A WEIRDO.
I JUST WANT TO MAKE CUTE, VIRTUAL GIRLS—THAT'S ALL.
I'M NOT INTERESTED IN ANYTHING ELSE.
SENSEI, DON'T YOU EVER PLAY AROUND WITH YOUR OWN AVATAR?
IS THIS FACE THE SAME AS YOUR REAL ONE?
YES, IT IS.
HMM.

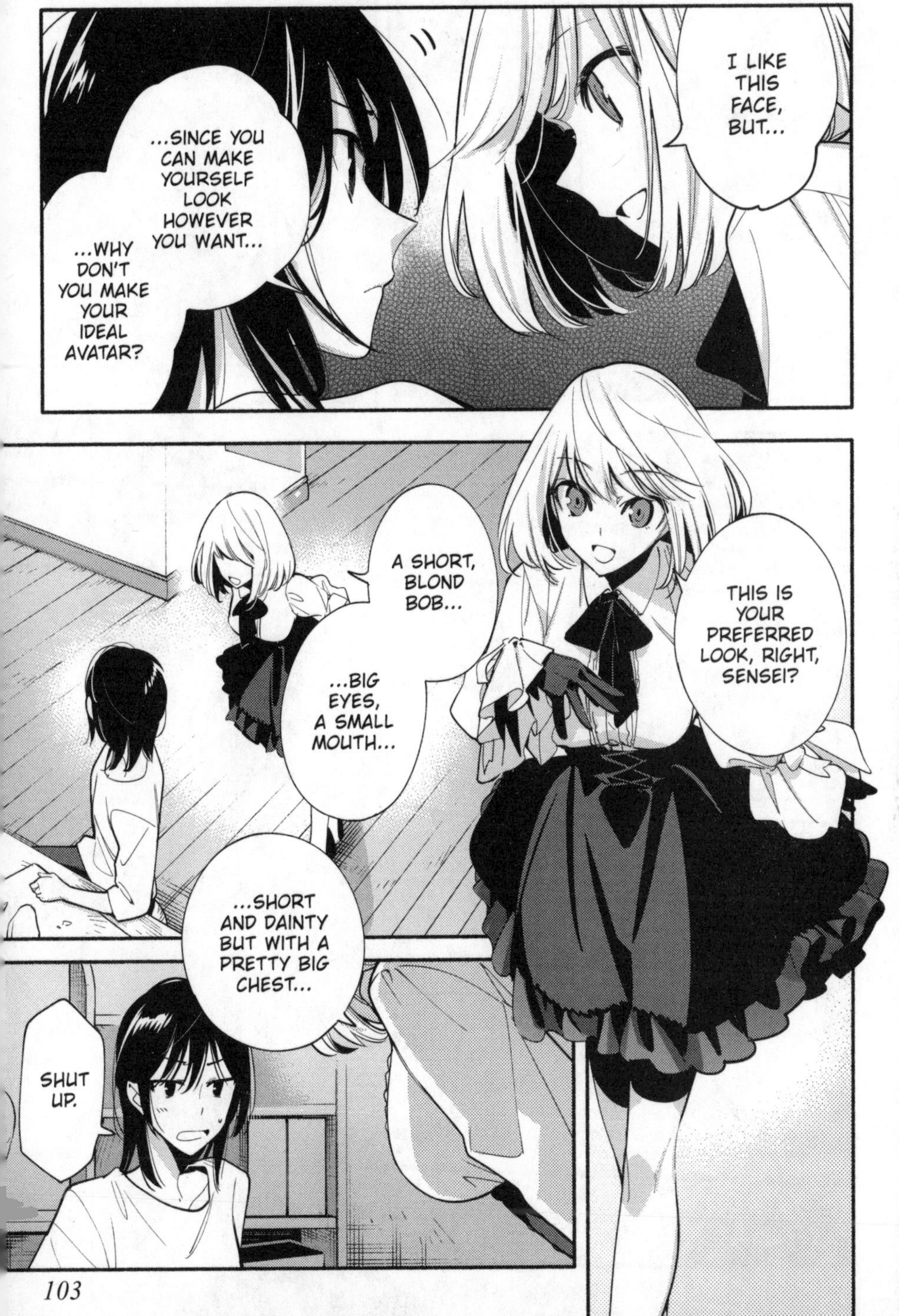
I LIKE THIS FACE, BUT...
...SINCE YOU CAN MAKE YOURSELF LOOK HOWEVER YOU WANT...
...WHY DON'T YOU MAKE YOUR IDEAL AVATAR?
THIS IS YOUR PREFERRED LOOK, RIGHT, SENSEI?
A SHORT, BLOND BOB...
...BIG EYES, A SMALL MOUTH...
...SHORT AND DAINTY BUT WITH A PRETTY BIG CHEST...
SHUT UP.

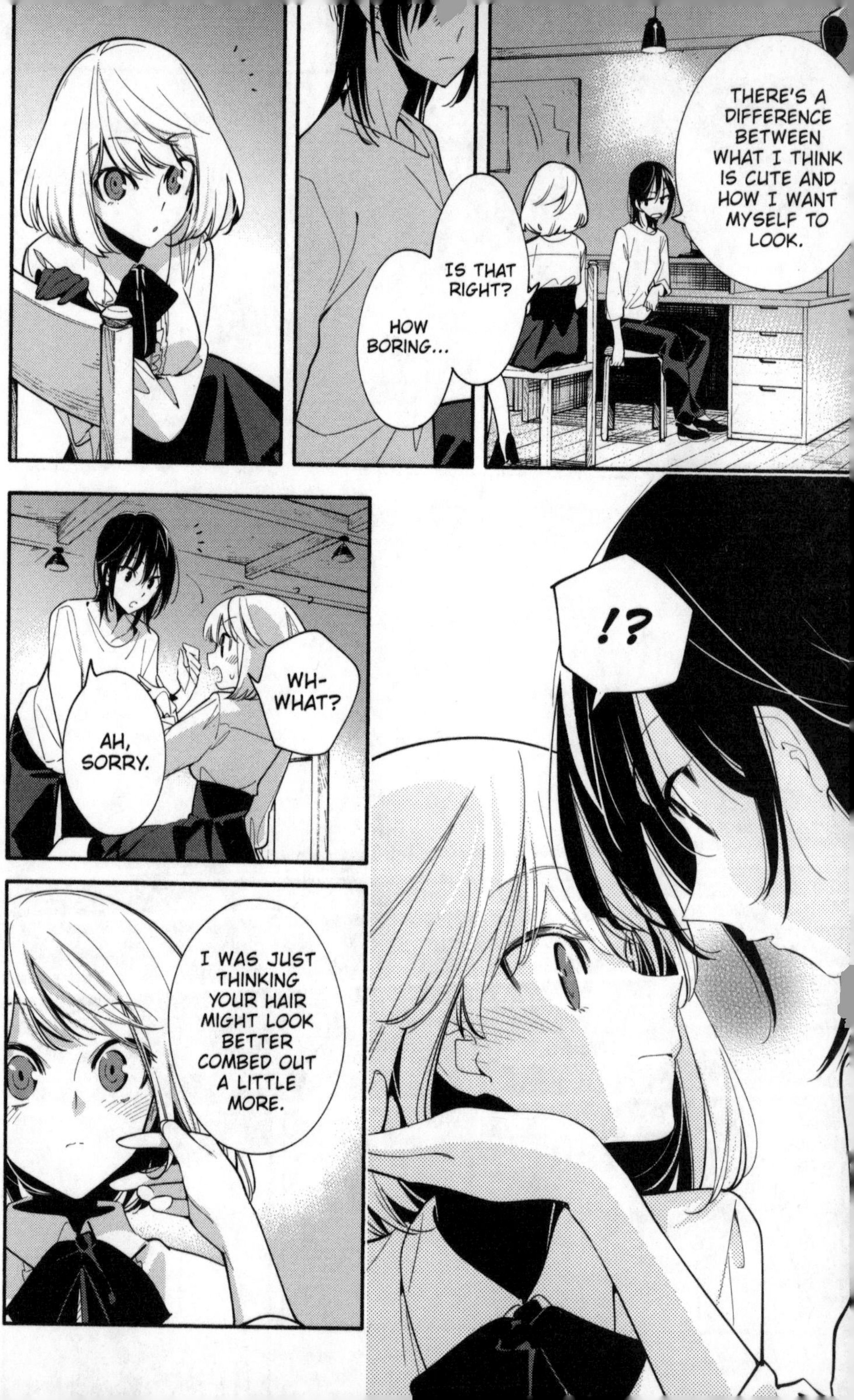
THERE'S A DIFFERENCE BETWEEN WHAT I THINK IS CUTE AND HOW I WANT MYSELF TO LOOK.
IS THAT RIGHT?
HOW BORING...
!?
WH-WHAT?
AH, SORRY.
I WAS JUST THINKING YOUR HAIR MIGHT LOOK BETTER COMBED OUT A LITTLE MORE.

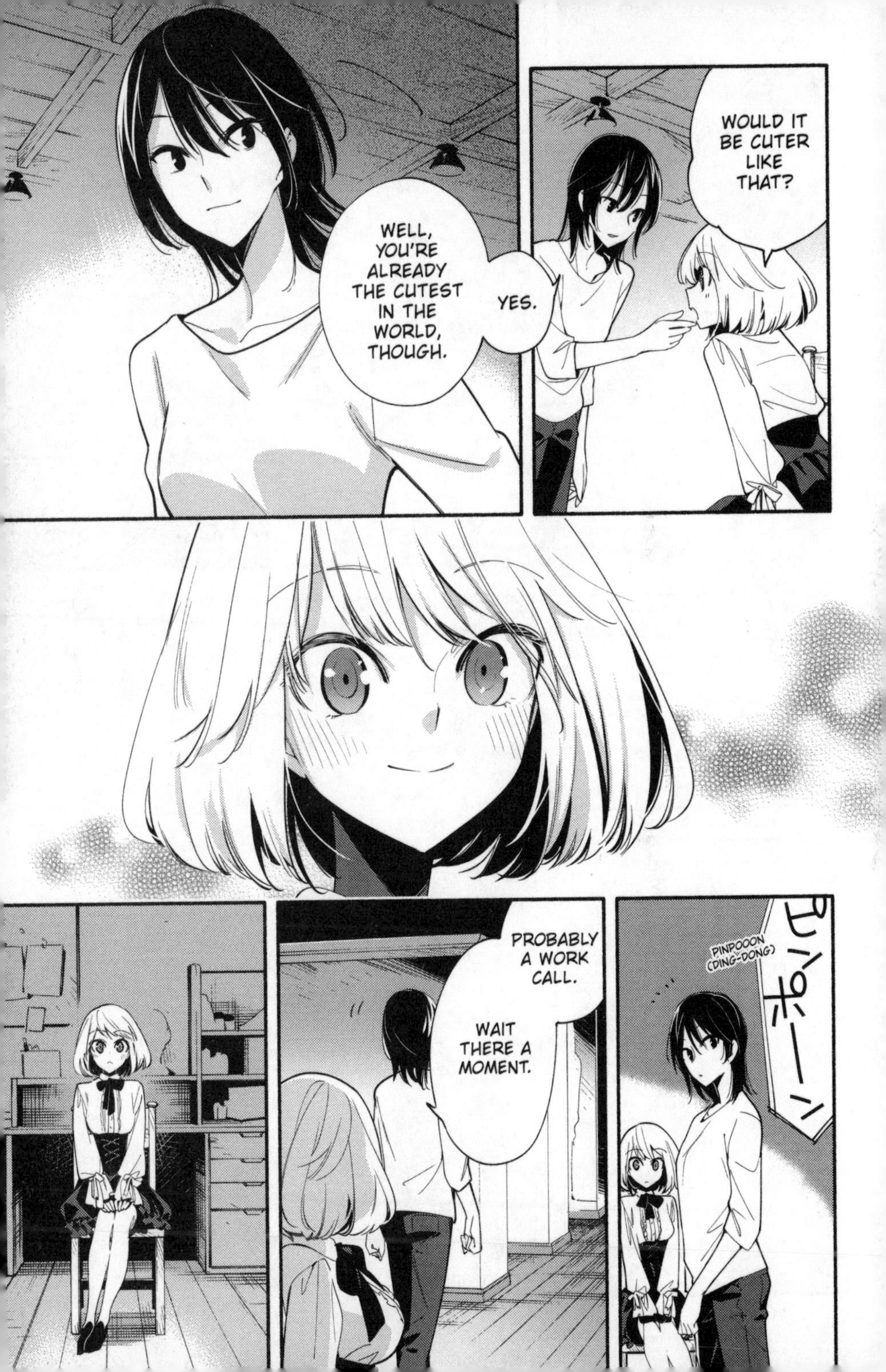
WOULD IT BE CUTER LIKE THAT?
YES.
WELL, YOU'RE ALREADY THE CUTEST IN THE WORLD, THOUGH.
ピンポーン
PINPOOON (DING-DONG)
...
PROBABLY A WORK CALL.
WAIT THERE A MOMENT.

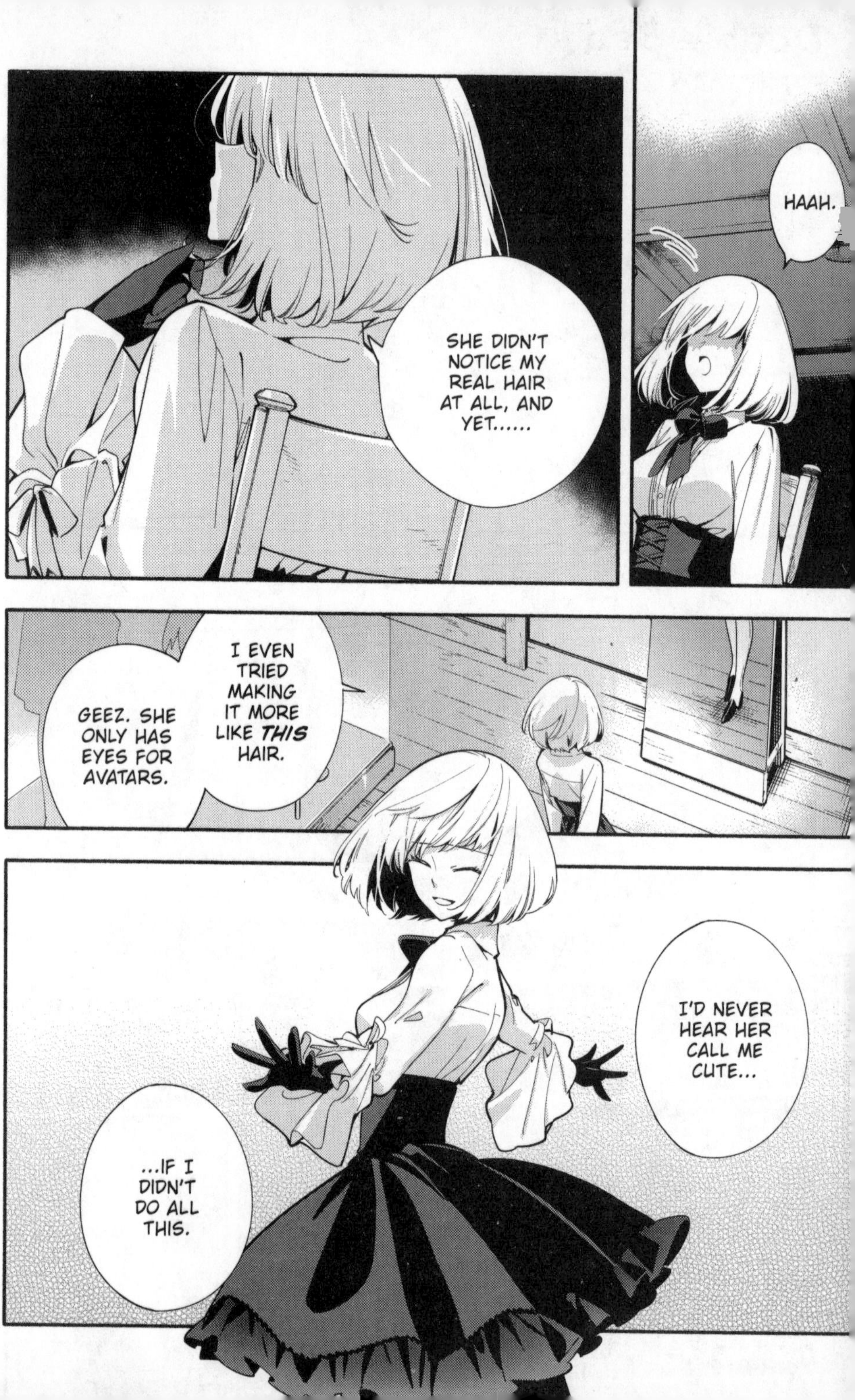
HAAH.
SHE DIDN'T NOTICE MY REAL HAIR AT ALL, AND YET......
I EVEN TRIED MAKING IT MORE LIKE *THIS* HAIR.
GEEZ. SHE ONLY HAS EYES FOR AVATARS.
I'D NEVER HEAR HER CALL ME CUTE...
...IF I DIDN'T DO ALL THIS.

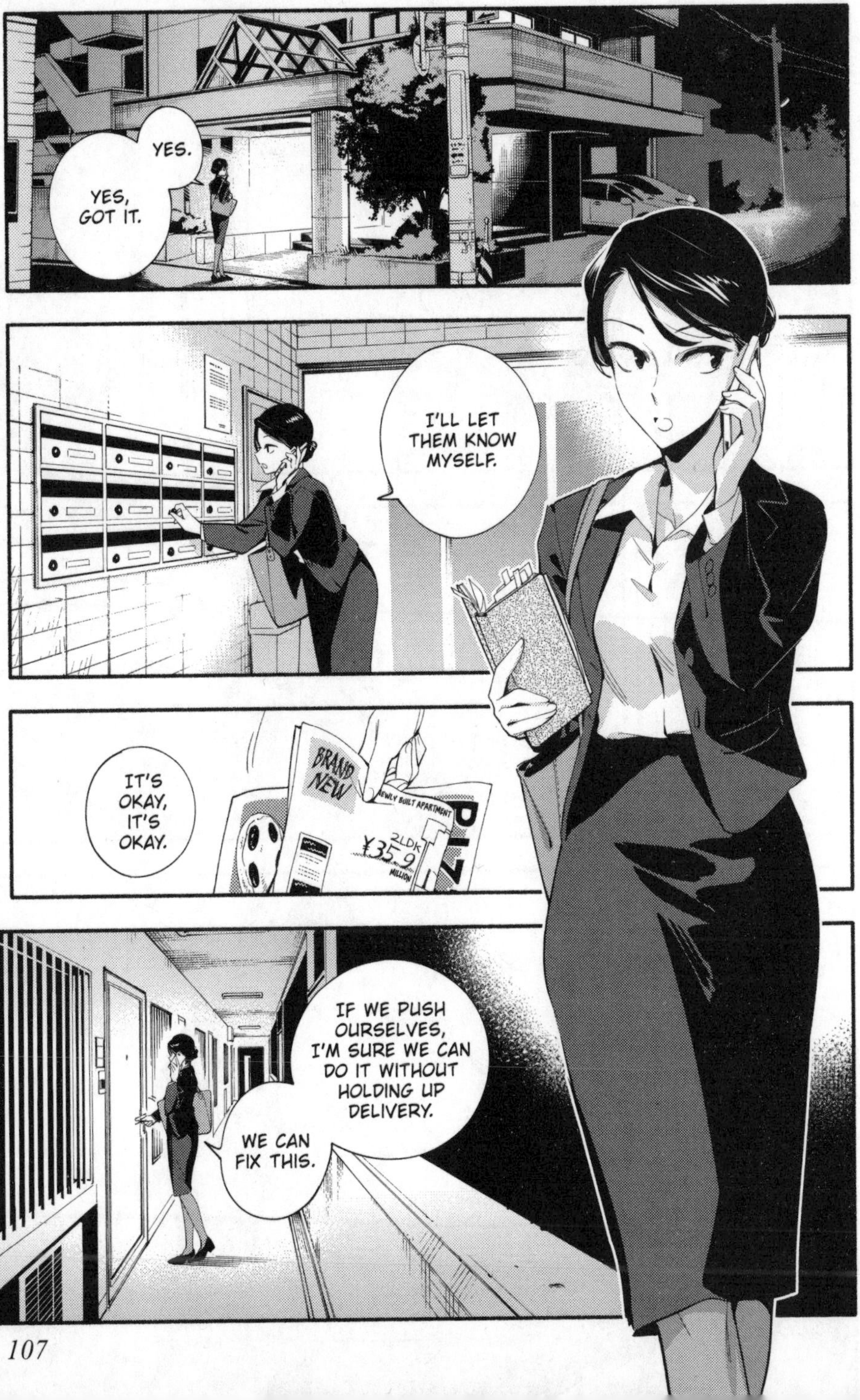
YES.
YES, GOT IT.
I'LL LET THEM KNOW MYSELF.
BRAND NEW
NEWLY BUILT APARTMENT
2LDK
¥35.9 MILLION
P17
IT'S OKAY, IT'S OKAY.
IF WE PUSH OURSELVES, I'M SURE WE CAN DO IT WITHOUT HOLDING UP DELIVERY.
WE CAN FIX THIS.

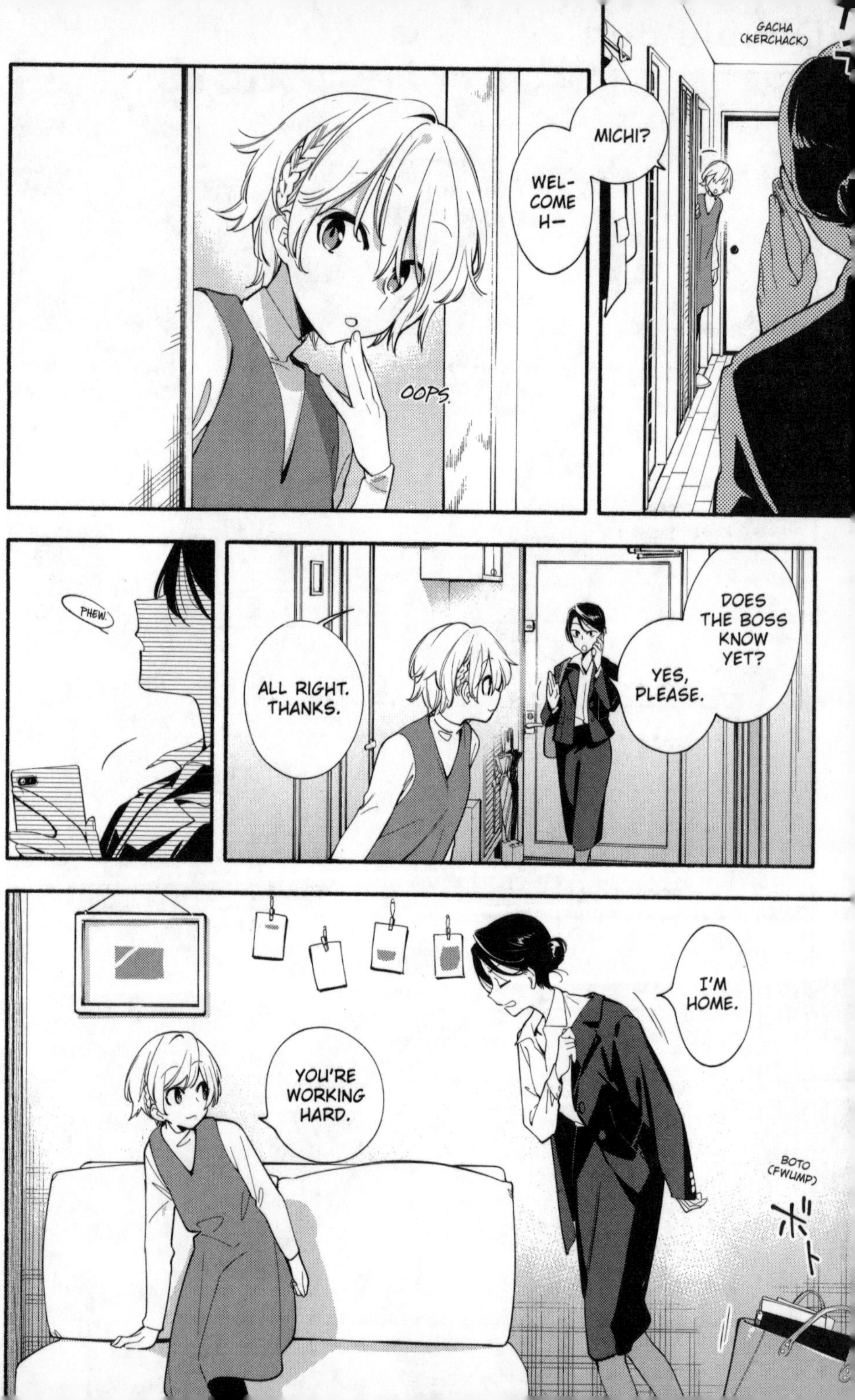
GACHA (KERCHACK)
MICHI?
WEL-COME H—
OOPS.
DOES THE BOSS KNOW YET?
YES, PLEASE.
ALL RIGHT. THANKS.
PHEW.
I'M HOME.
YOU'RE WORKING HARD.
BOTO (FWUMP)
ボト

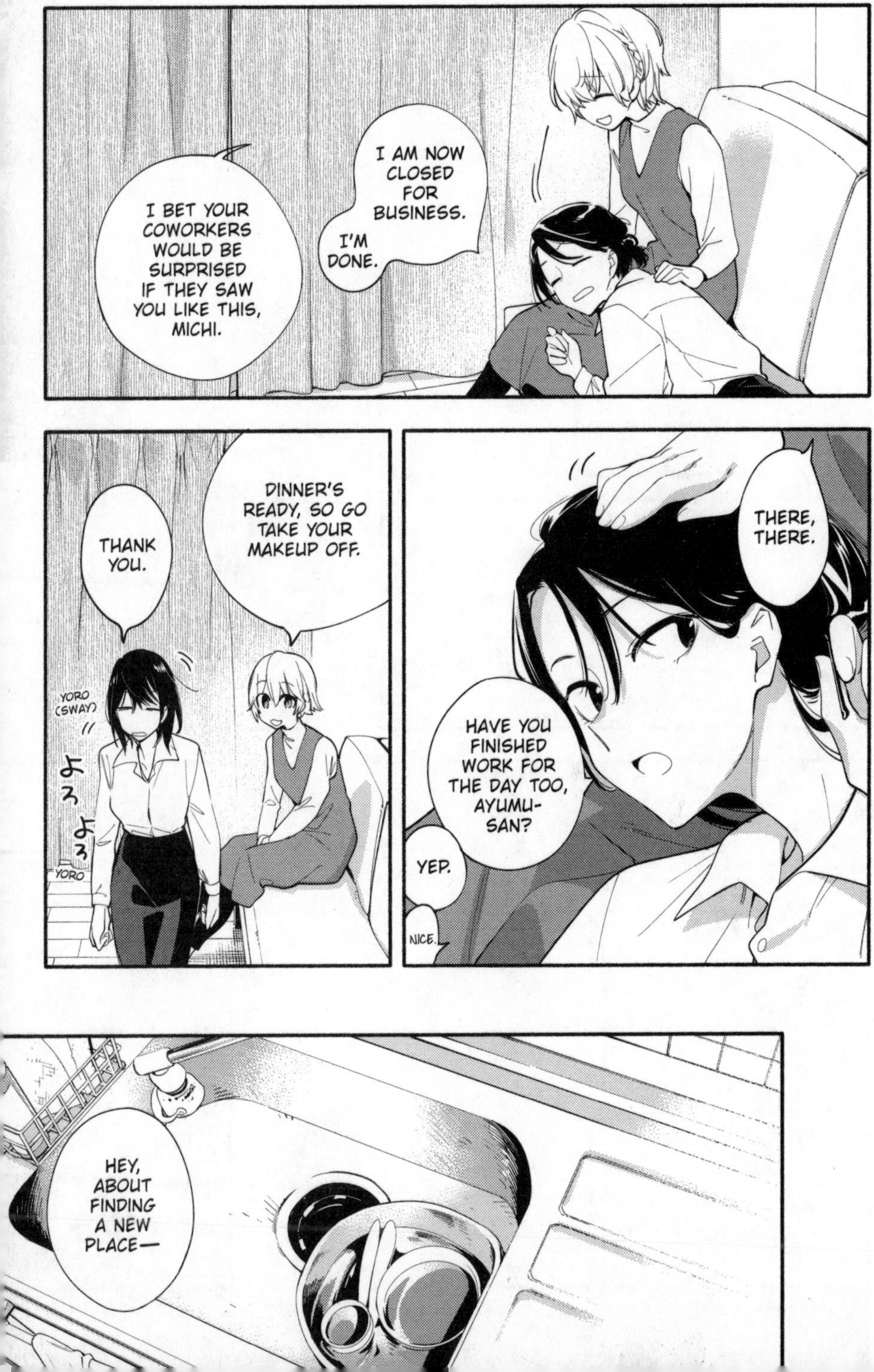
I AM NOW CLOSED FOR BUSINESS.
I'M DONE.
I BET YOUR COWORKERS WOULD BE SURPRISED IF THEY SAW YOU LIKE THIS, MICHI.
THERE, THERE.
HAVE YOU FINISHED WORK FOR THE DAY TOO, AYUMU-SAN?
YEP.
NICE.
DINNER'S READY, SO GO TAKE YOUR MAKEUP OFF.
THANK YOU.
よろよろ
YORO (SWAY)
YORO
HEY, ABOUT FINDING A NEW PLACE—

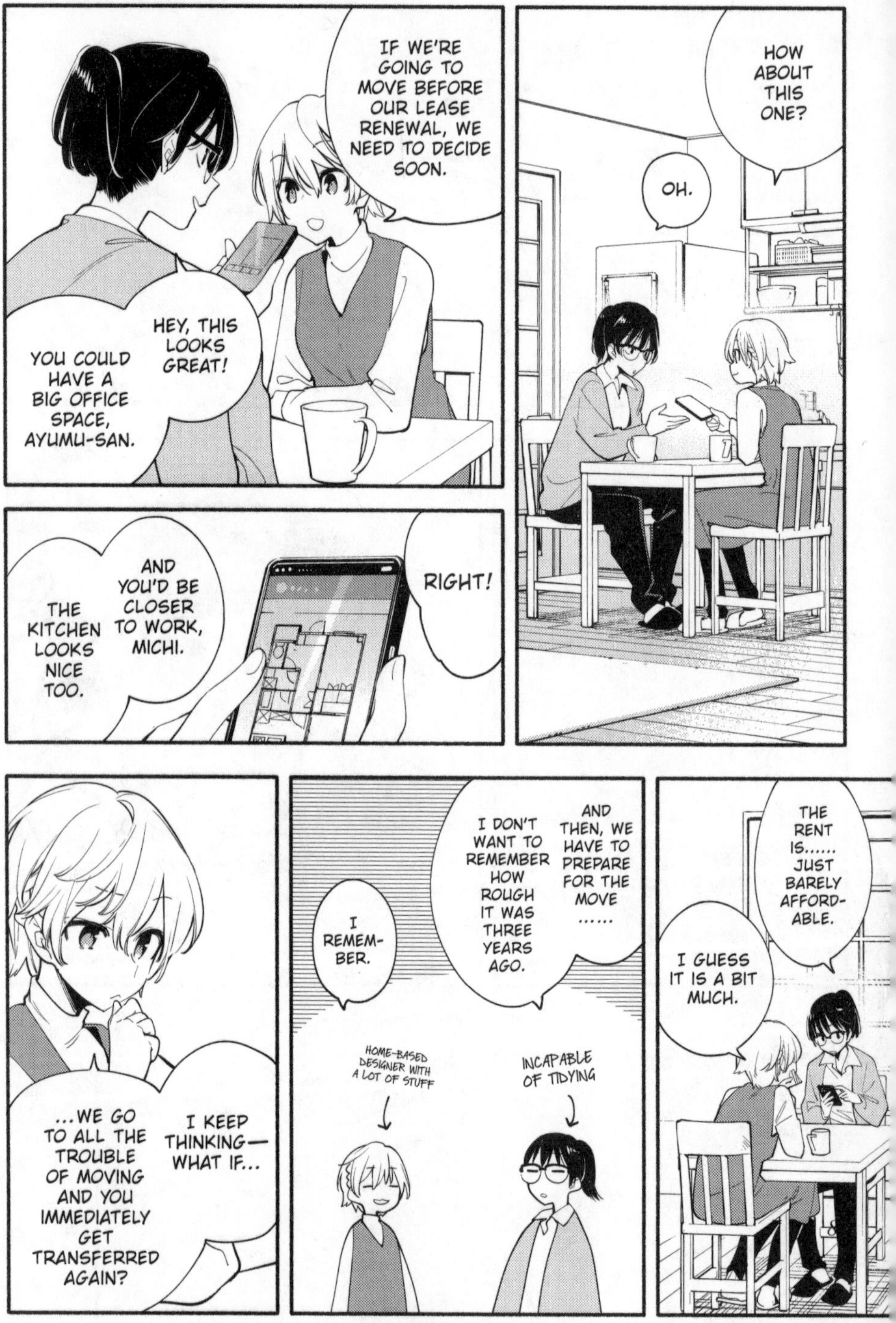
HOW ABOUT THIS ONE?
OH.
IF WE'RE GOING TO MOVE BEFORE OUR LEASE RENEWAL, WE NEED TO DECIDE SOON.
HEY, THIS LOOKS GREAT!
YOU COULD HAVE A BIG OFFICE SPACE, AYUMU-SAN.
RIGHT!
AND YOU'D BE CLOSER TO WORK, MICHI.
THE KITCHEN LOOKS NICE TOO.
THE RENT IS...... JUST BARELY AFFORDABLE.
I GUESS IT IS A BIT MUCH.
AND THEN, WE HAVE TO PREPARE FOR THE MOVE ......
I DON'T WANT TO REMEMBER HOW ROUGH IT WAS THREE YEARS AGO.
I REMEMBER.
INCAPABLE OF TIDYING
HOME-BASED DESIGNER WITH A LOT OF STUFF
I KEEP THINKING— WHAT IF...
...WE GO TO ALL THE TROUBLE OF MOVING AND YOU IMMEDIATELY GET TRANSFERRED AGAIN?

HMMMM...

......THERE'S NO NEED TO GO OUT OF OUR WAY TO MOVE AT RENEWAL TIME.

THERE'S NOT REALLY ANYTHING WRONG WITH OUR CURRENT PLACE.

...WELL.

	Dinner	Clean bath	Cle toi
Ayumu	卌 IIII	卌 IIII	卌 I
Michi	II	I	卌 卌

SURE......

SHALL WE JUST STAY HERE FOR NOW?

AH, OKAY.

LIGHTS-OUT!

GOOD NIGHT, MICHI.

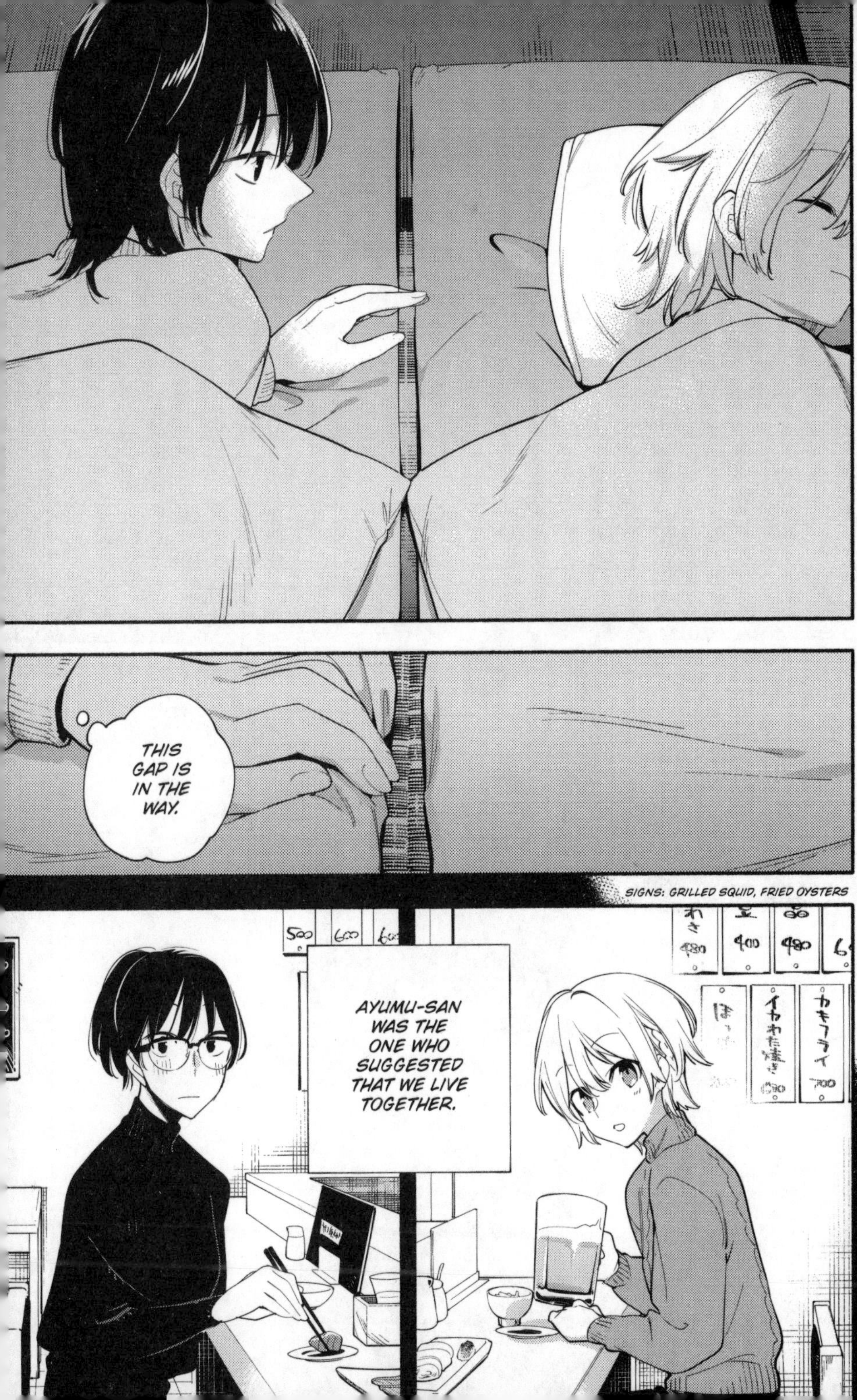
THIS GAP IS IN THE WAY.
SIGNS: GRILLED SQUID, FRIED OYSTERS
AYUMU-SAN WAS THE ONE WHO SUGGESTED THAT WE LIVE TOGETHER.

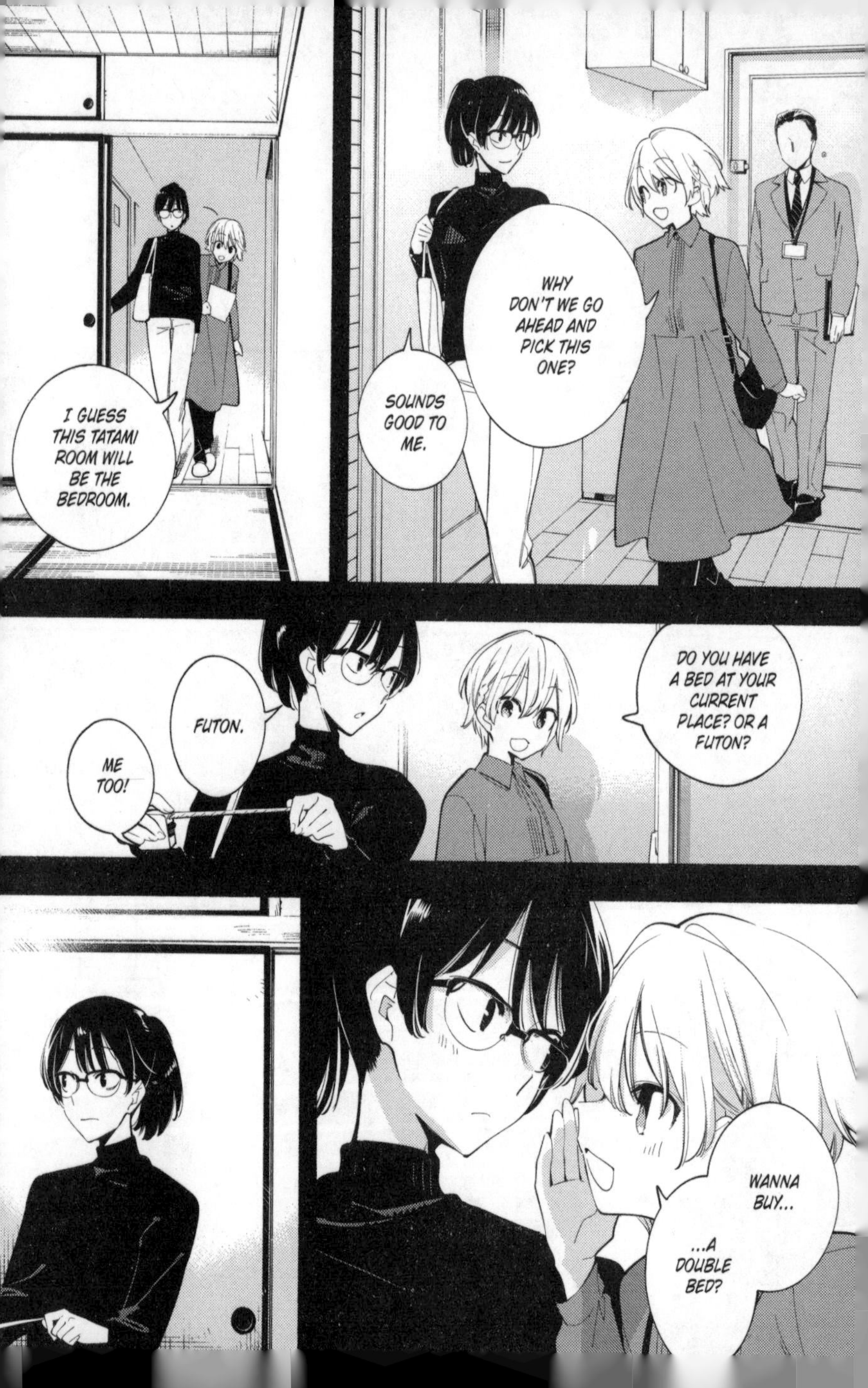
WHY DON'T WE GO AHEAD AND PICK THIS ONE?
SOUNDS GOOD TO ME.
I GUESS THIS TATAMI ROOM WILL BE THE BEDROOM.
DO YOU HAVE A BED AT YOUR CURRENT PLACE? OR A FUTON?
FUTON.
ME TOO!
WANNA BUY...
...A DOUBLE BED?

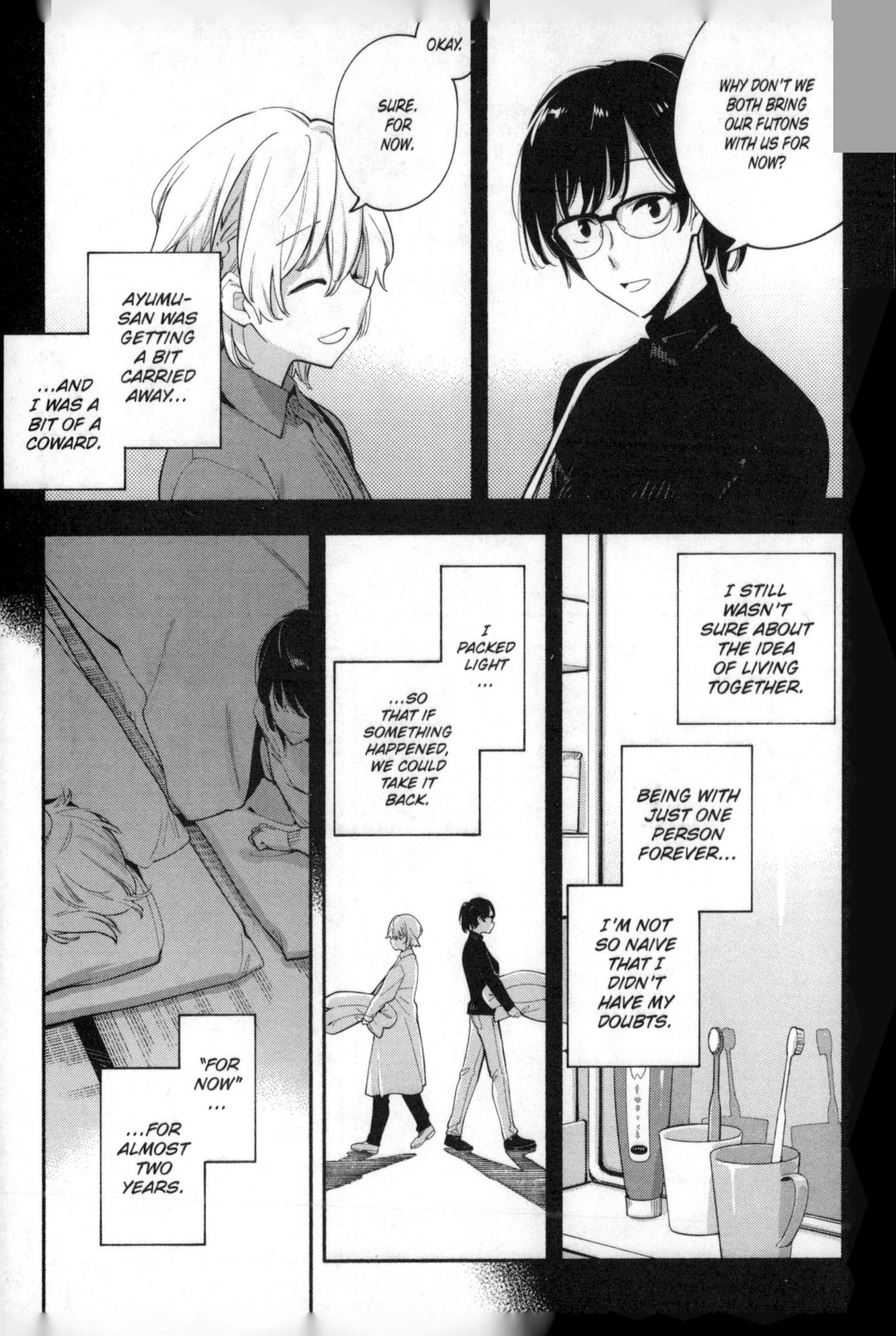
WHY DON'T WE BOTH BRING OUR FUTONS WITH US FOR NOW?
OKAY.
SURE. FOR NOW.
AYUMU-SAN WAS GETTING A BIT CARRIED AWAY...
...AND I WAS A BIT OF A COWARD.
I STILL WASN'T SURE ABOUT THE IDEA OF LIVING TOGETHER.
BEING WITH JUST ONE PERSON FOREVER...
I'M NOT SO NAIVE THAT I DIDN'T HAVE MY DOUBTS.
I PACKED LIGHT...
...SO THAT IF SOMETHING HAPPENED, WE COULD TAKE IT BACK.
"FOR NOW"...
...FOR ALMOST TWO YEARS.

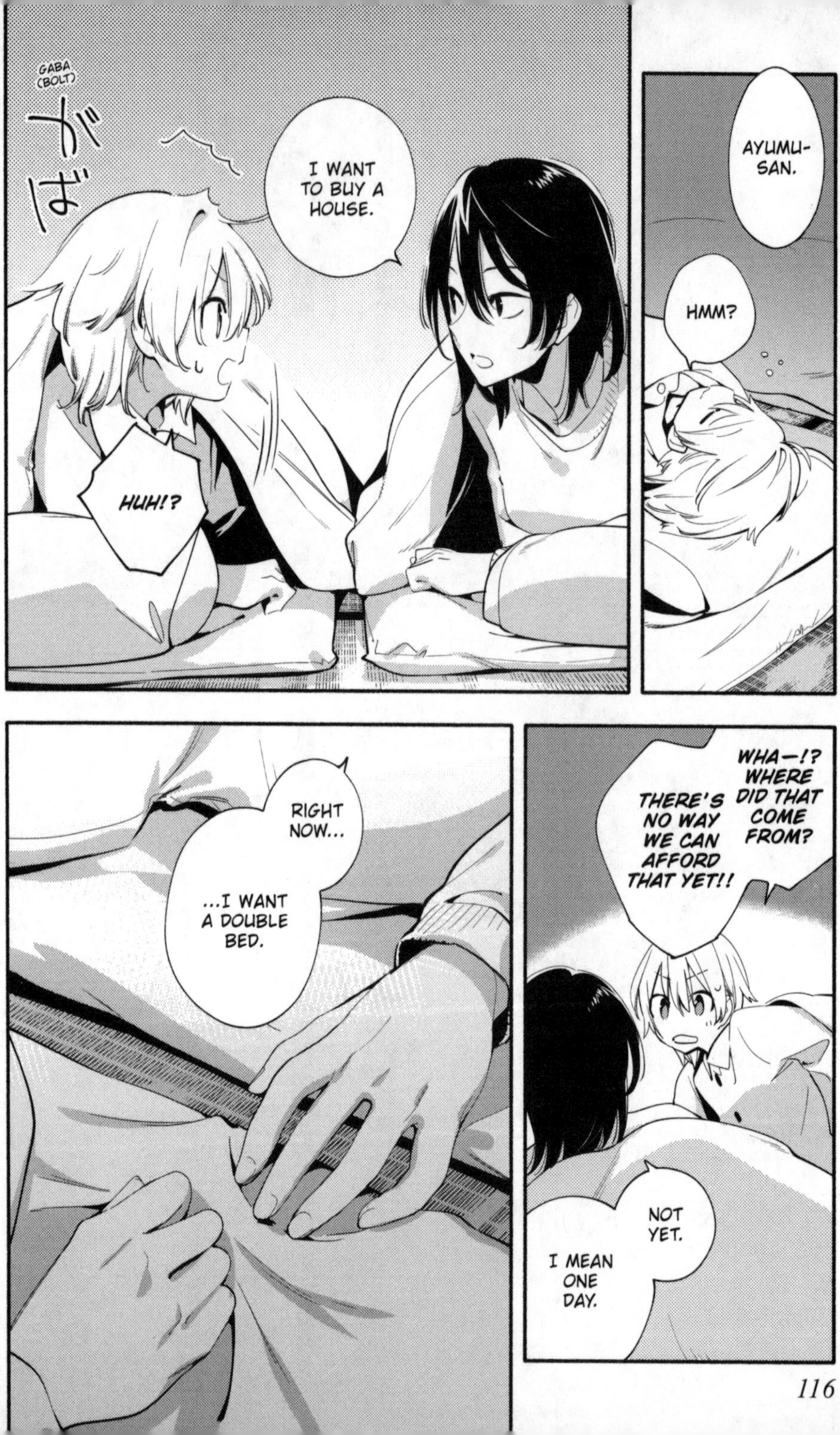
AYUMU-SAN.
HMM?
I WANT TO BUY A HOUSE.
GABA (BOLT)
がば
HUH!?
WHA—!? WHERE DID THAT COME FROM?
THERE'S NO WAY WE CAN AFFORD THAT YET!!
NOT YET.
I MEAN ONE DAY.
RIGHT NOW...
...I WANT A DOUBLE BED.

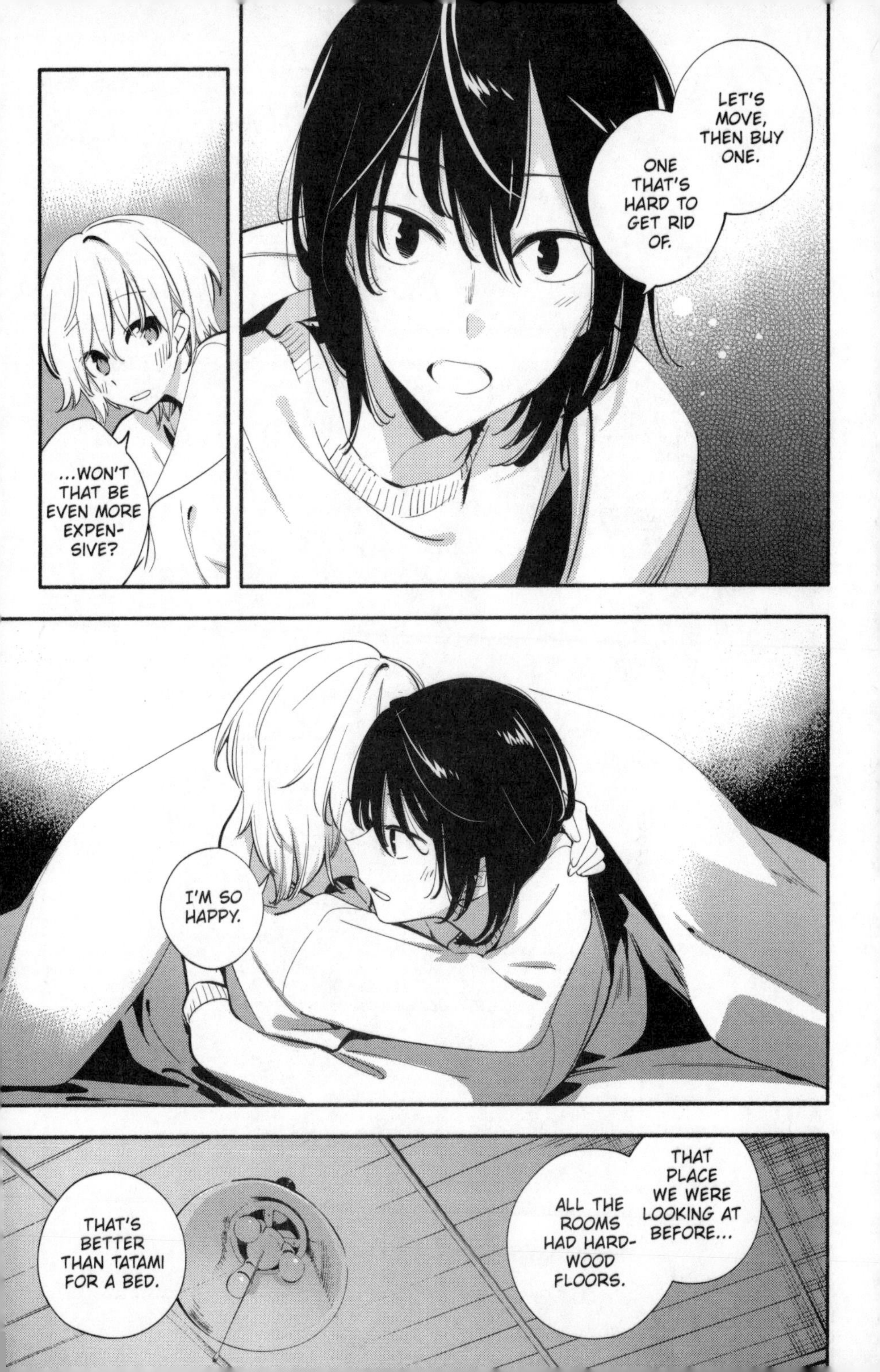
LET'S MOVE, THEN BUY ONE.
ONE THAT'S HARD TO GET RID OF.
...WON'T THAT BE EVEN MORE EXPEN-SIVE?
I'M SO HAPPY.
THAT PLACE WE WERE LOOKING AT BEFORE...
ALL THE ROOMS HAD HARD-WOOD FLOORS.
THAT'S BETTER THAN TATAMI FOR A BED.

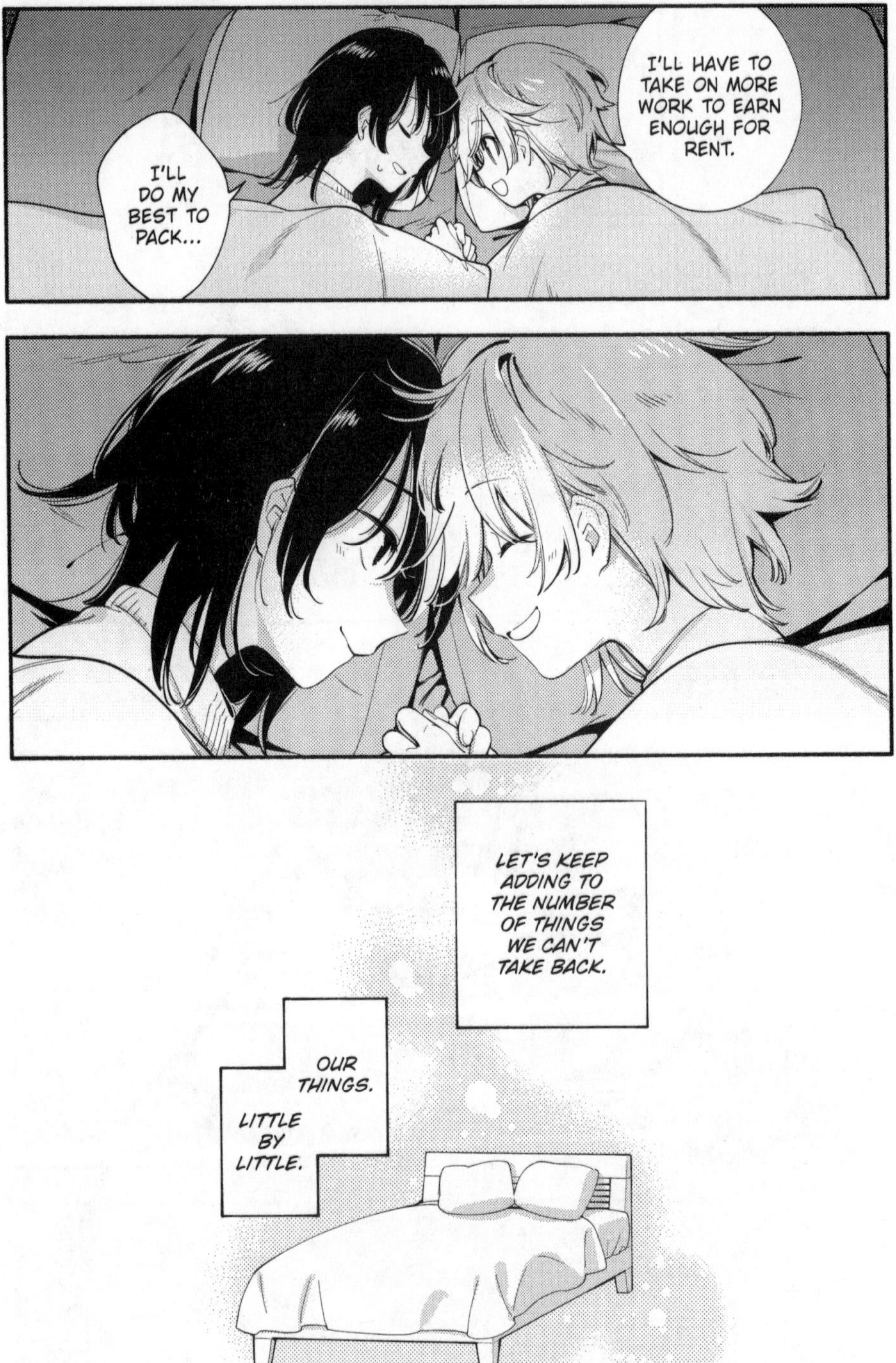
I'LL HAVE TO TAKE ON MORE WORK TO EARN ENOUGH FOR RENT.
I'LL DO MY BEST TO PACK...
LET'S KEEP ADDING TO THE NUMBER OF THINGS WE CAN'T TAKE BACK.
OUR THINGS.
LITTLE BY LITTLE.

【I Am Custom-Made】

This is from when I first got interested in VTubers, as you can tell. Girls' love is a prerequisite of short stories for the *Éclair* anthologies, but since I was in the middle of doing a series centering on the idea of girls' love itself, I started to play with little extra elements in more of my stories.

Initial release: *Éclair Rouge: A Girls' Love Anthology That Resonates in Your Heart*

【Double Bed】

I thought long and hard about how this couple met and all kinds of different settings, but in a one-shot, you can only actually write about a small part of all that. This story was printed in the edition of *Éclair* that went on sale at the same time as the final volume of *Bloom Into You*, and I think there is a very slight overlap in their themes.

Initial release: *Éclair Orange: A Girls' Love Anthology That Resonates in Your Heart*

Translation Notes:

Page 102
1 millimeter is approximately 0.04 inches.

Page 107
100 yen is approximately $1 USD.

Page 117
Tatami is a traditional style of Japanese flooring with mats made of dried rush grass. While it has its pros, it's also easily susceptible to damage, and heavy furniture can leave permanent indentations.

Farewell to My Alter

NIO NAKATANI SHORT STORY COLLECTION

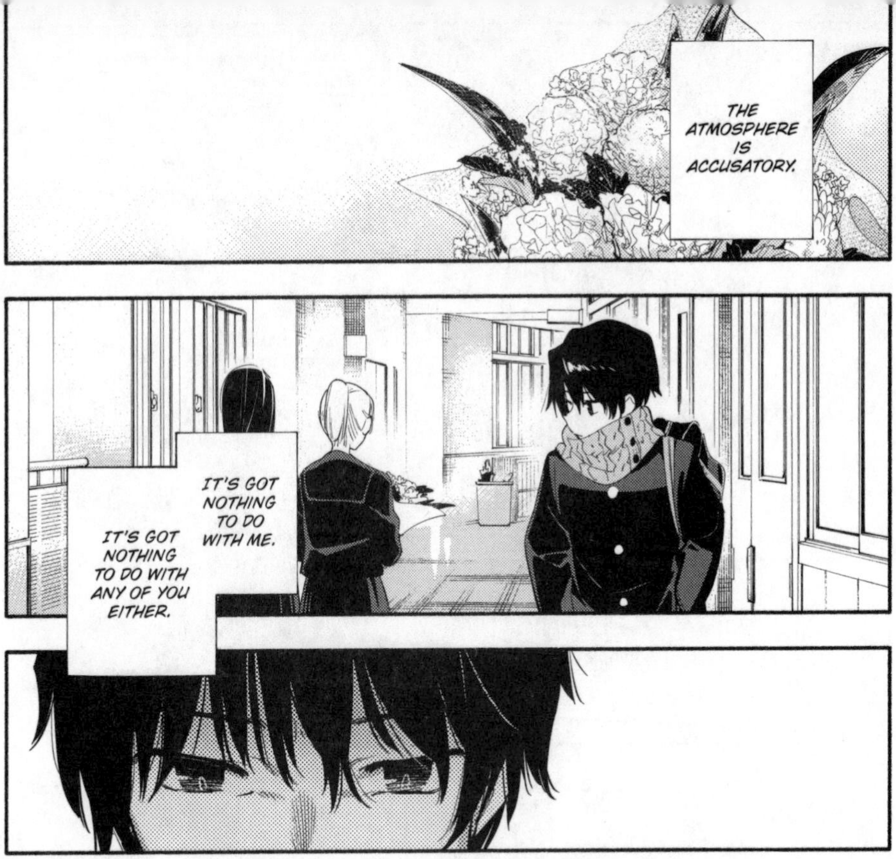
THE ATMOSPHERE IS ACCUSATORY.
IT'S GOT NOTHING TO DO WITH ME.
IT'S GOT NOTHING TO DO WITH ANY OF YOU EITHER.

I Want to Be Kind

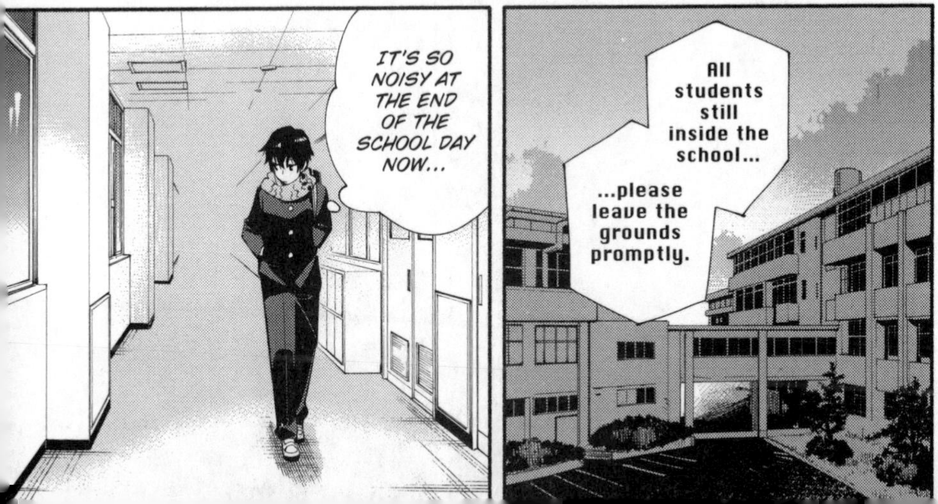
All students still inside the school...
...please leave the grounds promptly.
IT'S SO NOISY AT THE END OF THE SCHOOL DAY NOW...

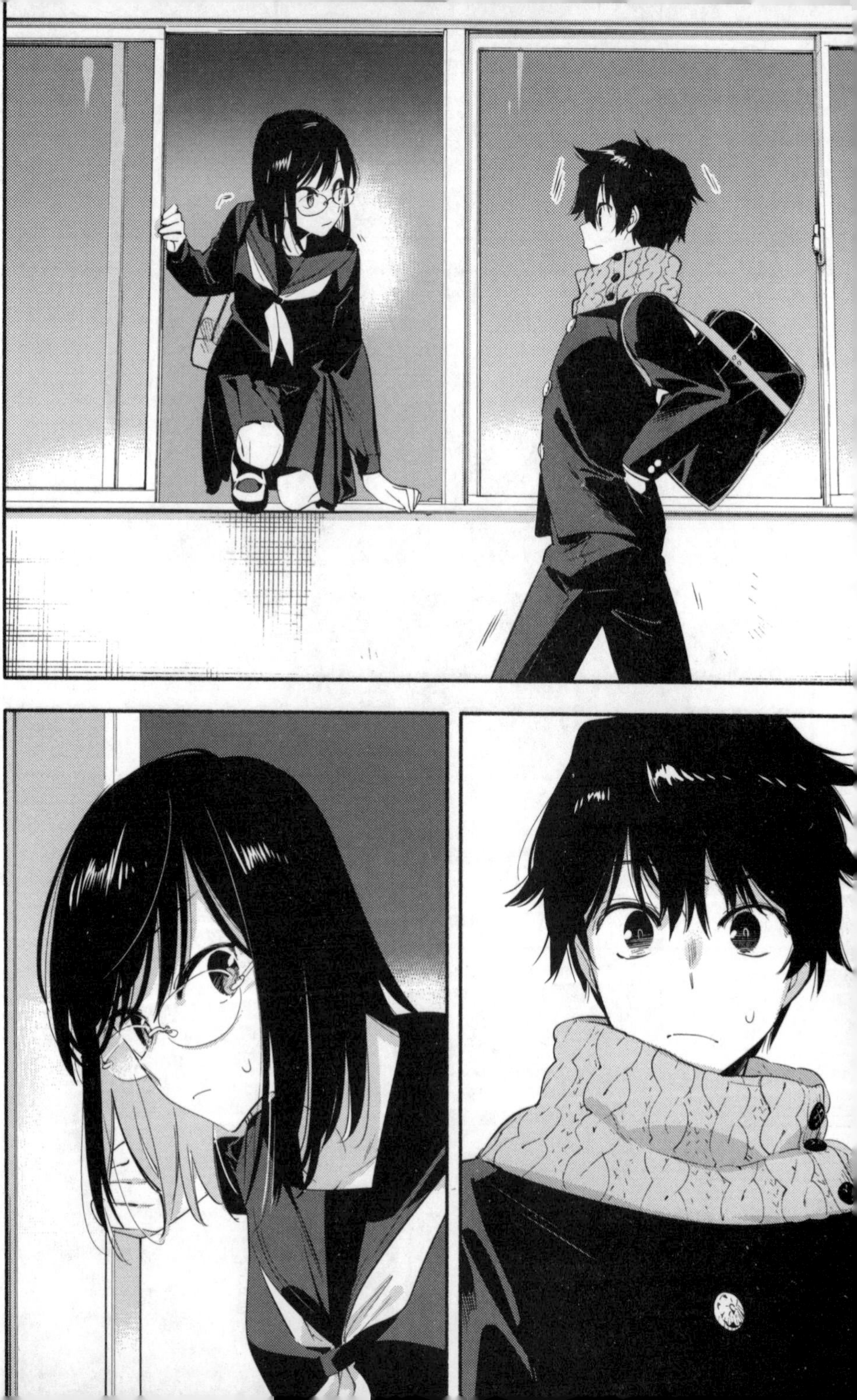

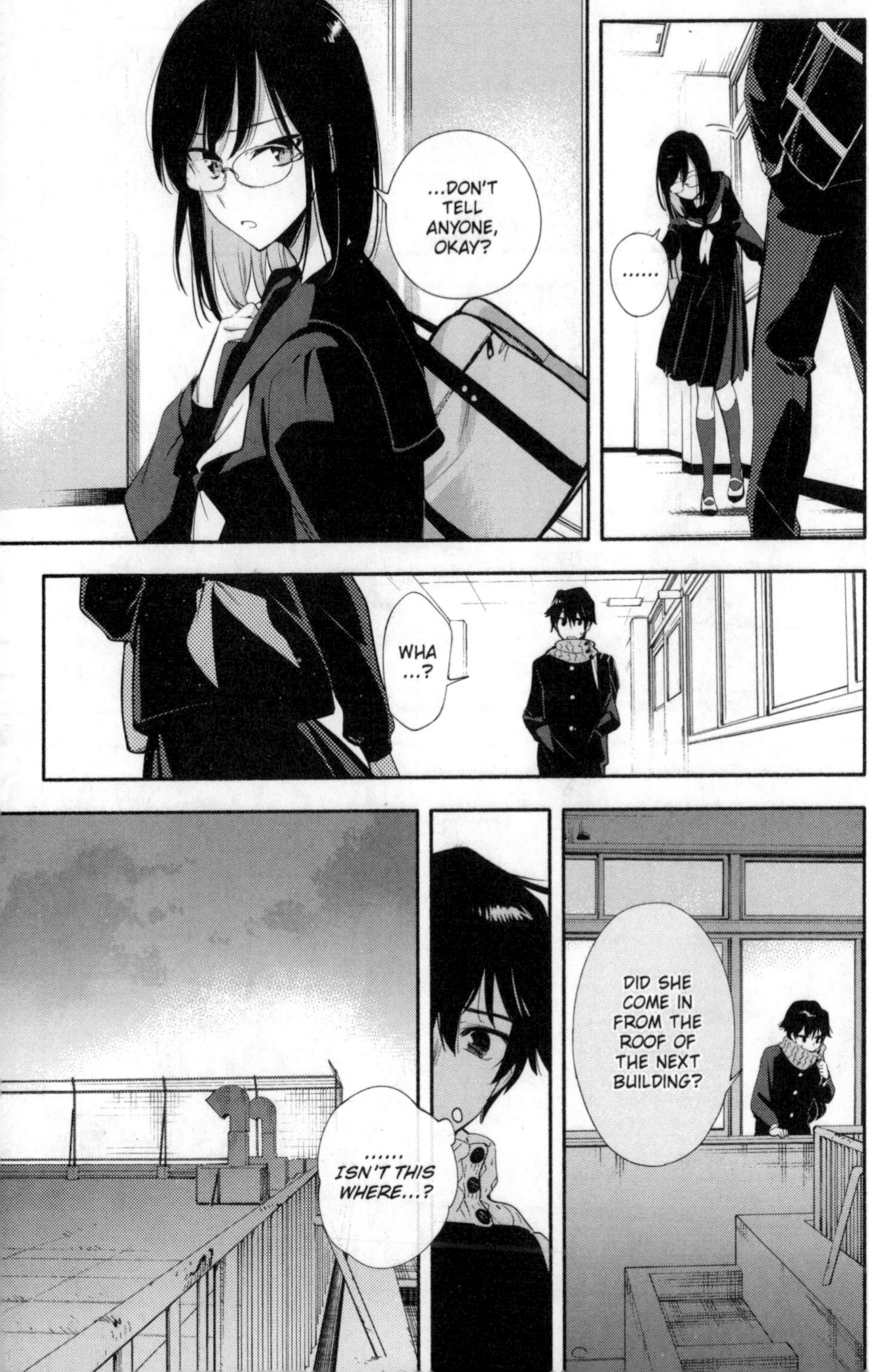
......
...DON'T TELL ANYONE, OKAY?
WHA ...?
DID SHE COME IN FROM THE ROOF OF THE NEXT BUILDING?
...... ISN'T THIS WHERE...?

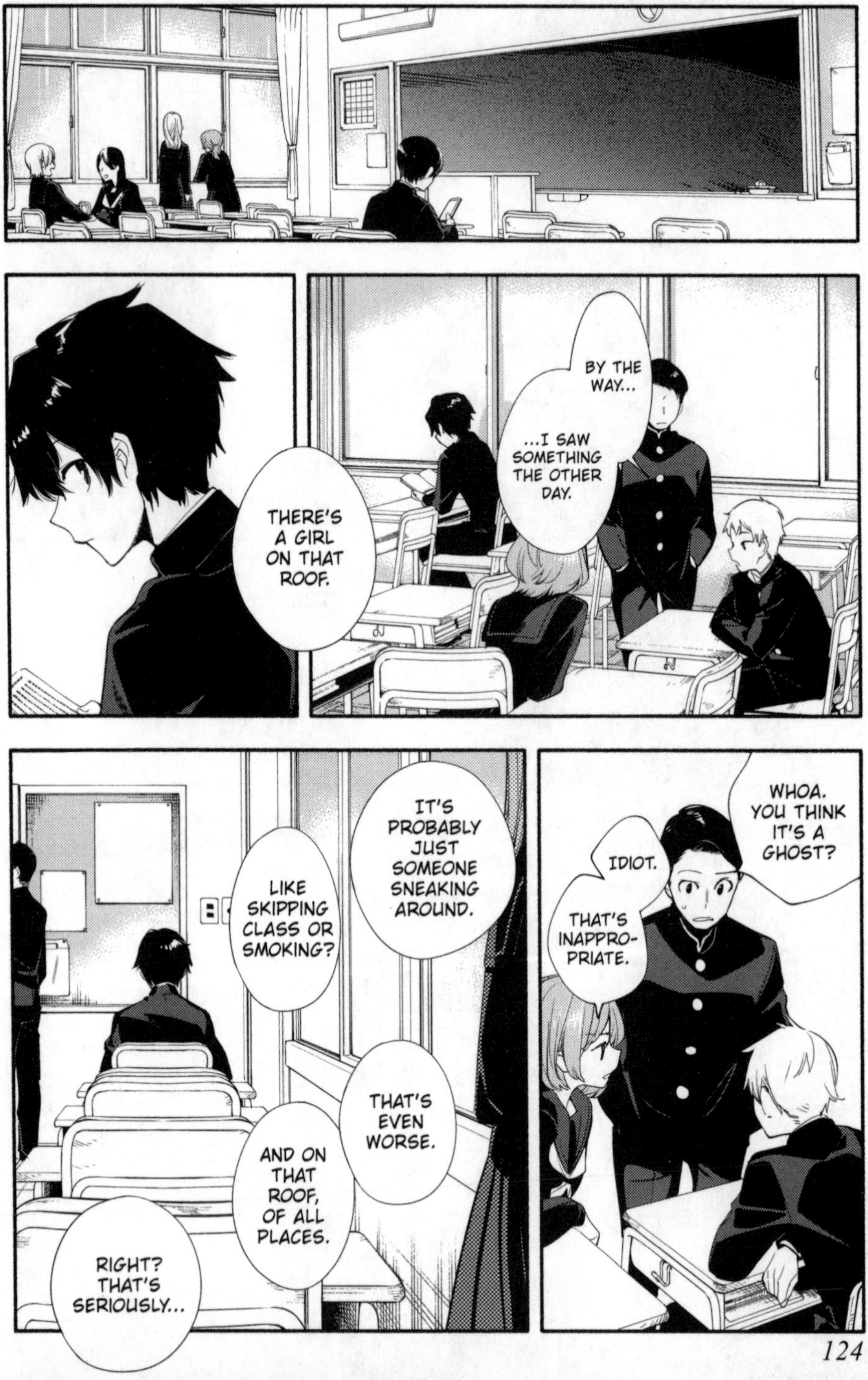
BY THE WAY...
...I SAW SOMETHING THE OTHER DAY.
THERE'S A GIRL ON THAT ROOF.
WHOA. YOU THINK IT'S A GHOST?
IDIOT.
THAT'S INAPPRO-PRIATE.
IT'S PROBABLY JUST SOMEONE SNEAKING AROUND.
LIKE SKIPPING CLASS OR SMOKING?
THAT'S EVEN WORSE.
AND ON THAT ROOF, OF ALL PLACES.
RIGHT? THAT'S SERIOUSLY...

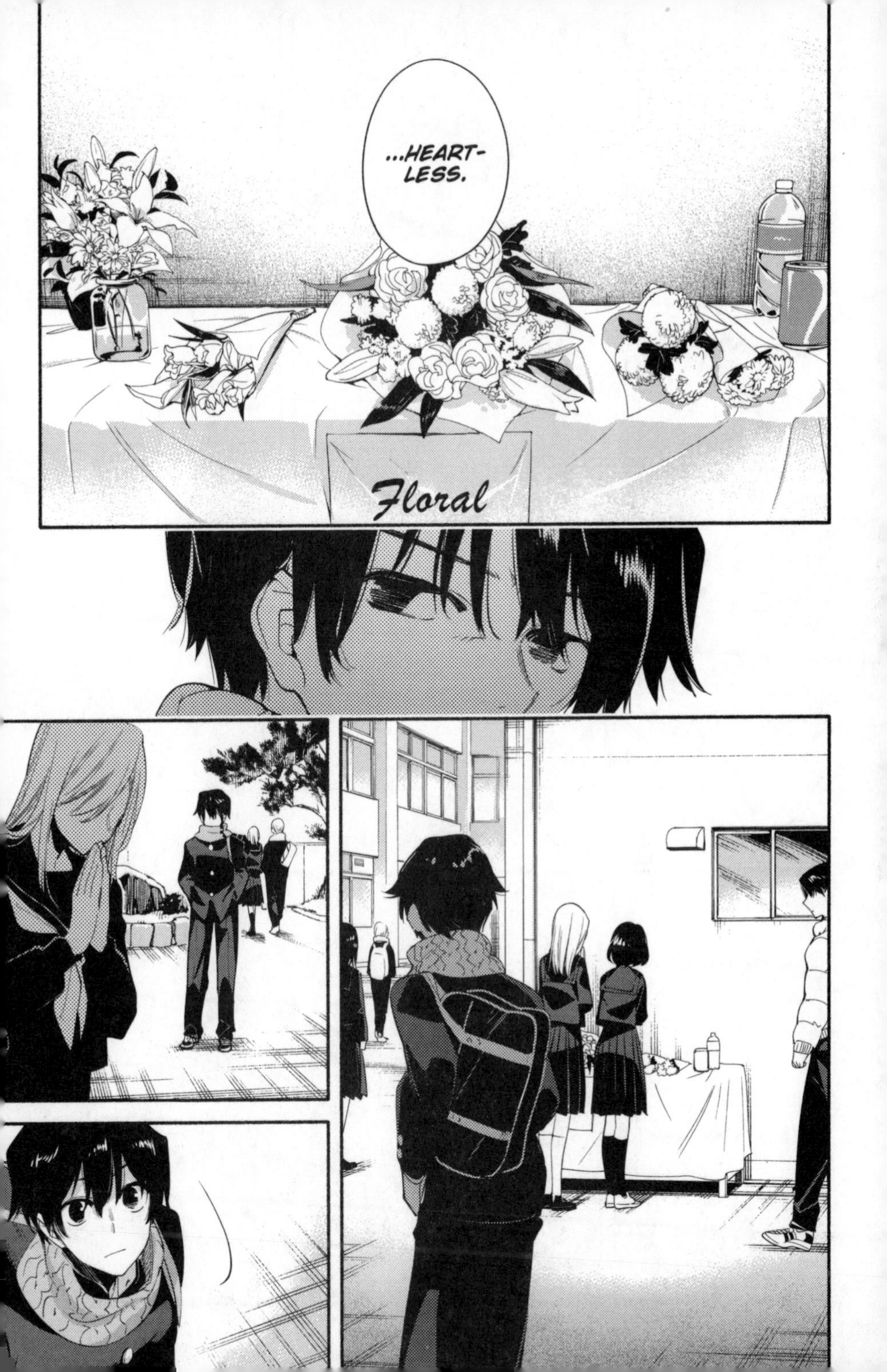
...HEART-
LESS.
Floral

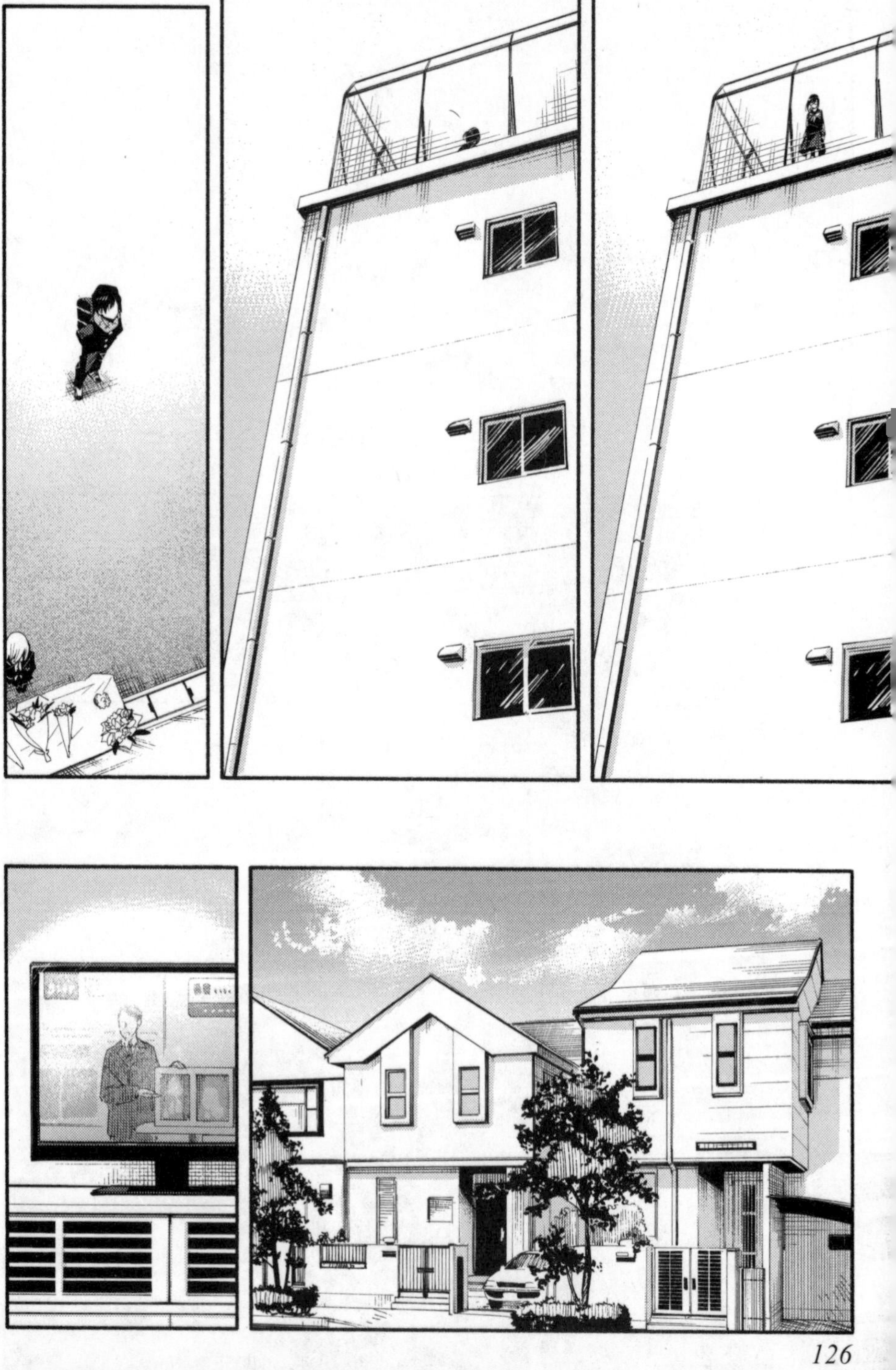

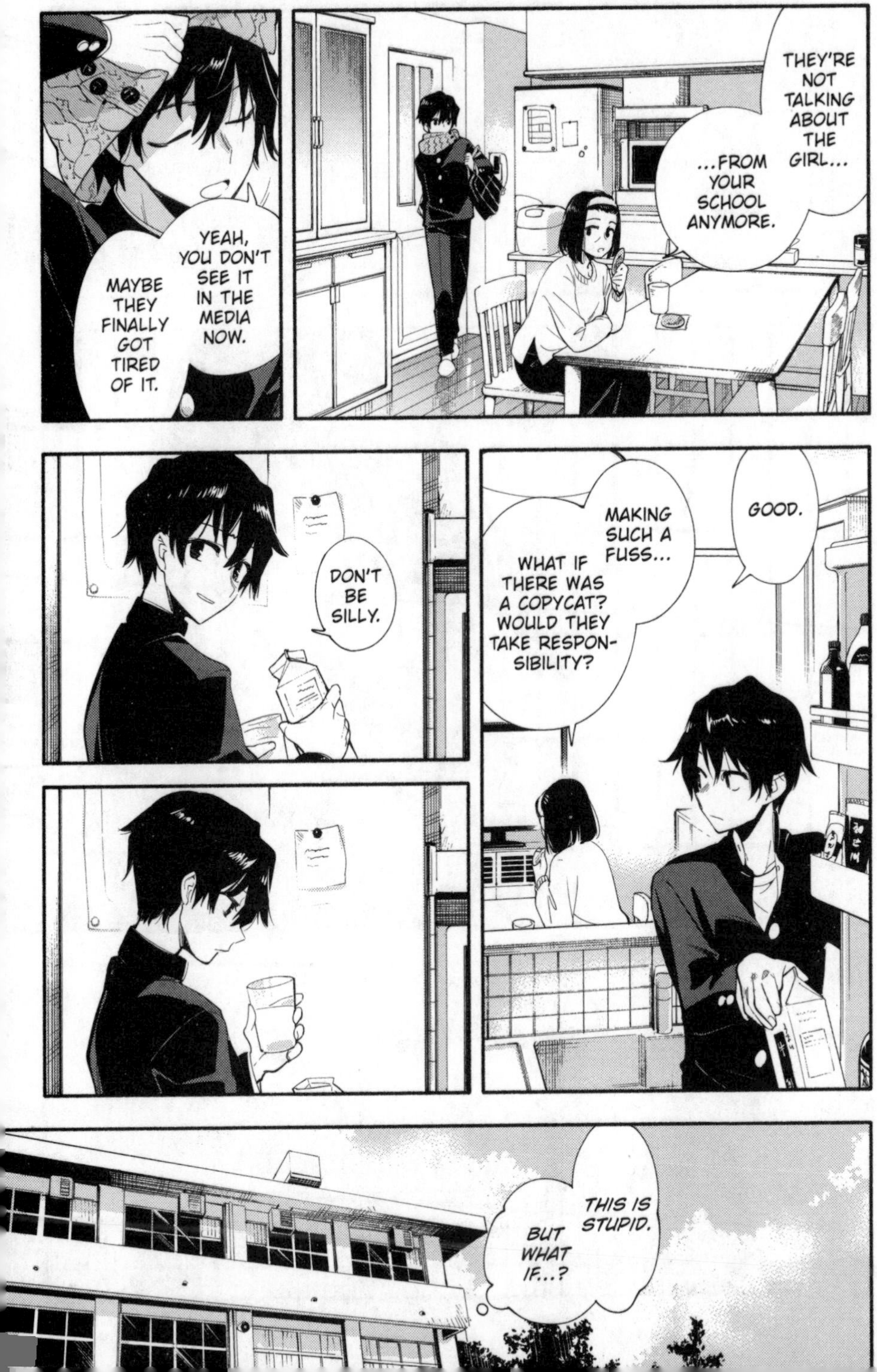
THEY'RE NOT TALKING ABOUT THE GIRL...
...FROM YOUR SCHOOL ANYMORE.
YEAH, YOU DON'T SEE IT IN THE MEDIA NOW.
MAYBE THEY FINALLY GOT TIRED OF IT.
GOOD.
MAKING SUCH A FUSS...
WHAT IF THERE WAS A COPYCAT? WOULD THEY TAKE RESPONSI-BILITY?
DON'T BE SILLY.
THIS IS STUPID.
BUT WHAT IF...?

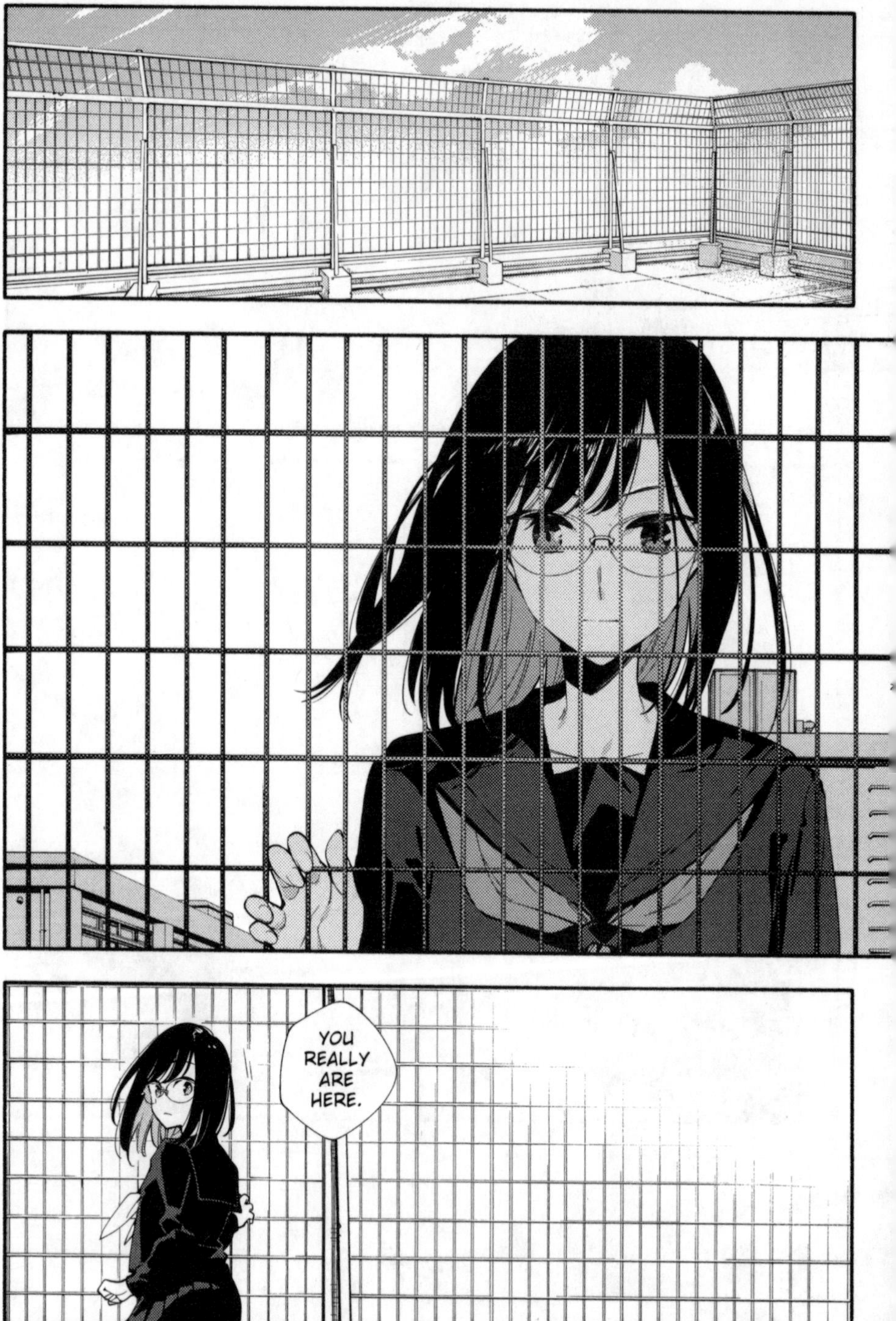
YOU REALLY ARE HERE.

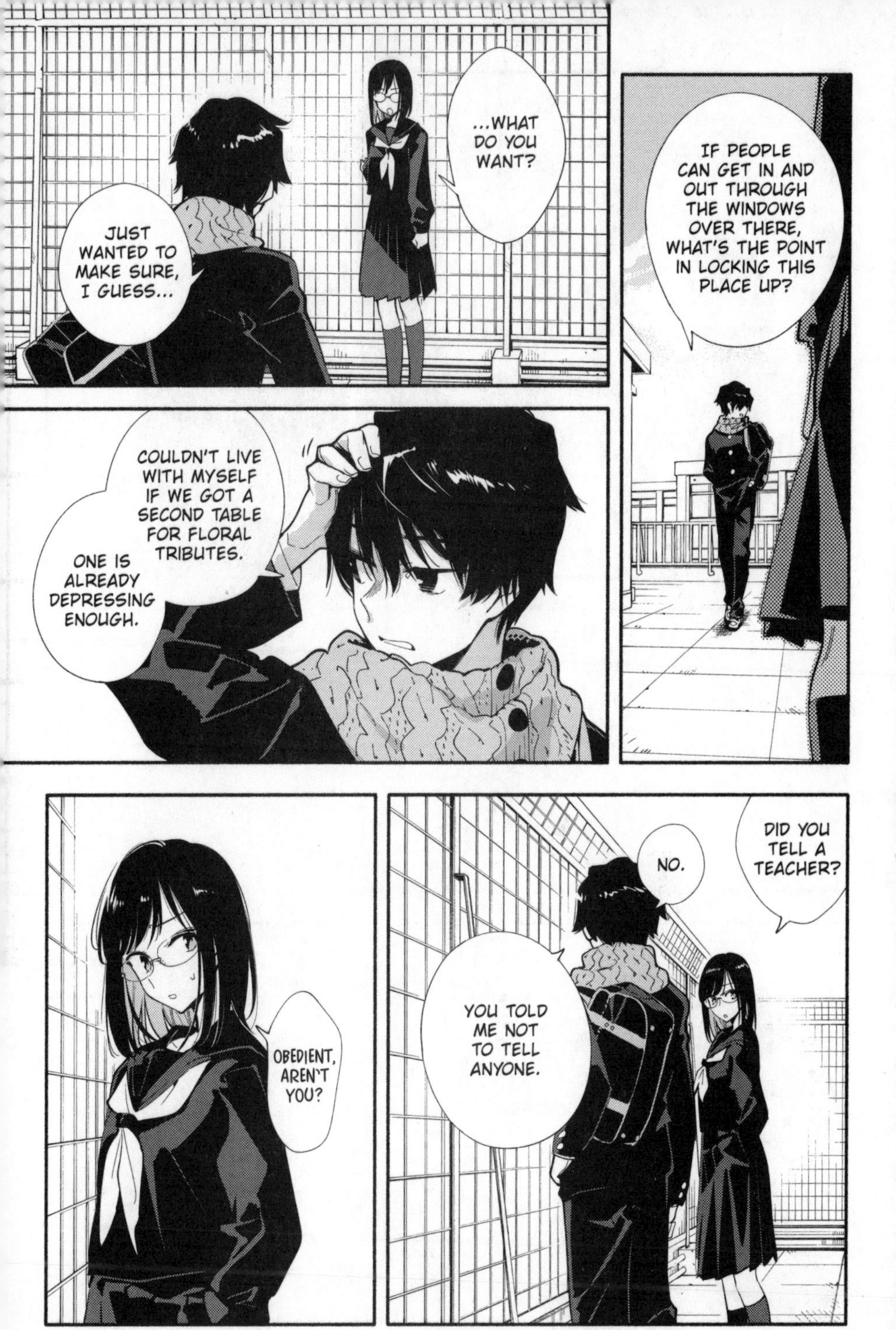
IF PEOPLE CAN GET IN AND OUT THROUGH THE WINDOWS OVER THERE, WHAT'S THE POINT IN LOCKING THIS PLACE UP?
...WHAT DO YOU WANT?
JUST WANTED TO MAKE SURE, I GUESS...
COULDN'T LIVE WITH MYSELF IF WE GOT A SECOND TABLE FOR FLORAL TRIBUTES.
ONE IS ALREADY DEPRESSING ENOUGH.
DID YOU TELL A TEACHER?
NO.
YOU TOLD ME NOT TO TELL ANYONE.
OBEDIENT, AREN'T YOU?

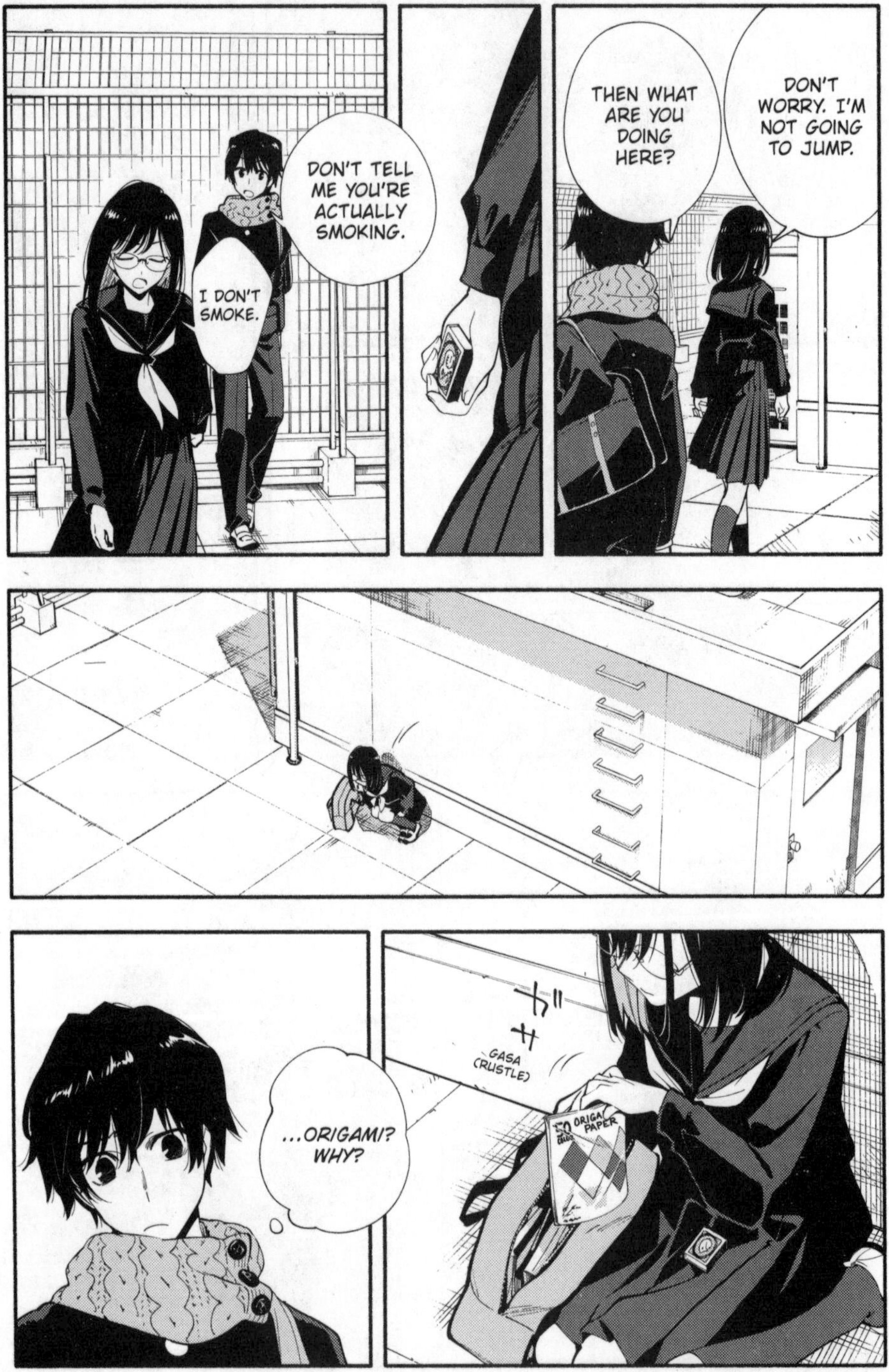
DON'T WORRY. I'M NOT GOING TO JUMP.
THEN WHAT ARE YOU DOING HERE?
DON'T TELL ME YOU'RE ACTUALLY SMOKING.
I DON'T SMOKE.
ガサ
GASA (RUSTLE)
...ORIGAMI? WHY?

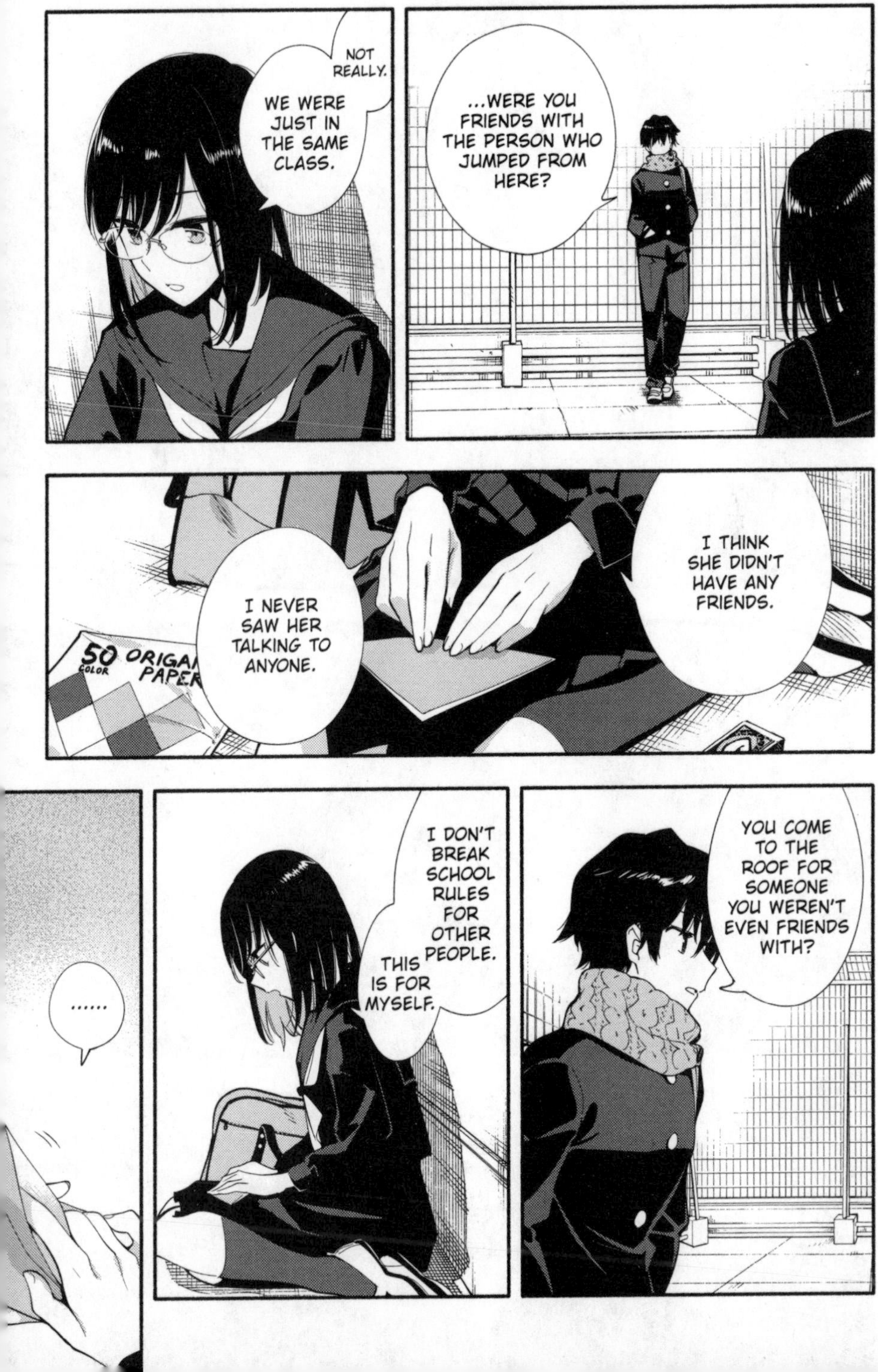
...WERE YOU FRIENDS WITH THE PERSON WHO JUMPED FROM HERE?
NOT REALLY.
WE WERE JUST IN THE SAME CLASS.
I THINK SHE DIDN'T HAVE ANY FRIENDS.
I NEVER SAW HER TALKING TO ANYONE.
50 COLOR
YOU COME TO THE ROOF FOR SOMEONE YOU WEREN'T EVEN FRIENDS WITH?
I DON'T BREAK SCHOOL RULES FOR OTHER PEOPLE.
THIS IS FOR MYSELF.
......

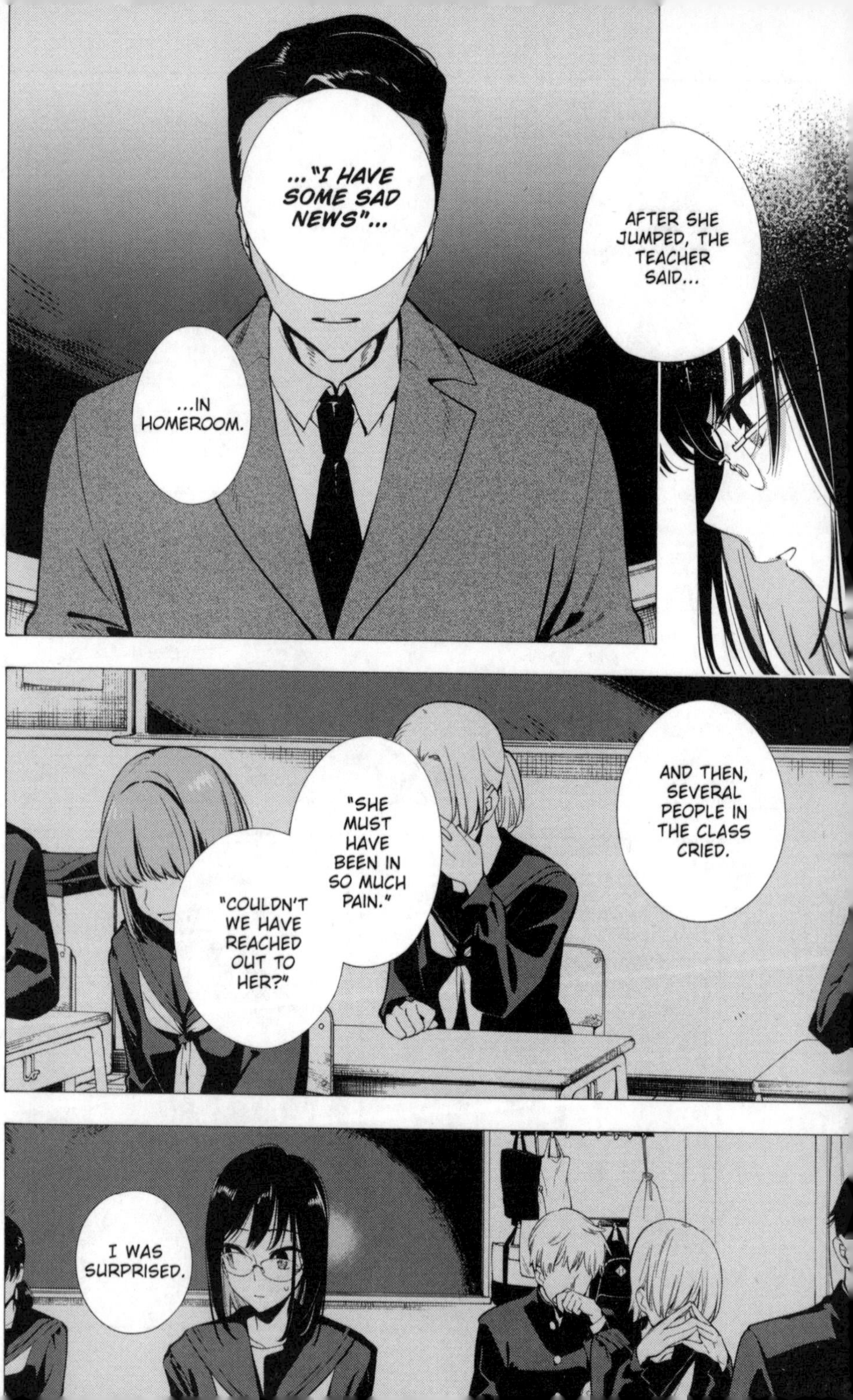
AFTER SHE JUMPED, THE TEACHER SAID...
..."I HAVE SOME SAD NEWS"...
...IN HOMEROOM.
AND THEN, SEVERAL PEOPLE IN THE CLASS CRIED.
"SHE MUST HAVE BEEN IN SO MUCH PAIN."
"COULDN'T WE HAVE REACHED OUT TO HER?"
I WAS SURPRISED.

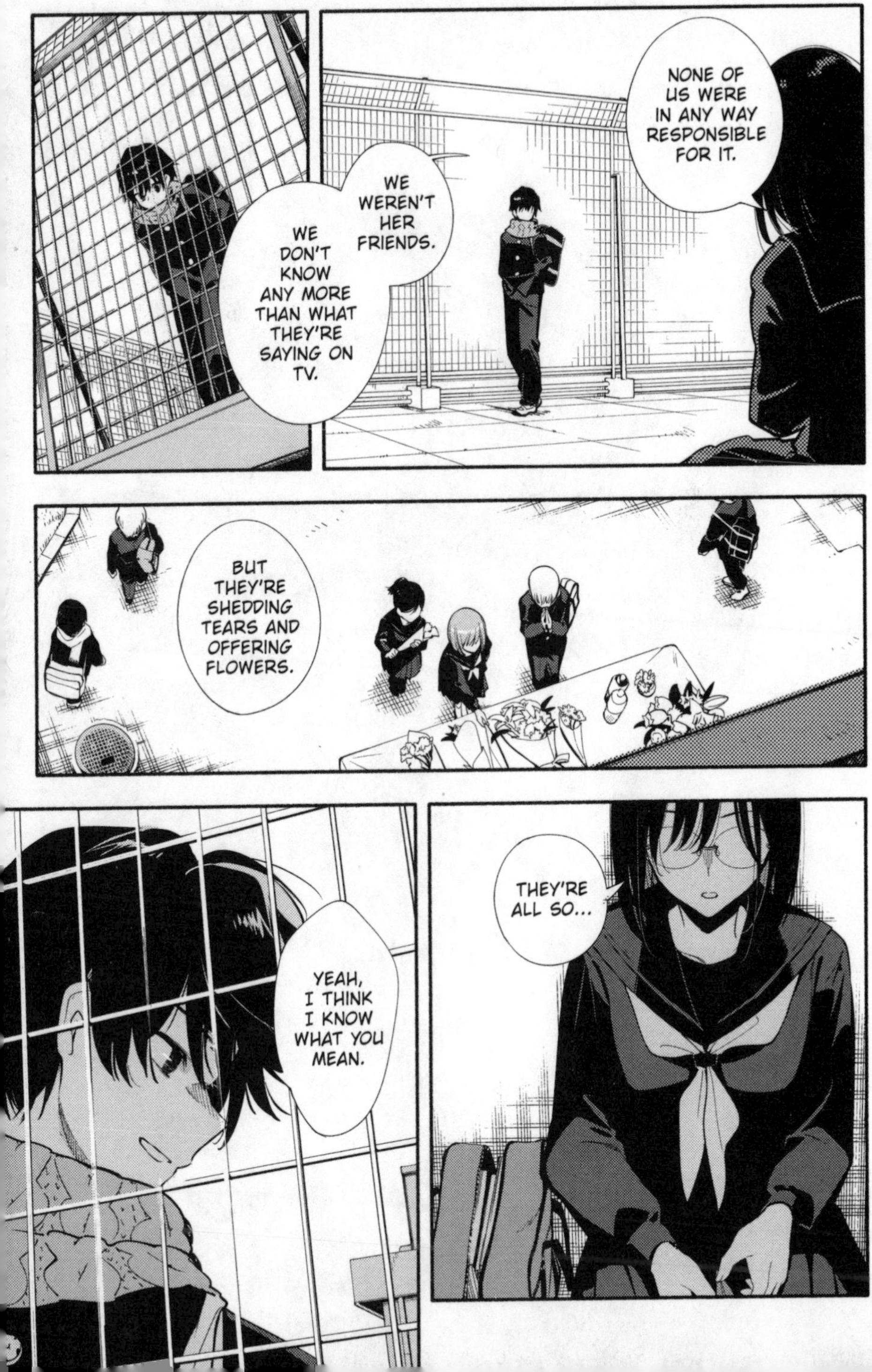
NONE OF US WERE IN ANY WAY RESPONSIBLE FOR IT.
WE WEREN'T HER FRIENDS.
WE DON'T KNOW ANY MORE THAN WHAT THEY'RE SAYING ON TV.
BUT THEY'RE SHEDDING TEARS AND OFFERING FLOWERS.
THEY'RE ALL SO...
YEAH, I THINK I KNOW WHAT YOU MEAN.

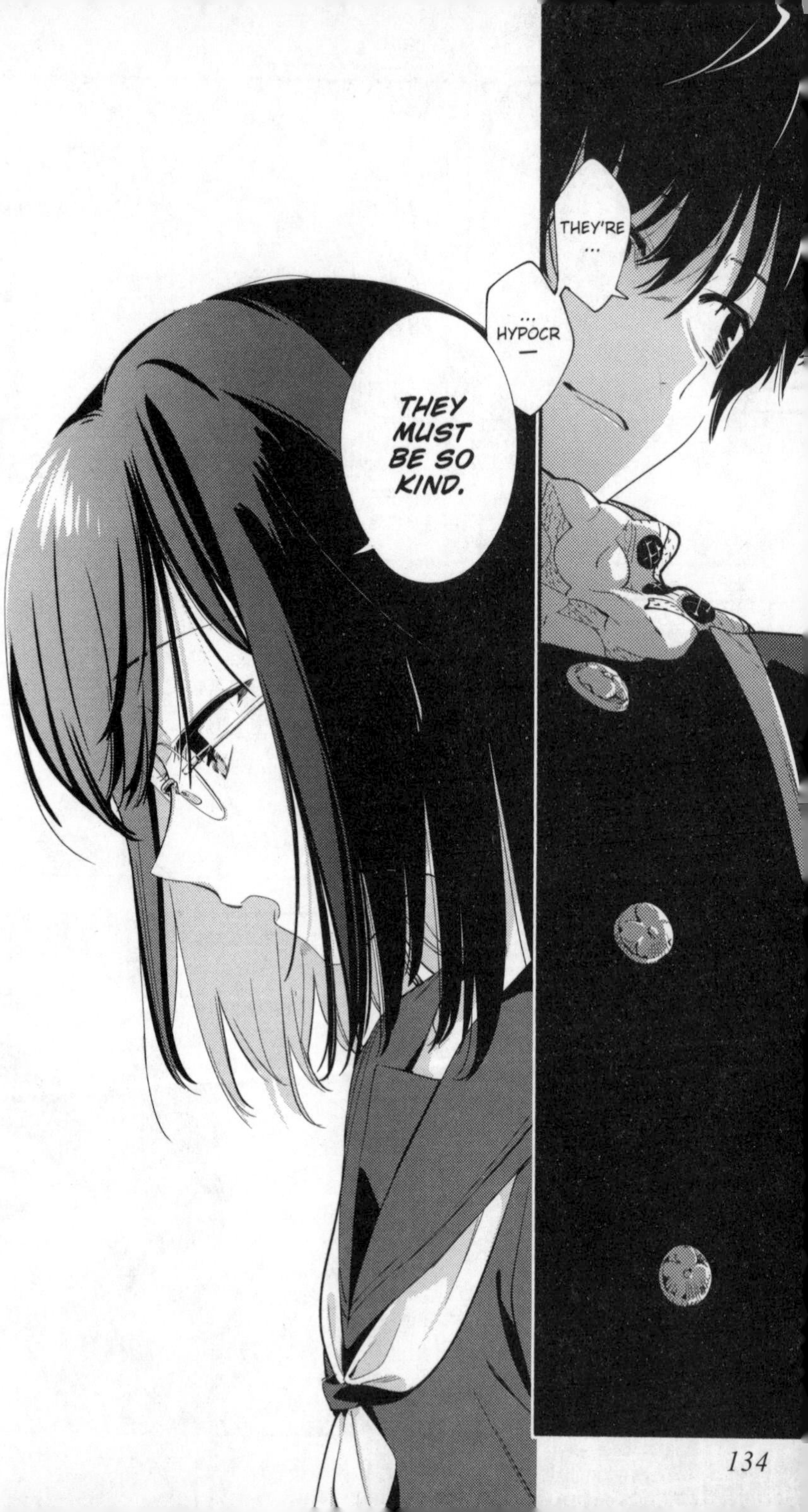
THEY'RE ...
... HYPOCR—
THEY MUST BE SO KIND.

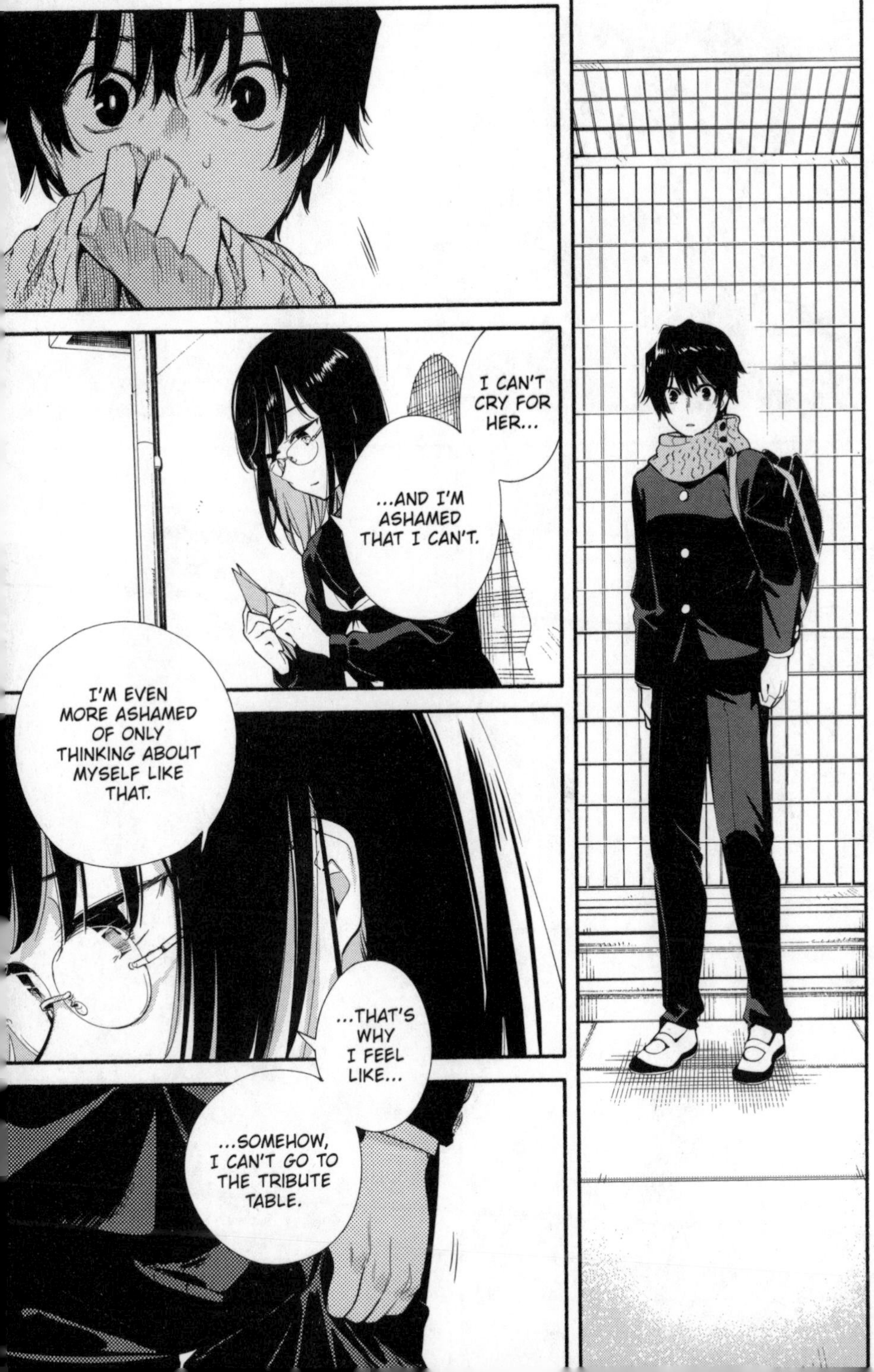
I CAN'T CRY FOR HER...
...AND I'M ASHAMED THAT I CAN'T.
I'M EVEN MORE ASHAMED OF ONLY THINKING ABOUT MYSELF LIKE THAT.
...THAT'S WHY I FEEL LIKE...
...SOMEHOW, I CAN'T GO TO THE TRIBUTE TABLE.

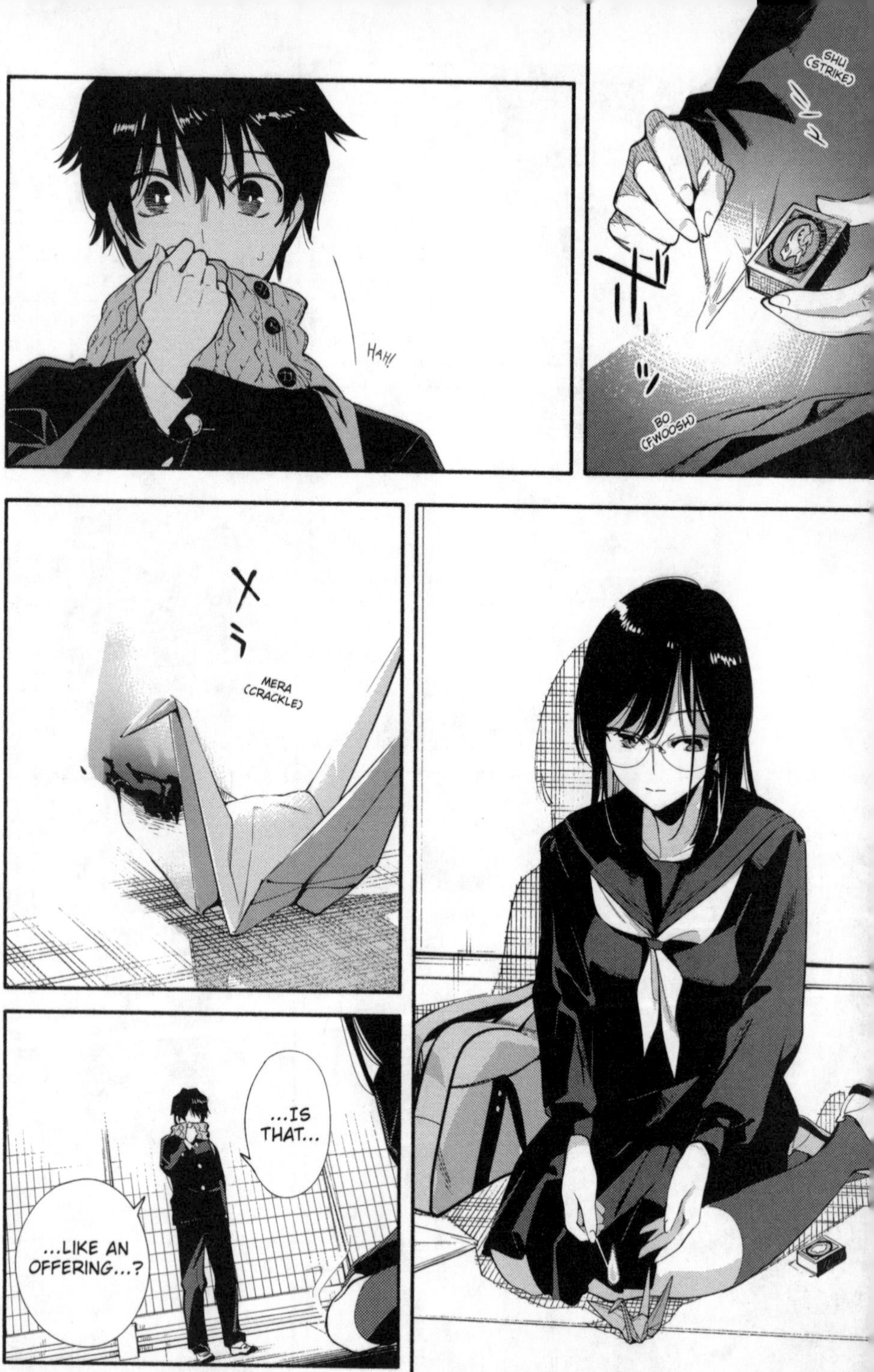
シュッ
SHU (STRIKE)
ボッ
BO (FWOOSH)
HAH!
メラ
MERA (CRACKLE)
...IS THAT...
...LIKE AN OFFERING...?

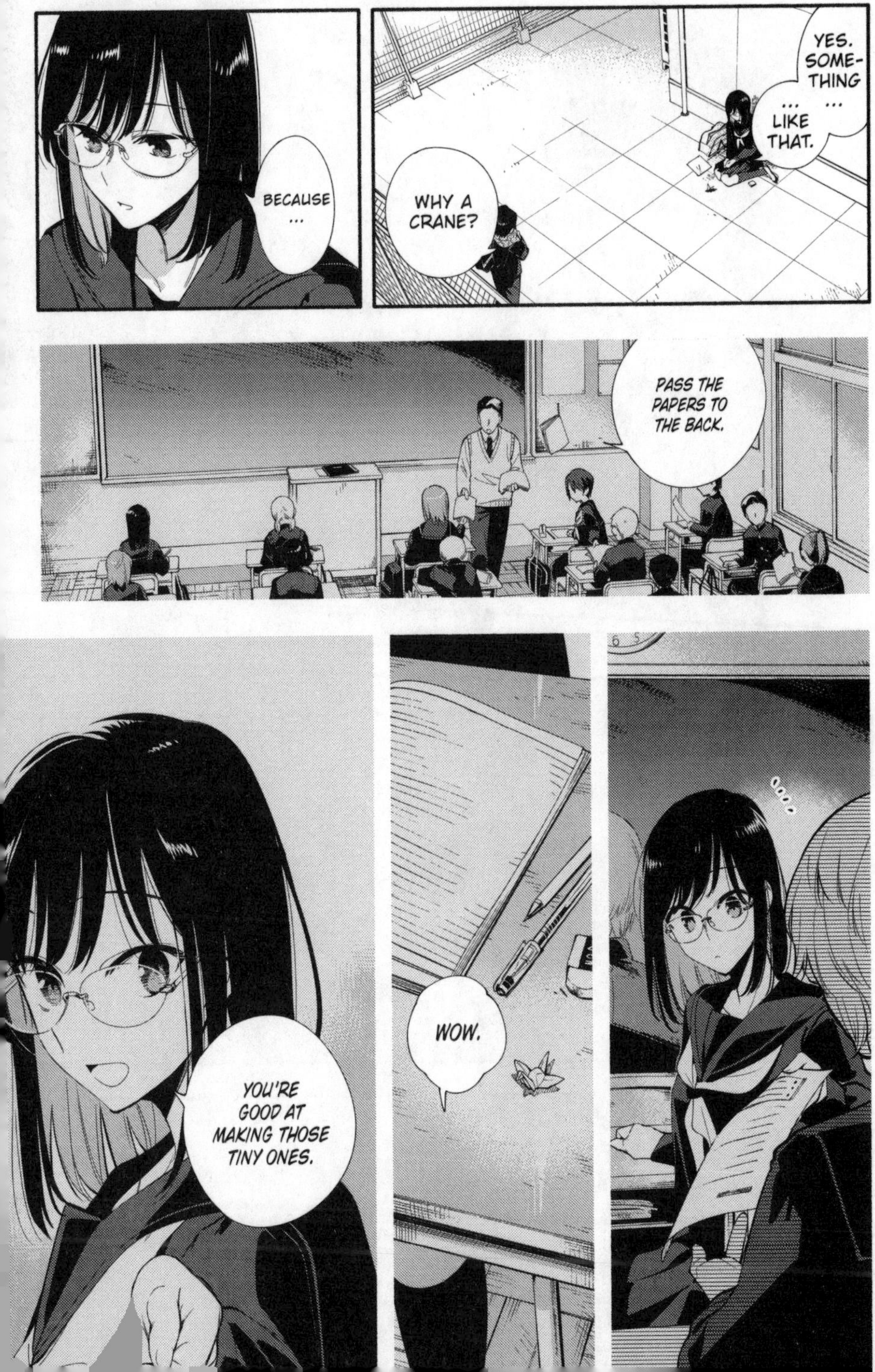
YES. SOMETHING ...
... LIKE THAT.
WHY A CRANE?
BECAUSE ...
PASS THE PAPERS TO THE BACK.
....
WOW.
YOU'RE GOOD AT MAKING THOSE TINY ONES.

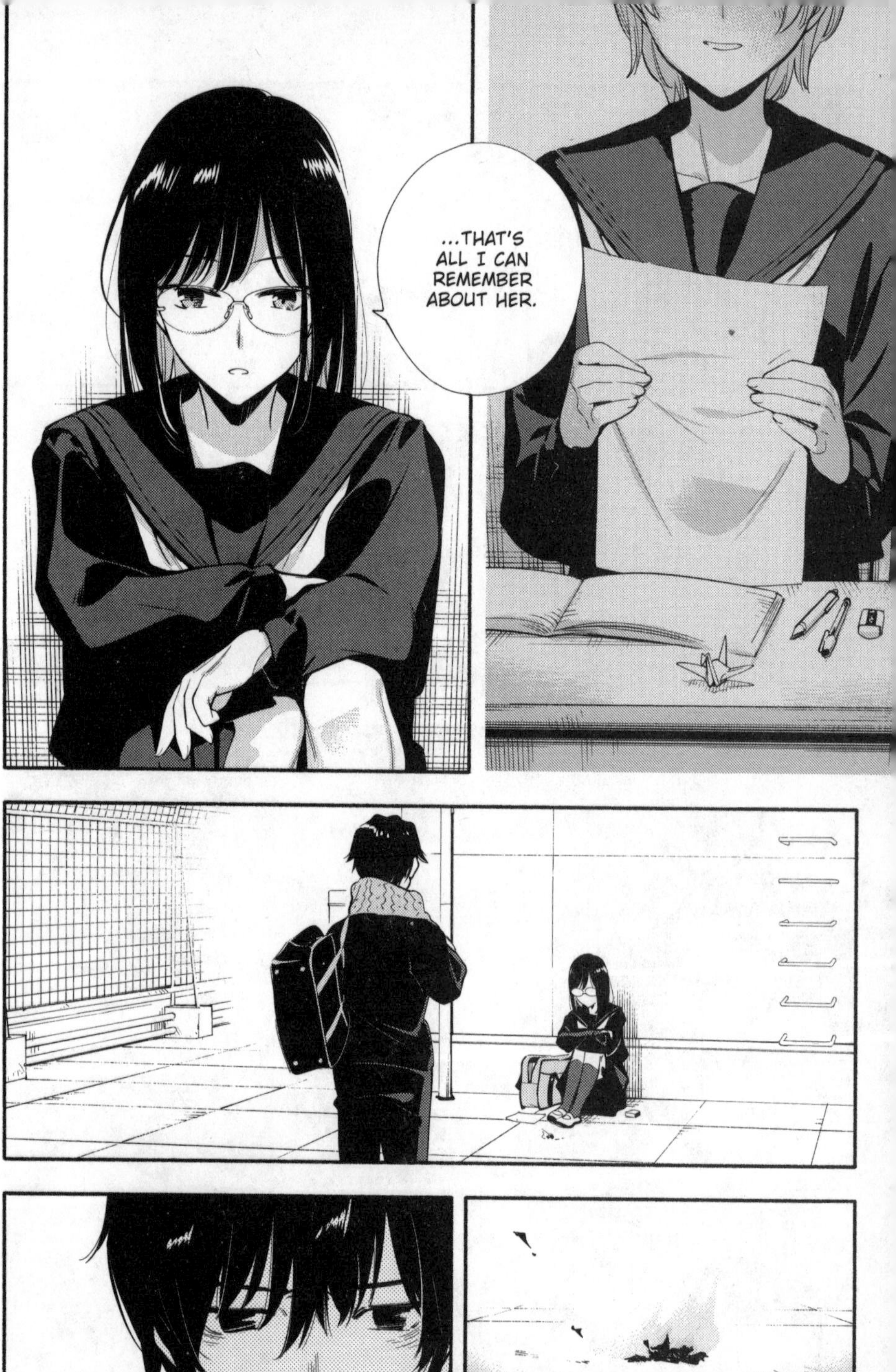
...THAT'S ALL I CAN REMEMBER ABOUT HER.

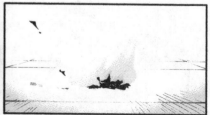

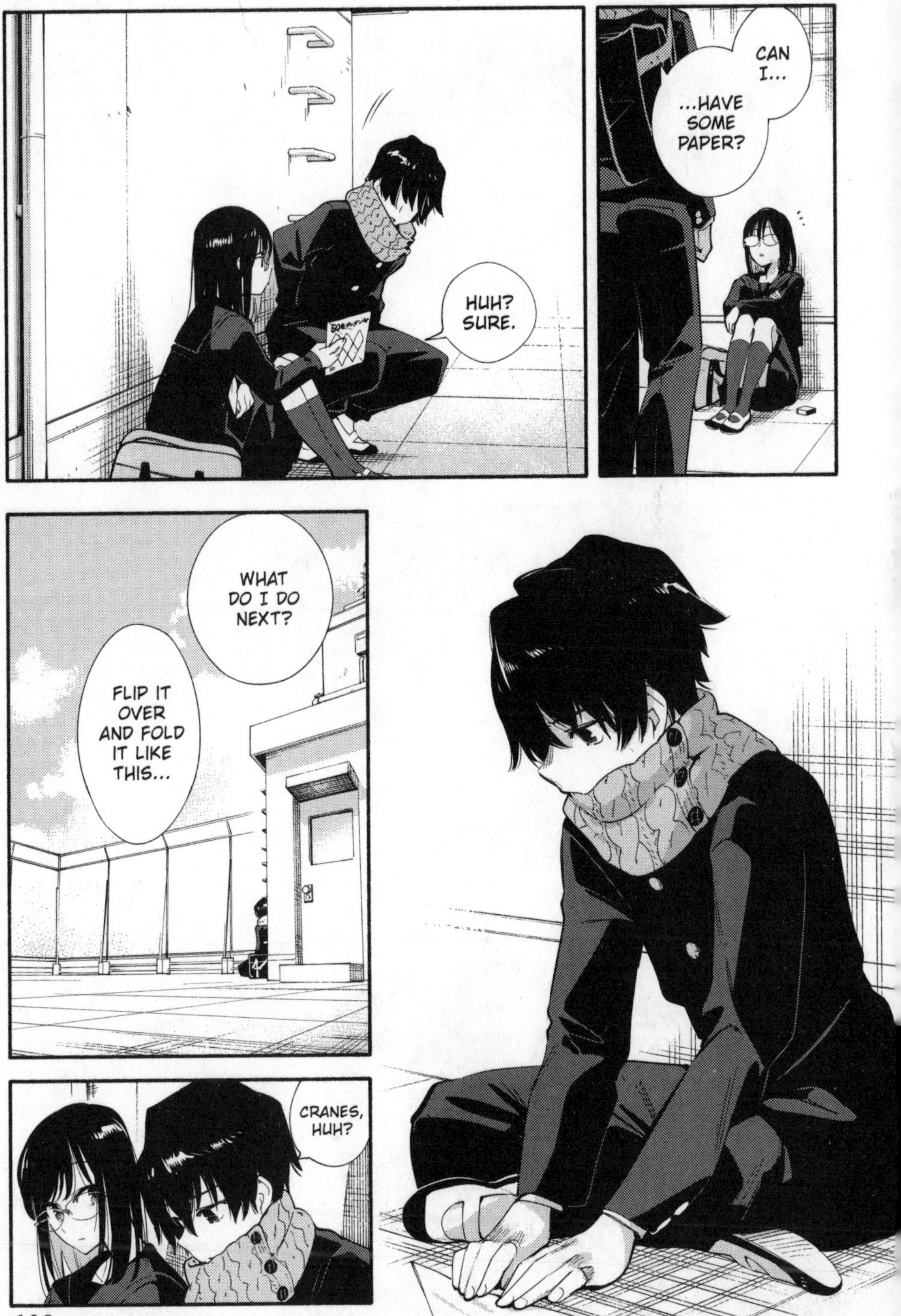
CAN I...
...HAVE SOME PAPER?
HUH? SURE.
WHAT DO I DO NEXT?
FLIP IT OVER AND FOLD IT LIKE THIS...
CRANES, HUH?

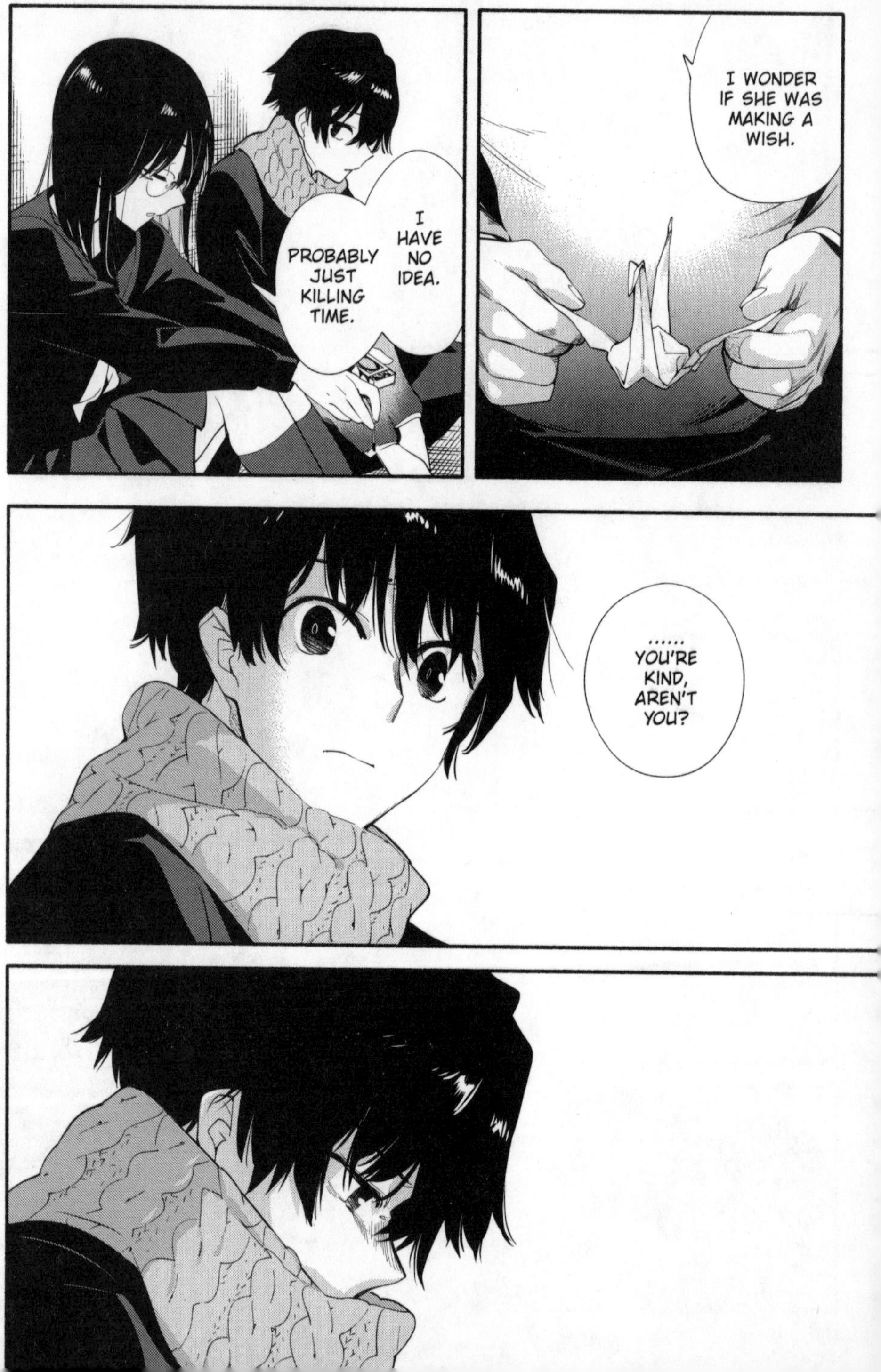
I WONDER IF SHE WAS MAKING A WISH.
I HAVE NO IDEA.
PROBABLY JUST KILLING TIME.
...... YOU'RE KIND, AREN'T YOU?

I...

...WAS JUST COPYING YOU.

IF I WAS GOING TO MAKE A WISH...

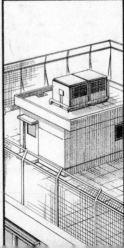

...IT WOULD BE THAT...

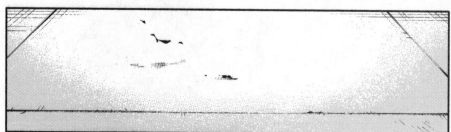

...I WANT TO BE KIND.

【I Want to Be Kind】

It's hard when you're allowed to write about anything you want. I tried writing some science fiction at first, but it wouldn't come together, so in the end, I wrote a story very close to my heart. I am also a coldhearted person, so I too would like to become kind.

Initial release: new story written for this book

Translation Note:

Page 140
There's an old belief in Japan that, if you fold a thousand paper cranes, your wish will come true.

AFTERWORD

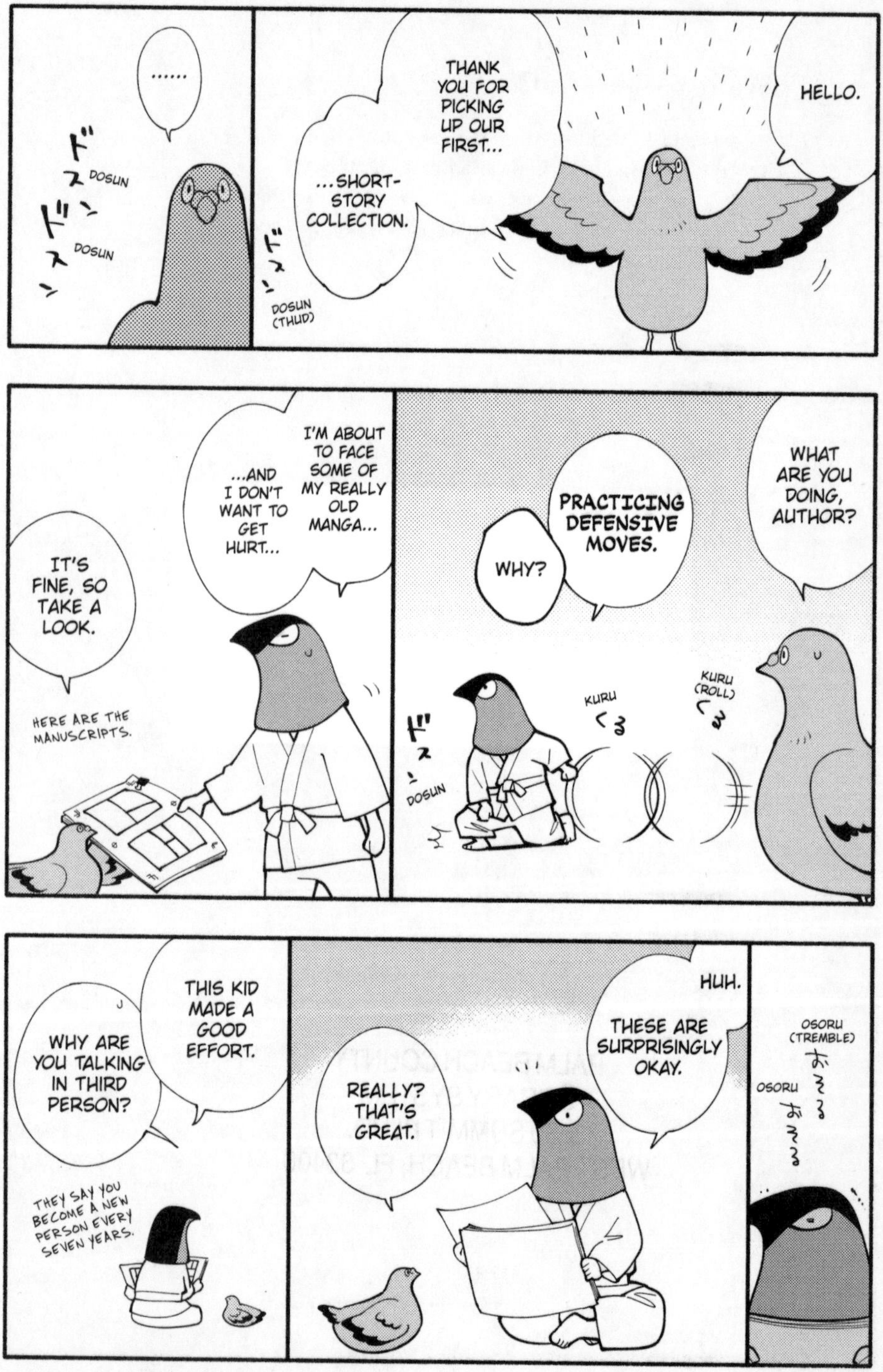
HELLO.
THANK YOU FOR PICKING UP OUR FIRST...
...SHORT-STORY COLLECTION.
DOSUN (THUD)
......
DOSUN
DOSUN
WHAT ARE YOU DOING, AUTHOR?
PRACTICING DEFENSIVE MOVES.
WHY?
KURU (ROLL)
KURU
DOSUN
I'M ABOUT TO FACE SOME OF MY REALLY OLD MANGA...
...AND I DON'T WANT TO GET HURT...
IT'S FINE, SO TAKE A LOOK.
HERE ARE THE MANUSCRIPTS.
OSORU (TREMBLE)
OSORU
HUH.
THESE ARE SURPRISINGLY OKAY.
REALLY? THAT'S GREAT.
THIS KID MADE A GOOD EFFORT.
WHY ARE YOU TALKING IN THIRD PERSON?
THEY SAY YOU BECOME A NEW PERSON EVERY SEVEN YEARS.

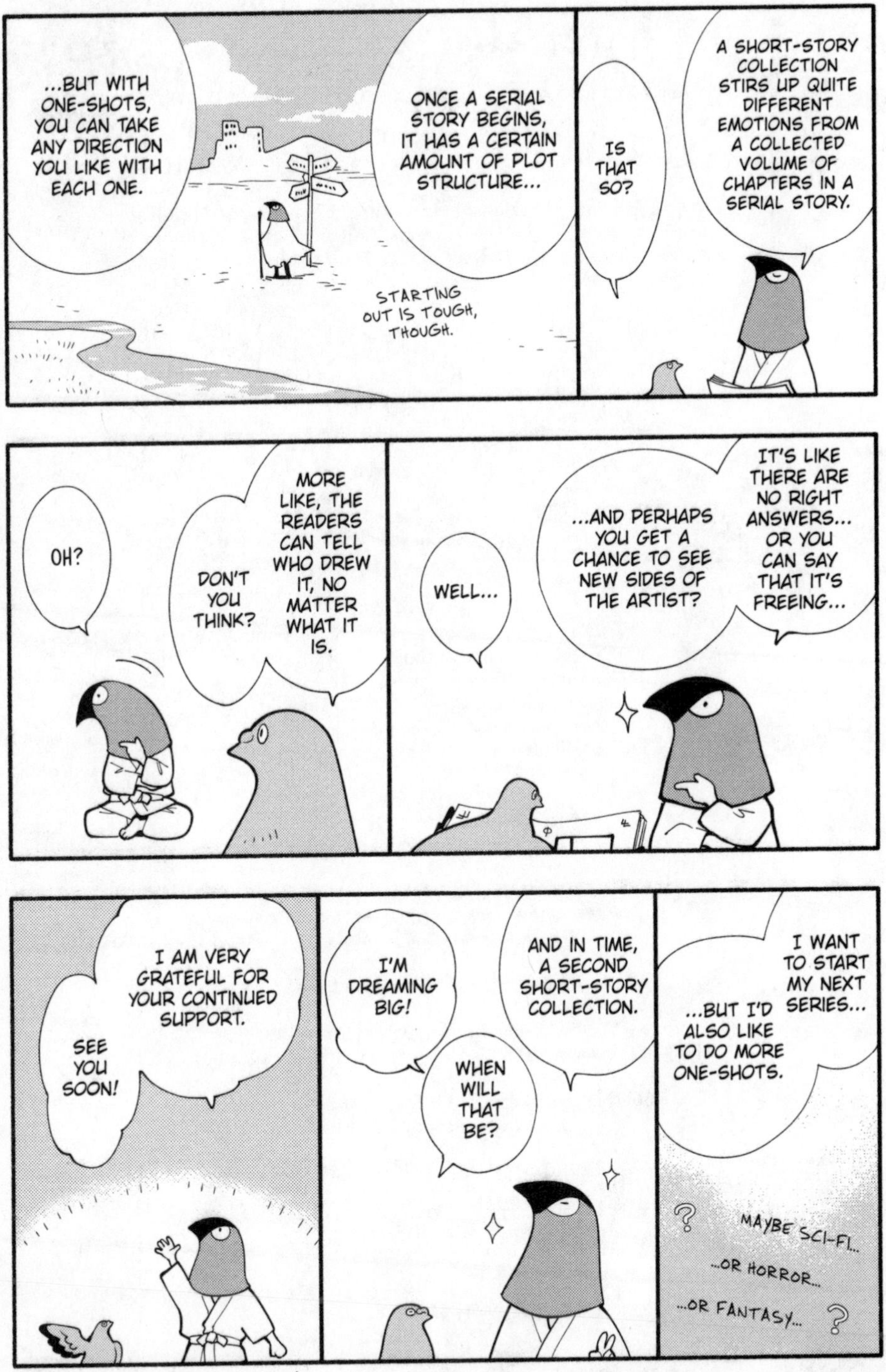
A SHORT-STORY COLLECTION STIRS UP QUITE DIFFERENT EMOTIONS FROM A COLLECTED VOLUME OF CHAPTERS IN A SERIAL STORY.
IS THAT SO?
ONCE A SERIAL STORY BEGINS, IT HAS A CERTAIN AMOUNT OF PLOT STRUCTURE...
STARTING OUT IS TOUGH, THOUGH.
...BUT WITH ONE-SHOTS, YOU CAN TAKE ANY DIRECTION YOU LIKE WITH EACH ONE.
IT'S LIKE THERE ARE NO RIGHT ANSWERS... OR YOU CAN SAY THAT IT'S FREEING...
...AND PERHAPS YOU GET A CHANCE TO SEE NEW SIDES OF THE ARTIST?
WELL...
MORE LIKE, THE READERS CAN TELL WHO DREW IT, NO MATTER WHAT IT IS.
DON'T YOU THINK?
OH?
I WANT TO START MY NEXT SERIES...
...BUT I'D ALSO LIKE TO DO MORE ONE-SHOTS.
MAYBE SCI-FI...
...OR HORROR...
...OR FANTASY...
AND IN TIME, A SECOND SHORT-STORY COLLECTION.
I'M DREAMING BIG!
WHEN WILL THAT BE?
I AM VERY GRATEFUL FOR YOUR CONTINUED SUPPORT.
SEE YOU SOON!

THANK YOU SO MUCH!

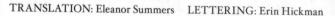

Farewell to My Alter

NIO NAKATANI SHORT STORY COLLECTION

TRANSLATION: Eleanor Summers   LETTERING: Erin Hickman

NAKATANI NIO TANPENSHU SAYONARA ORUTA
©Nakatani Nio 2020
First published in Japan in 2020 by KADOKAWA CORPORATION, Tokyo.
English translation rights arranged with KADOKAWA CORPORATION,
Tokyo, through Tuttle-Mori Agency, Inc.

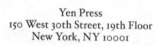

Yen Press
150 West 30th Street, 19th Floor
New York, NY 10001

Visit us at yenpress.com • facebook.com/yenpress •
twitter.com/yenpress • yenpress.tumblr.com •
instagram.com/yenpress

First Yen Press Edition: June 2021

Yen Press is an imprint of Yen Press, LLC.
The Yen Press name and logo are trademarks of Yen Press, LLC.

Library of Congress Control Number: 2021935483

ISBNs: 978-1-9753-2125-3 (paperback)
       978-1-9753-2126-0 (ebook)

10 9 8 7 6 5 4 3 2 1

WOR

Printed in the United States of America